After Bakhtin

If the 1960s was the decade of structuralism, and the 1970s the decade of deconstruction, then the 1980s have been dominated by the discovery and dissemination of Mikhail Bakhtin's work.

Now widely regarded as one of the most important thinkers of the twentieth century, the Russian writer Mikhail Bakhtin was silenced by political censorship and persecution for most of his life.

In *After Bakhtin* David Lodge sketches Bakhtin's extraordinary career, and explores the relevance of his ideas on the dialogic nature of language, on the typology of fictional discourse, and on the carnivalesque – to the writings of authors as diverse as George Eliot, James Joyce, D. H. Lawrence, Fay Weldon and Martin Amis. Further essays study particular texts – by Elizabeth Gaskell, Jane Austen, Henry James, Rudyard Kipling and Milan Kundera – illustrative of the development of the novel in its classic, modernist and post-modernist phases. Two final essays reflect on the current state of academic criticism.

David Lodge is Honorary Professor of Modern English Literature at the University of Birmingham. He is the author of several novels, most recently *Nice Work*, which won the Sunday Express Book of the Year Award in 1988. Among his works of literary criticism are *Language of Fiction* (1966), *The Novelist at the Crossroads* (1971), *The Modes of Modern Writing* (1977) and *Working with Structuralism* (1981). In 1986 he published a collection of occasional essays, *Write On*.

After Bakhtin

Essays on fiction and criticism

David Lodge

ROUTLEDGE

London and New York

First published 1990
by Routledge
11 New Fetter Lane, London EC4P 4EE

Simultaneously published in the USA and Canada
by Routledge
a division of Routledge, Chapman and Hall, Inc.
29 West 35th Street, New York, NY 10001

Typeset in 10/12 Garamond by Input Typesetting Ltd, London
Printed in Great Britain by Richard Clay Ltd, Bungay, Suffolk

British Library Cataloguing in Publication Data
Lodge, David
  After Bakhtin : essays on fiction and criticism.
  1. Literature. Critical studies
  I. Title
  809

Library of Congress Cataloging in Publication Data
Lodge, David
  After Bakhtin: essays on fiction and criticism/David Lodge.
    p. cm.
  1. Bakhtin, M. M. (Mikhail Mikhaïlovich), 1895–1975–Influence.
  2. English fiction–19th century–History and criticism. 3. English
  fiction–20th century–History and criticism. 4. Fiction–20th
  century–History and criticism. 5. Criticism–History–20th
  century. I. Title.
  PG2947.B3L63 1990
  801′.95′092–dc20 89–70160
  ISBN 0 415 05037 5
  ISBN 0 415 05038 3 pbk

To Bernard and Anne,
and in memory of Gabriel

Contents

Introduction

A majority of the essays in this book were influenced to a greater or lesser extent by the work of the Russian literary critic and theorist, Mikhail Bakhtin, and apply some of his ideas and methods of analysis to literary materials mostly unknown to him. I have called the collection *After Bakhtin* partly in homage, as painters acknowledge the masters they imitate. But, as the title essay suggests, those who are learning from Bakhtin today are very conscious of working 'after' him in the most literal sense. Most literary critics enjoy whatever fame they achieve in their own lifetimes; their ideas are publicly discussed and debated with their contemporaries, and their influence tends to wane rapidly on their decease. Bakhtin's work, in contrast, was hardly known outside a small group of friends for most of his life, and it is only since his death that he has begun to emerge as, in the words of his biographers, Katerina Clark and Michael Holquist, 'one of the leading thinkers of the twentieth century'.[1]

Mikhail Mikhaïlovitch Bakhtin was born in 1895 in Orel, a provincial town south of Moscow, the son of a bank manager whose family name was ancient and distinguished. He was educated at the universities of Odessa and St Petersburg, and graduated from the latter in 1918, in the first year of the Russian Revolution. It was an exciting, and dangerous, time and place to be a young intellectual. For a while the political ferment encouraged innovation and experiment in art and ideas. Russia became a creative centre of modernism. Futurist poets, constructivist artists and architects, rallied to the cause of the Revolution. In criticism, the Russian formalists provided a theoretical justification for avant-garde writing by their emphasis on the 'defamiliarizing' function of all art. But under Stalin the Soviet state became increasingly intolerant of aesthetic and intellectual individualism. Socialist realism superseded modernism as the politically acceptable mode of artistic production. In the late twenties, and throughout the thirties, the poets and artists, the critics and theorists, were imprisoned, exiled, exterminated or driven to suicide.

As far as we can tell, Bakhtin identified himself with the renewal of Russian society promised by the Revolution in its early years, working as a humble schoolteacher, and pursuing his intellectual interests through informal discussion groups with like-minded friends. But he was unusual in retaining his Christian faith, in the Russian Orthodox tradition. A fascinating newspaper report of a debate in which he participated in 1918 says of Bakhtin, 'At some points he did recognize, and even expressed appreciation of socialism, but he complained of, and worried about, the fact that socialism had no care for the dead.'[2] But if Bakhtin was unable to espouse a completely materialist, political philosophy of life, he was, as a literary theorist, equally critical of the Russian formalists' argument that change in literary fashion was a purely formal, internal process, driven by a cyclical need to find new styles to replace exhausted ones, rather than by developments in history and culture at large. Formalist literary theory was derived (through the mediation of the Moscow Linguistic Circle) from the linguistics of Ferdinand de Saussure, which described language (*langue*) as a system of differences with no positive terms. Both Saussure and the formalists tried, heroically, to make their respective disciplines 'scientific' by excluding the semantic dimension of language from consideration, or treating it as a function of purely formal relationships. Bakhtin's critique of Russian formalism was based on an alternative linguistics of language as speech (*parole*): language not as system, but as social activity, 'dialogue'.

The Russian formalists were on a collision course with the ideology of Stalinism, as they soon discovered. Bakhtin's approach was, on the surface, much more compatible with dialectical materialism, and in the 1920s it was articulated with a Marxist gloss in the publications of Bakhtin's friends and associates, P. N. Medvedev and V. Volosinov. Much controversy and uncertainty surrounds the question of how much of works such as Medvedev's *The Formal Method in Literary Scholarship* (1928) and Volosinov's *Marxism and the Philosophy of Language* (1929) was actually written by Bakhtin himself; but undoubtedly he was, directly or indirectly, the source of their most original (and least Marxist) parts. The Marxist gloss did not, in any case, save Bakhtin (or, in due course, his friends) from the disapproval of the state. In 1929, the year in which he published his first book under his own name, *Problems of Dostoevsky's Art*, Bakhtin was arrested, and exiled to the remote province of Kazakhstan. Later he was allowed to move back to a provincial town near Moscow. But throughout the thirties he worked in humble teaching and clerical jobs, unable to publish his work. As far as literary criticism was concerned (by no means his only field of research) this was an increasingly ambitious attempt to rewrite the history of Western European literature in the light of two interconnected ideas: the dialogic nature of language and the carnivalesque tradition in culture. As these ideas are summarized and explored in several of the essays collected below, I shall not discuss them further here.

Amazingly, Bakhtin survived the Stalinist purges of the thirties, the dangers and privations of the Second World War, and chronic osteomyelitis which required the amputation of a leg in 1938. In 1946 he was allowed, after much opposition, to defend his seminal doctoral thesis on Rabelais. In the post-Stalinist thaw, Bakhtin enjoyed a measure of rehabilitation, and his work began to be published and translated in the 1960s and 1970s, to an ever-increasing chorus of admiration and excitement. The long-delayed publication of *Rabelais and His World* (1966) was a landmark in that respect. Bakhtin retired from his post at the Saransk Teachers Training College in 1961, and was allowed to settle in Moscow in 1969, where he received a growing stream of visitors. He died in March 1975, at the age of 80, and was buried according to the rites of the Russian Orthodox Church.

It is an extraordinary story of outstanding intellectual achievement in the teeth of every imaginable obstacle and discouragement; and it has a poignant echo in the parallel story of Mikhail's elder brother, Nikolai, who broke off his classical studies at St Petersburg in 1916 to join the Russian Army. For reasons of chance circumstance and impulse rather than conviction, Nikolai was drawn into fighting on the White Russian side in the civil war which broke out in 1918, a step he later deeply regretted. He was forced to flee from Russia, enlisted in the French Foreign Legion in Constantinople while under the influence of drink, was wounded and invalided out of the Legion, and lived for some years in extreme poverty in Paris, freelancing as a lecturer and writer, until some British friends and admirers started him on an academic career which led, via a PhD in classics at Cambridge, to appointments at Southampton University in 1935, and then Birmingham University in 1938. He lectured in classics, modern Greek and linguistics at Birmingham, becoming eventually a one-man Department of Linguistics. He died suddenly from a heart attack, at the age of 54, in 1950, ten years before I was appointed to the same Faculty. The testimony of those who knew Nikolai and heard him lecture suggests that he had a share of his brother's genius, but he left very little permanent record of his achievements: a little-known, though highly regarded, *Introduction to the Study of Modern Greek*, and a handful of occasional essays and papers collected posthumously by friends at the University of Birmingham.[3] There seems to have been no communication between Nikolai and his brother after the early 1920s. Nikolai did not know of his brother's first book on Dostoevsky until he came across it by chance in a Paris bookshop in 1930. He did not learn of Mikhail's arrest in 1929 until some time in the 1940s, and assumed that Mikhail had perished in the purges of the 1930s. It seems likely that Mikhail for his part received no information about his brother's life in exile until long after the latter's death.[4] As Clark and Holquist observe, it is ironic that Mikhail should have achieved so much more than Nikolai in circumstances so much less conducive to scholarly work; but he did not suffer the trauma of exile from his native language and culture. Those of us who have pursued our literary and academic careers in less interesting times (to invoke a well-known Chinese proverb) can only contemplate the lives of these two scholars with humility and awe.

If, in the small world of academic literary criticism, the 1960s was the decade of structuralism, and the 1970s the decade of deconstruction and other varieties of post-structuralism, then the 1980s have arguably been dominated by the discovery and dissemination of Mikhail Bakhtin's work, partly as a means of countering or transcending the impact of those afore-mentioned developments in the human sciences on the study of literature. It has been Bakhtin's ironic fate to be invoked as a counterforce to move-ments that arose 'after' him. Bakhtin is sometimes described as a 'post-formalist', and his critique of formalism (as inferred from Medvedev and Volosinov) is parallel at several points to the post-structuralist critique of structuralism. But this did not lead him, as it has led the exponents of deconstruction, into an antihumanist scepticism about meaning, communi-cation, and the value of the western cultural tradition. 'The two pillars upon which a theory of criticism must rest,' said I. A. Richards, 'are an account of value and an account of communication.'[5] Bakhtin's theory has both these essential components and has therefore given new hope to literary critics who were beginning to wonder whether there was a life after post-structuralism. To those of a Marxist persuasion he has restored a non-vulgar concept of the socially constructive function of language and literature; to liberal humanist scholars he has restored the legitimacy of a diachronic, philologically based study of literature; to formalists he has opened up new possibilities of analysing and categorizing narrative discourse.

My own critical interests straddle these last two categories. Most of my academic criticism could be described as an attempt to ground historical, evaluative and interpretative criticism of the novel in its form, rather than its content or context. Since the medium of the novel is the written word, this seemed the best place to start. In my first book, *Language of Fiction* (1966), I argued:

> that if we are right to regard the art of poetry as an art of language, then so is the art of the novel; and that the critic of the novel has no special dispensation from that close and sensitive engagement with language we naturally expect from the critic of poetry.[6]

I would still stand by that assertion as a general principle, but not by the inference I drew from it in that book (and defended with a certain desper-ation in an essay, 'Towards a poetics of fiction: an approach through language', in my next one, *The Novelist at the Crossroads*; 1971): namely, that all critical questions about a novel are reducible to questions about language. For narrative is itself a kind of language that functions indepen-dently of specific verbal formulations. Some of the meanings attributable to a narrative will remain constant when it is translated from one natural language to another, or from one medium to another, and some of the crucial decisions by which a narrative is produced, such as the writer's choice of narrative point of view, or the treatment of time, are in a sense made prior to, or at a deeper level than, the articulation of the text in a sequence of sentences. All this now seems so obvious that the question arises as to why I was so concerned to suppress or deny it in my early theoretical speculations (in practical criticism, I was not always consistent with my principles, as some reviewers noted). What I did not see at that time was the possibility of a formalist criticism of the specifically narrative elements of a literary text, perhaps because those elements had been down-graded by the Anglo-American New Criticism in whose methods of 'close reading' I had been trained, or had trained myself. The credo quoted above from *Language of Fiction* derives from a statement by Mark Schorer in his influential essay, 'Technique as discovery':

> technique [in fiction] is thought of in blunter terms than those which one associates with poetry, as such relatively obvious matters as the arrangement of events to create plot; or, within plot, of suspense and climax; or as the means of revealing character motivation, relationships and developments, or the use of point of view.[7]

This dismissive attitude to what are in fact far from obvious matters is probably traceable to the fact that the New Criticism was partly motivated by a desire to justify the experiments of modernist writing, and that the modernist novel seemed, superficially at least, to be uninterested in narrative as such, and to foreground stylistic experiment. Virginia Woolf's attack on the well-made novels of Bennett and Wells, and her praise of Joyce's stream-of-consciousness writing in her essay 'Modern fiction' (1919) is echoed forty years later by Mark Schorer's unfavourable comparison of Wells's *Tono-Bungay* with Joyce's *A Portrait of the Artist as a Young Man* in 'Technique as discovery'. In my own chapter on *Tono-Bungay* in *Language of Fiction*, I tried to correct the modernist bias of Schorer's stylistic criticism; but what was really needed was a more comprehensive theory of 'technique' – a poetics of fiction which would allow the critic to move freely between the 'deep structure' of a text, where the raw story-stuff is organized in terms of sequence, point of view, etc., to its surface realization in a specific verbal form.

Such a poetics of fiction exists. Pioneered by the Russian formalists, such as Viktor Shklovsky and Boris Tomashevsky, developed and elaborated by the French critics of the 1960s and 1970s, such as Tzvetan Todorov, A. H. Greimas, Gérard Genette and Roland Barthes, incorporating some of the ideas of linguistic and anthropological structuralism as practised by Roman Jakobson and Claude Lévi-Strauss, it has since been assimilated and synthes-ized with Anglo-American criticism in such books as Seymour Chatman's *Story and Discourse* (1978). I spent much of the 1970s familiarizing myself with this work, and applying it in various essays, some collected in *Working With Structuralism* (1981) and some in the present volume (especially those on Jane Austen and Kipling).

In pursuing this research I came across Roman Jakobson's distinction between metaphor and metonymy, two figures of speech which are models of the two ways in which any discourse is structured: by relationships of similarity and by relationships of continuity. I was particularly struck by his almost throwaway remark that, 'Following the path of contiguous relationships, the realist author metonymically digresses from the plot to the atmosphere and from the characters to the setting in space and time. He is fond of synecdochic details.'[8] Metaphor has always been the key trope of lyric poetry, and the New Criticism (like much old criticism) had always privileged lyric poetry. When critics like Mark Schorer did stylistic criticism of the novel, they instinctively looked for metaphorical features, and the realist novel was either downgraded or distorted in the process. Jakobson's category of metonymy opened up the possibility of a formalist criticism of the realistic novel that would not inevitably find it aesthetically wanting. In *The Modes of Modern Writing* (1977) I applied the metaphor–metonymy typology to twentieth-century English and American writing, and suggested that literary fashion had oscillated periodically between the two poles.

The metaphor–metonymy distinction is a powerful tool for analysing and categorizing literary discourse, but *The Modes of Modern Writing* is not entirely free from the tendency of most stylistic criticism to treat the language of a novel as if it were a homogeneous entity. That is to say, in determining whether a given text is structured predominantly by the principle of metaphor or metonymy, one is tempted to ignore, or at least marginalize, the non-dominant element. Yet every text must contain both, and it may be that the tension or 'dialogue' between them is one of the most significant features of a text. Indeed dialogue in the ordinary sense of that term – the interchange of direct speech between individual characters – is a vital component of the novel which a stylistics of dominance is particularly ill-equipped to deal with. This of course is where Bakhtin comes in, explaining that there is no such thing as *the* style, *the* language of a novel, because a novel is a medley of many styles, many languages – or, if you like, voices.

The point was made long ago by Plato, in Book III of *The Republic*, where Socrates distinguishes between two ways of representing action in words: by diegesis (the poet's speech) and/or mimesis (the imitated speech of characters). I was directed to this fascinating passage by the always illuminating Gérard Genette, and it led me to Bakhtin, whose typology of narrative discourse is essentially a more sophisticated and comprehensive version of Plato's. (It is, incidentally, a remarkable fact that almost nothing of interest was written on the subject of narrative theory between ancient

Greece and twentieth-century Russia.) There is one passage in particular in Bakhtin which had on me the same effect, as of a light-bulb being switched on in one's head, as Jakobson's remark about metonymy. It is quoted in a condensed form in several of the essays quoted below:

> The possibility of employing on the plane of a single work discourses of various types, with all their expressive capacities intact, without reducing them to a single common denominator – this is one of the most fundamental characteristics of prose. Herein lies the profound distinction between prose style and poetic style . . . For the prose artist the world is full of other people's words, among which he must orient himself and whose speech characteristics he must be able to perceive with a very keen ear. He must introduce them into the plane of his own discourse, but in such a way that this plane is not destroyed. He works with a very rich verbal palette.[9]

The relevance of this insight to the ongoing critical project which I have just described, is obvious. If I had known it when I wrote *Language of Fiction* it would have diverted me from some theoretical cul-de-sacs. But the passage struck me with equal force in relation to my own experience of writing novels. It explained to me why I was a novelist rather than a poet. It explained to me why, as a novelist, I have been drawn to pastiche, parody and travesty – often of the very kind of discourse I produce in my capacity as an academic critic. Much later I came across another comment of Bakhtin's which encapsulates even more succinctly his understanding of the creative process: 'The writer is a person who knows how to work language while remaining outside of it; he has the gift of indirect speech.'[10]

Perhaps in the end Bakhtin's greatest contribution to contemporary criticism is, through the historical irony of his long obscurity and posthumous fame, to have made a timely reaffirmation of the writer's creative and communicative power. This is an idea that structuralism (implicitly), and post-structuralism (explicitly) have sought to discredit and replace with theories about the autonomous productivity of texts and their readers. Readers outside the academy, however, continue to believe in the existence and importance of authors. This is one of several issues that have created a barrier of non-comprehension between academic and non-academic discussion of literature – a matter that concerns me greatly, and that is touched on in several of the essays collected here.

I have always regarded myself as having a foot in both camps – the world of academic scholarship and higher education, and the world of literary culture at large, in which books are written, published, discussed and consumed for profit and pleasure in all senses of those words. Over many years I have published a book of criticism and a work of fiction in alternation. I took a keen interest in the developments in literary theory that arose out of European structuralism – learned from them, applied them, domesticated and cannibalized them in criticism and literary journalism, and satirized and carnivalized them in my novels, all in an effort (not always conscious) to encourage the circulation of ideas between the two worlds of discourse. But undoubtedly this bridging posture has become increasingly difficult to maintain as the professionalization of academic criticism has opened up a widening gap between it and 'lay' discussion of literature.

A few years ago, for a number of converging reasons, I retired from my post at the University of Birmingham, to pursue the career of a freelance writer. I retain an honorary academic title, I still keep up my university contacts, and give the occasional lecture or conference paper. But inevitably I feel myself drifting away from the academic institution, and its institutional stimuli, satisfactions and incentives. Without them, a lot of academic literary criticism and theory – the kind published in learned journals and by American university presses – frankly no longer seems worth the considerable effort of keeping up with it. A vast amount of it is not, like the work of Bakhtin, a contribution to human knowledge, but the demonstration of a professional mastery by translating known facts into more and more arcane metalanguages. This is not an entirely pointless activity – it sharpens the wits and tests the stamina of those who produce and consume such work – but it seems less and less relevant to my own writing practice. Though I intend to go on writing literary criticism, I doubt whether it will be 'academic' in the way most of the essays included in this book are academic. If the title *After Bakhtin* has a faintly elegiac ring, then, that is not entirely inappropriate.

All the essays collected here have been published before, sometimes in slightly different forms, and/or under different titles. They are arranged in a thematic order, rather than in order of composition, moving from fairly broad-ranging exercises in Bakhtinian criticism to studies of particular texts and authors illustrative of developments in the novel between the nineteenth and twentieth centuries, and concluding with reflections on the current state of academic criticism. The first essay acts as a kind of overture. I have taken advantage of this opportunity to revise or expand some parts of the original texts; and I have made various cuts in order to reduce (but not entirely remove) the repetition of explanations and illustrations of certain key terms and concepts. I have also deleted, in most cases, references to the occasions or contexts to which these pieces originally belonged, and by which their form and content were partly determined. I am grateful to all the editors, conference organizers, universities and publishers concerned in the instigation and/or first publication of these essays.

'The novel now: theories and practices' was the keynote address of a conference entitled 'Why the novel matters: a post-modern perplex', organized by the journal *Novel* at Brown University, Providence R.I., in 1987, and was subsequently published in *Novel*, vol. 21 (1988). 'Mimesis and diegesis in modern fiction' was contributed to a symposium held in Lausanne under the auspices of the Swiss Association of University Teachers in 1981, and subsequently published in *Contemporary Approaches to Narrative*, ed. Anthony Mortimer, Tubingen, 1984. In its present form it incorporates part of a paper on 'Joyce and Bakhtin' delivered at the eighth international James Joyce Symposium held in Dublin in 1982, and subsequently published in the *James Joyce Broadsheet*, No. 11, in 1983. '*Middlemarch* and the idea of the classic realist text' was originally presented at the George Eliot Centenary Conference held at Leicester University in July 1980, some six months before Colin MacCabe, of whose work it is in part a critique, became the centre of a widely publicized controversy at the University of Cambridge. I draw attention to the sequence of events to make clear that my essay should not be read as an oblique comment on the Cambridge 'affair' or a taking of sides in relation to it. The essay was later published in *The Nineteenth Century Novel: Critical Essays and Documents*, ed. Arnold Kettle, Open University Press, 1982. 'Lawrence, Dostoevsky, Bakhtin', was first published in the D. H. Lawrence Centenary issue of *Renaissance and Modern Studies* vol. 29 (1985), guest editor James T. Boulton, and, in its present form, in *Rethinking Lawrence*, ed. Keith Brown, Open University Press, 1990. 'Dialogue in the modern novel' was delivered as the E. J. Pratt Memorial Lecture at the Memorial University of Newfoundland in 1985, and subsequently published as a pamphlet by that University. 'After Bakhtin' was delivered as a paper at a conference entitled 'The linguistics of writing' at Strathclyde University in 1986, and was published in *The Linguistics of Writing: Arguments between Language and Literature*, ed. Nigel Fabb, Derek Attridge, Alan Durant and Colin MacCabe, Manchester University Press, 1987. 'Crowds and power in the early Victorian novel' was first published in *The French Revolution and British Culture*, ed. Ian Small and Ceri Crossley, Oxford University Press, 1989. 'Composition, distribution, arrangement: form and structure in Jane Austen's novels' was first published in *The Jane Austen Handbook*, ed. J. David Grey, A. Walton Litz and Brian Southam, Macmillan, New York, 1986. 'The art of ambiguity: *The Spoils of Poynton*' was the Introduction to my edition of Henry James's novel in the Penguin Classics series, Harmondsworth, 1987. 'Indeterminacy in modern narrative: reading off "Mrs Bathurst" ' was originally delivered as a paper at a symposium on modern British literature organized by the English Language and Literature Association of Korea, held in Seoul in 1982, and in its present form was published in *Kipling Considered*, ed. Philip Mallett, Macmillan, 1989. 'Milan Kundera and the idea of the author in modern criticism' was first published in *The Critical Quarterly*'s twenty-fifth anniversary issue, vol. 26 (1984). 'Reading and writhing in a double-bind' was first published in the *Times Literary Supplement*, April 23, 1982. 'A kind of business: the academic critic in America' was first published in the Australian journal *Scripsi*, vol. 5, no. 1,

1988. This Introduction incorporates some passages from the Afterword to the Second Edition of my *Language of Fiction*, Routledge, 1984.

The place of publication of books cited is London unless otherwise indicated.

Birmingham, July 1989

Chapter 1

The novel now
Theories and practices

When I began the twin careers of novelist and academic critic some thirty
years ago, the relationship between fiction and criticism was comparatively
unproblematical. Criticism was conceived of as a second-order discourse
dependent on the first-order discourse of fiction. Novelists wrote novels
and critics criticized them. This latter activity was usually described as a
combination of description, interpretation and evaluation of texts, with
different schools striking a different balance between the terms of this
formula. The function of theory was to provide a more and more comprehensive and refined methodology for carrying out this work, and in the
1960s in England and America this task was seen as very much a matter of
bringing novel criticism up to a level of formal sophistication comparable
to that achieved by the New Criticism (from, say, William Empson to W.
K. Wimsatt) in relation to poetry.

This critical activity also had an ideological function, seldom overtly
acknowledged, namely, the maintenance of a canon. The storehouse of
fiction has many floors, but it is shaped like a ziggurat, or pyramid. There
is a lot of space on the ground floor for contemporary work, but much of
it is speedily dumped in the trash cans outside the back door, without ever
having been shelved upstairs in the storeys reserved for 'serious' writing.
As authors are promoted higher and higher up the scale of value, and
recede into the historical past, their number becomes fewer and fewer, the
accommodation for them more limited. The top floor, reserved for the
classics, is very small indeed. The English Victorian novel, for instance, is
represented by the work of perhaps a dozen novelists, out of the thousand
or more who actually wrote novels in that period. This is inevitable: the
collective consciousness can store only a finite number of texts; when one
is added, another must drop out to make room for it.

The higher you go up the storeys of the ziggurat, the more evident it is
that the process of selection and exclusion is controlled by academic critics,
rather than by reviewers, literary journalists and writers themselves. This
is because the academic study of literature depends crucially on the existence
of a canon. Without a common body of texts to refer to and compare, the

subject would become impossible to teach or learn. Teachers who set out
to subvert the idea of the literary canon are obliged to provide an alternative
one, usually of theoretical texts. And if critics need a canon, novelists need
a tradition. You cannot begin to write novels without having read at least
one, and probably hundreds; without defining yourself in relationships of
apprenticeship, discipleship, rivalry, and antagonism with precursors and
peers. Sometimes, for instance in the hey-day of modernism, a realignment
of writers in relation to tradition is carried over into a revision of the
academic canon, which in turn affects the reading of the next generation of
aspirant writers. The comparative rarity of such cross-fertilization in today's
literary culture is one of its more worrying symptoms.

The traditional model of the relationship between fiction and criticism is
not, then, entirely disinterested. It privileges the novelist in the sense that
he or she is seen as the creative source without whom the critic would have
nothing to criticize, but it is used to police the work of contemporary
writing in a way that can be oppressive. It is an author-centred model –
the history of the English or American novel is seen as the story of excep-
tionally gifted writers who handed on the great tradition of fiction, each
adding some distinctive contribution of their own. But it is also self-centred,
since the process of sifting and evaluating and interpreting the classic or
potentially classic texts serves the purpose of the academic institution.
Academic critics have great respect for the canonical novelists, but not
much for novelists who don't seem to be interested in getting into the
canon. One gets the impression from a good deal of traditional academic
criticism, certainly that associated with the name of F. R. Leavis, that it is
a finer thing to be a critic working on a major novelist than to be oneself
a good minor novelist. This is not generally true of reviewers, who are
more generous in their reception of new fiction. Indeed, one of the functions
academic critics have often seen themselves as performing is to counteract
the inflated currency of journalistic reviewing. But both kinds of critic have,
until recently, shared the same implied aesthetic, which a contemporary
academic theorist, Catherine Belsey, has labelled 'expressive realism'.[1] That
is to say, they have interpreted and evaluated novels as more or less powerful
expressions of a unique sensibility or world-view – the author's – and as
more or less truthful representations of reality.

   This traditional, or as it is sometimes called, humanist model of the
relationship between fiction and criticism is still widely subscribed to.
However, in the last twenty years or so it has sustained a number of attacks
from within the academic institution as the latter has become increasingly
dominated by structuralist and post-structuralist theory. The effect has been
to throw academic literary studies into a state of exciting intellectual ferment
or terminal crisis, according to your point of view. But as far as I can see
it has had little effect on the ground floor of the ziggurat, that is to say on

the reception of new writing, at least in England and America. Whether it has had any effect on novelists themselves, and whether such an effect is or might be either liberating or inhibiting are questions worth considering.

It all started, of course, with the impact of structuralism on literary criticism in the 1960s. In its classic form, structuralism seeks to understand culture in terms of the systems of signification that underlie it: the emphasis is on the system, not individual realizations of the system. In this respect it modelled itself on the linguistics of Saussure, who maintained that linguistic science should concern itself with the finite system of *langue*, not the infinite variety of *parole*. Another of Saussure's seminal ideas, much misunderstood, and often vulgarized, was that the relationship between the two aspects of the verbal sign, the signifier and the signified, is arbitrary. It is not the relationship between words and things that allows language to signify, but the difference between elements of the linguistic system. Language, in the famous phrase, is a system of differences.

It is easy to see why this way of thinking, when applied to literature, diverted attention away from what was unique to texts and towards what they have in common: codes, conventions, rules; why it reduced the originating power of the author, and elevated the importance of the reader, in the production of meaning; why it subverted the privileged status of the literary canon, since the beauty of semiotic systems could be demonstrated as well, or better, by reference to anonymous folk tales and myths, or the products of popular culture like thrillers, advertising and fashion; why it subverted the notion of realism, exposing it as an art of bad faith because it seeks to disguise or deny its own conventionality. In short, although structuralism in its classical form was a rather conservative methodology, seeking to interpret rather than change the world (to invoke Marx's formula), it was capable of being co-opted, in the revolutionary atmosphere of the 1960s, to a radical intellectual critique of traditional humanistic ideas about literature and culture.

At that time there *was* some creative interaction between the new structuralist-influenced criticism and the production and reception of new writing. In France the *nouvelle critique* provided a basis for defending and interpreting the *nouveau roman*. In America and to a lesser extent in Britain, various kinds of post-modernist experiments in fiction seemed to derive from or at least could be explained in terms of the new critical attacks upon realism. But, as structuralism pursued its own premises and problems into a second phase of debate and speculation generally called 'post-structuralism', it became more and more scholastic, esoteric and inward-looking in its concerns, and had less and less to do with the encouragement or criticism of new imaginative writing – unless you regard it as a form of avant-garde literature in its own right. The tendency of post-structuralist theory has certainly been to abolish the conceptual boundary between creative and critical discourse which was one of the basic assumptions of the traditional humanist model. The most influential figures in this post-structuralist phase – Lacan, Derrida, Althusser, Foucault – were not literary critics by discipline. And although their theories have had a profound effect upon academic literary studies, it is not one which, at first glance, seems likely to inspire or encourage the writer who practises his art outside the academy.

Unfortunately, this discourse is so opaque and technical in its language that the first glance – baffled, angry, or derisive – is likely to be the last one. An unhappy consequence of recent developments has certainly been the loss of a common language of critical discourse which used to be shared between academic critics, practising writers, literary journalists and the educated common reader. Thirty or forty years ago, a reader of the book pages of the London *Observer* or the *New York Times Book Review* could pick up a copy of *Scrutiny* or the *Sewanee Review* and be able to take an intelligent interest in most of what he found in those university-based journals. If such a reader were to pick up their equivalents today – *Critical Inquiry*, say, or the *Oxford Review* – he would in all probability be totally baffled and bewildered, unable to make any sense at all of what purports to be literary criticism. Nor would he find there much comment on contemporary imaginative writing. Critics these days are too busy keeping up with each other's work.

Perhaps this discontinuity between the most advanced and innovative discourse about literature and the production and reception of new writing matters more to someone like me, who has a foot in both worlds, than it does to writers who have no connection with the academic world and are free to ignore its abstruse debates, or to academics who take for granted that the high ground of aesthetics will always be accessible only to a small minority. But I can't believe that this is a healthy situation, and I do believe that contemporary theory has something useful and important to say about what Poe called the philosophy of composition, alien as it may seem to the creative writer at first sight.

Let me try and illustrate the point by citing two statements by two eminent modern theorists, Roland Barthes and Paul de Man, on two issues, the idea of the author, and the relationship between fiction and reality, which have been central both to the practice of fiction writing and the reception and criticism of fiction in modern culture. The idea of the author as a uniquely constituted individual subject, the originator and in some sense owner of his work, is deeply implicated in the novel as a literary form and historically coincident with the rise of the novel; so is an emphasis on the mimetic function of verbal art, its ability to reflect or represent the world truthfully and in detail. Both these principles are called into question in the statements I wish to cite.

The first is from Roland Barthes's essay, 'The death of the author' (1968). He seeks to replace 'author' with the term 'scriptor':

The Author, when believed in, is always conceived of as the past of his own book: book and author stand automatically on a single line divided into a *before* and an *after*. The Author is thought to *nourish* the book, which is to say that he exists before it, thinks, suffers, lives for it, is in the same relation of antecedence to his work as a father to his child. In complete contrast, the modern scriptor is born simultaneously with the text, is in no way equipped with a being preceding or exceeding the writing, is not the subject with the book as predicate; there is no other time than that of the enunciation and every text is eternally written *here and now* . . .

   We know now that a text is not a line of words releasing a single 'theological' meaning (the 'message' of the Author-God) but a multi-dimensional space in which a variety of writings, none of them original, blend and clash.[2]

The second quotation is from Paul de Man's essay, 'Criticism and crisis', in *Blindness and Insight* (1971):

That sign and meaning can never coincide is what is precisely taken for granted in the kind of language we call literary. Literature, unlike every-day language, begins on the far side of this knowledge; it is the only form of language free from the fallacy of unmediated expression . . . The self-reflecting mirror effect by means of which a work of fiction asserts, by its very existence, its separation from empirical reality, its divergence, as a sign, from a meaning that depends for its existence on the constitutive activity of this sign, characterises the work of literature in its essence. It is always against the explicit assertion of the writer that readers degrade the fiction by confusing it with a reality from which it has forever taken leave.[3]

Now my first reaction as a novelist is to contest these remarks – to say to Barthes that I *do* feel a kind of parental responsibility for the novels I write, that the composition of them *is*, in an important sense, my past, that I do think, suffer, live for a book while it is in progress; and to say to de Man that my fiction has not 'for ever taken leave of reality' but is in some significant sense a representation of the real world, and that if my readers did not recognize in my novels some truths about the real behaviour of, say, academics or Roman Catholics, I should feel I had failed, and so would my readers.

   Certainly the way in which fiction is produced and circulated and received in our culture is totally at odds with the assertions of Barthes and de Man. The reception of new writing has in fact probably never been more obsessively author-centred than it is today, not only in reviewing, but in supplementary forms of exposure through the media – interviews and pro-files in the press and on TV, prizes, public readings and book launches and so on. All this attention is focused on the author as a unique creative self, the mysterious, glamorous origin of the text; and the questions one is asked on these occasions invariably emphasize the mimetic connection between fiction and reality which de Man denies exists: what is your book *about*? Is it autobiographical? Is such and such a character based on a real person? Do academics/Catholics really behave like that? and so on. Let it not be supposed that such questions come only from naive or uneducated readers. Some of the most committed post-structuralists among my acquaintances are also the most determined to read my novels as *romans à clef*.

I suppose most novelists have had this experience, and found it an uncomfortable one. Then the extreme formulations of Barthes and de Man about the impersonality and fictiveness of literary discourse begin to look rather attractive, and one may appeal to something like them in order to discourage a reductively empiricist reading of one's work. For what is objectionable about such a reading is that it seems to treat the text as a sign of something more concrete, more authentic, more real, which the writer could, if he or she cared to, hand over in its raw and naked truth. Even much more sophisticated criticism based on the same assumptions can seem oppressive to the author, delving into the biographical origins of one's fiction, seeking to establish a perfect fit between the novelist's personal identity and his *oeuvre*. Graham Greene has a nice passage in *Ways of Escape* where he says that there comes a time when the established writer

> is more afraid to read his favourable critics than his unfavourable, for with terrible patience they unroll before his eyes the unchanging pattern of the carpet. If he has depended a great deal on his unconscious, and his ability to forget even his own books when they are once on the public shelves, his critics remind him – this theme originated ten years ago, that simile which came so unthinkingly to his pen a few weeks back was used nearly twenty years ago . . . [4]

Greene's insistence on the need of the novelist to forget his own books, and in a sense his own past, sounds surprisingly close to Barthes's concept of the modern scriptor who only exists at the moment of composition. But in the same book Greene claims a documentary truthfulness for his fiction that neither Barthes nor de Man would allow:

> Some critics have referred to a strange violent 'seedy' region of the mind . . . which they call Greeneland, and I have sometimes wondered whether they go round the world blinkered. 'This is Indo-China,' I want to exclaim, 'this is Mexico, this is Sierra Leone carefully and accurately described.' [5]

The closer we come to the actual experience of writing, the more we encounter paradox and contradiction. Are books made out of the writer's observation and experience, or out of other books? Does the writer write his novel or does the novel 'write' the writer? Is the implied author of a novel – the creative mind to whom we attribute its existence, and whom we praise or blame for its successes and failures – the 'same' as the actual historical individual who sat at his desk and wrote it, and who has his own life before and after that activity, or an identity who exists only at the moment of composition? Can a novel be 'true to life' or does it merely create a 'reality effect'? Is reality itself such an effect? Is the absence of the writer from his own text that which spurs him to refine and polish his language so that his meaning will be effectively communicated without the supplementary aids of voice, gesture, physical presence, etc., which assist communication in ordinary speech? Or is the association of meaning with presence a fallacy which writing, through its inherent ambiguity and open-ness to a variety of interpretations, helps to expose?

Structuralists and post-structuralists will give one set of answers to these questions and humanist or expressive realist critics another set. Most wri-ters, I suspect – certainly I myself – would be inclined to say in each case, 'Yes and no', or 'Both alternatives are true'. But the expressive realist theses (that novels arise out of their authors' experience and observation of life, that they are works of verbal mimesis, and so on) are based on common sense, the grounds for believing them are self-evident. The grounds for believing the antithetical propositions are not self-evident, and the value of contemporary literary theory may be that by articulating them it prevents – or would prevent if it were more accessible – the total dominance of our literary culture by expressive realism.

It is not fortuitous, I think, that the anxieties generated by modern critical theory weigh more heavily, or press more sharply, upon writers and critics of prose fiction than upon poets and dramatists and their critics. The novel came into existence under the sign of contradiction, as Lennard J. Davis has argued in his stimulating book, *Factual Fictions: The Origins of the English Novel*.[6] It emerged, he argued, from a new kind of writing which he calls 'news/novels discourse', the earliest manifestations of that journalistic, documentary reporting of recent or current events which we take for granted in the modern era, but which was virtually unknown before the Renaissance because it depended upon the invention of the printing press. As Davis points out (he is not of course the first to do so, but he gets more mileage out of the idea than earlier critics), most of the early English novelists had close connections with the world of printing and/or journal-ism, and framed their fictitious narratives with avowals that these were factual documents (letters, confessions, etc.) of which they were merely the editors. Novelists perceived that by imitating the form of documentary or historical writing they could exert an exciting new power over their readers, obtaining total faith in the reality of fictitious characters and events. (There was no way, Davis plausibly argues, by which an eighteenth-century reader could be sure whether *Robinson Crusoe* or *Pamela* were true stories or not.) By the same means they threw a defensive smoke screen around the contradictory demands made upon them as storytellers – on the one hand the traditional aesthetic imperative that literature should embody general truths about human nature, and on the other hand the audience's appetite for the truth-is-stranger-than-fiction particularity of journalistic reportage.

Like Ian Watt's, Davis's theory of the rise of the novel applies more obviously to Defoe and Richardson than it does to Fielding, who mocked the technique of pseudo-documentary reporting in *Shamela* and *Joseph Andrews*. But Davis points out that Fielding was a journalist before he was a novelist and that he integrated the facts of a real historical event (the Jacobite Rising of 1745) into his fictional *History of Tom Jones* with unprecedented care and attention to detail. He was also attacked (ironically enough by Richardson among others) for basing his characters transparently upon real people.

Davis's thesis may be overstated, but he is certainly on to something. The ambivalent and sometimes contradictory relationship between fact and fiction in the early novel persists into its classic and modern phases. Think for instance of Dickens's Preface to *Bleak House*, where he insists that 'everything set forth in these pages concerning the Court of Chancery is substantially true and within the truth', and assures his readers that there are 'about thirty cases on record' of spontaneous combustion, while at the same time saying, 'I have purposely dwelt on the romantic side of familiar things'. Or consider the work of James Joyce. Almost every incident and character in his novels and stories can be traced back to some fact of his own life and experience, and he boasted that if the city of Dublin were to be destroyed it could be reconstructed from his books, yet at the same time he made large implicit and explicit claims for the timeless and universal significance of those narratives. Novelists are and always have been split between, on the one hand, the desire to claim an imaginative and representative truth for their stories, and on the other the wish to guarantee and defend that truth-claim by reference to empirical facts: a contradiction they seek to disguise by elaborate mystifications and metafictional ploys such as framing narratives, parody and other kinds of intertextuality and self-reflexivity or what the Russian formalists called 'baring of the device'. These ploys are not, as is sometimes thought, absent from the classic realist novel – one finds examples in for instance, *The Heart of Midlothian*, *Northanger Abbey* and *Vanity Fair*; but they do seem to be particularly marked in contemporary fiction, as if in response to or defence against the epistemological scepticism of contemporary critical theory.

I recently taught, at the University of Birmingham, a short seminar course on contemporary British fiction. Taking Kingsley Amis's *Lucky Jim* as a benchmark to represent the kind of social realism typical of British fiction in the fifties, I selected seven texts to illustrate subsequent developments: *A Clockwork Orange* by Anthony Burgess; *The French Lieutenant's*

Woman by John Fowles; *Not to Disturb* by Muriel Spark; *Briefing for a Descent into Hell* by Doris Lessing; *The White Hotel* by D. M. Thomas; *The History Man* by Malcolm Bradbury and *Money* by Martin Amis. Five of these texts introduce their author, or a thinly disguised surrogate for him or her, into the text itself in order to raise questions about the ethics and aesthetics of the novel form; and the other two (the Lessing and the Thomas) incorporate documentary sources into their fictional stories in ways which transgress the conventional distinction between factual and fictional narrative. Martin Amis actually has his hero, or anti-hero, who is called John Self, meet *him*self, that is to say, a character called Martin Amis, a novelist. John Self asks the question that everybody asks novelists ' "Hey," I said, "When you [write], do you sort of make it up, or is it just, you know, like what happens?" ' The Martin Amis character answers: 'Neither'.[7]

In the passage I quoted earlier, Paul de Man referred to 'the self-reflecting mirror effect by means of which a work of fiction asserts, by its very existence, its separation from empirical reality, its divergence, as a sign, from a meaning that depends for its existence on the constitutive activity of [that] sign'. What is self-evident to the deconstructionist critic is, in fact, by no means obvious to the average novel reader. But by arranging an encounter – indeed, several encounters – between himself and his character within the story he is writing, Martin Amis makes that 'self-reflecting mirror effect' concrete and explicit. So do, in different ways, the other writers I mentioned.

I do not mean to suggest that such metafictional devices are mandatory for the contemporary novelist. The vitality and viability of the realist tradition in fiction continues to surprise those who have pronounced obsequies over it. Indeed it would be false to oppose metafiction to realism; rather, metafiction makes explicit the implicit problematic of realism. The foregrounding of the act of authorship within the boundaries of the text which is such a common feature of contemporary fiction, is a defensive response, either conscious or intuitive, to the questioning of the idea of the author and of the mimetic function of fiction by modern critical theory.

Having mentioned Lennard Davis's *Factual Fictions*, I must take note of his latest book, *Resisting Novels*, which articulates a critique of the traditional humanist conception of the novel that comes from the ideological rather than the semiotic wing of post-structuralist theory. The book is in a sense the confessions of a justified sinner. Davis writes as a long-term addict of fiction who has come to the conclusion that novel-reading is bad for us. 'We can no longer smugly think of the novel as the culmination of the human spirit or the height of mimetic accomplishment,' he says.[8] 'Novels are not life, their situation of telling their stories is alienated from lived experience, their subject matter is heavily oriented towards the ideological, and their function is to help humans adapt to the fragmentation and isolation of the modern world' (p. 12). 'Novel reading as a social behaviour helps prevent change' (p. 17).

What Davis does is to draw out the ideological implications of the formal conventions of the novel. The novelistic handling of space encouraged the fetishization of objects and personal property. The complexity of characters in the classic novel is actually an illusion made possible by the very *few* traits of which they are composed and the codes of consistency and relevancy which bind them together. This novelistic concept of character has the ideological function of reconciling us to the alienation of modern existence. The novel cannot deal easily with group action, on which political change depends – or even group discussion. Dialogue in novels bears very little resemblance to real speech not only because it is grammatically well-formed but because it lacks the negotiated turn-taking of real conversation. And so on.

Davis's polemic in many ways resembles the critique of the classic realist text initiated by Roland Barthes and carried on by British critics of a left-wing political persuasion, for example Terry Eagleton, Catherine Belsey and Colin MacCabe. But whereas these critics usually bring forward the modernist or post-modernist text as a kind of fiction which avoids complicity with the ideology of bourgeois capitalism, Davis will make no such exceptions. His comment on modern fiction is that 'change is now removed even from the realm of the personal and psychological, as it had already been from the historical. Change becomes valenced by purely aesthetic categories – an aestheticism approved and promulgated by much of modern criticism' (p. 221).

Davis's book expresses a view antithetical to that put forward by D. H. Lawrence in his famous essay. 'Why the novel matters'. To Lawrence the novel mattered because of all forms of human discourse and cognition it was the only one which could embrace the totality of human experience, the whole of man alive:

> being a novelist, I consider myself superior to the saint, the scientist, the philosopher, and the poet, who are all great masters of different bits of man alive, but never get the whole hog.
>
> The novel is the one bright book of life. Books are not life. They are only tremulations on the ether. But the novel as a tremulation can make the whole man alive tremble. Which is more than poetry, philosophy, science, or any other book-tremulation can do.[9]

Notice that Lawrence emphasizes that 'books are not life'. This is something Davis cannot forgive them for. He yearns nostalgically for a more primitive or organic culture in which narrative was not commodified in the form of a printed book, and consumed in silence and privacy, but exchanged orally in a real social encounter. The metaphysics of presence returns with a vengeance, not to bolster up the novel, but to sweep it away.

In one sense there is no answer to Davis's polemic. If you oppose life to art, acting to reading, rather than including the second term of these pairs in the first, if you think that the important thing is not to interpret the world but to change it, then the novel will seem at best an irrelevance, at worst an obstacle. But the logical conclusion of Davis's argument is that he should stop being a literary critic and become a political activist. His reluctance to do so leaves him floundering in his last chapter, hoping rather lamely that 'resisting the novel may in fact be a way of reforming the novel . . .' (p. 239). One might argue that this is precisely what novelists themselves have always done, from Cervantes to Martin Amis: reformed the novel by building resistance to fictional stereotypes and conventions into the novel itself.

If we are looking for a theory of the novel that will transcend the opposition of humanist and post-structuralist viewpoints and provide an ideological justification for the novel that will apply to its entire history, the most likely candidate is the work of Mikhail Bakhtin. In their recent study of his life and work, Katerina Clark and Michael Holquist observe:

> Bakhtin's view of language differs from two other current conceptions of language . . . Personalists [i.e. humanists] maintain that the source of meaning is the unique individual. Deconstructionists locate meaning in the structure of the general possibility of difference underlying all particular differences. Bakhtin roots meaning in the social, though the social is conceived in a special way.[10]

The special way is Bakhtin's concept of language as essentially dialogic: that is, the word is not, as in Saussure, a two-sided sign – signifier and signified – but a two-sided *act*. Bakhtin's linguistics is a linguistics of *parole*. The words we use come to us already imprinted with the meanings, intentions and accents or previous users, and any utterance we make is directed towards some real or hypothetical Other. 'The word in living conversation is directly, blatantly, oriented toward a future answer word,' says Bakhtin. 'It provokes an answer, anticipates it and structures itself in the answer's direction.'[11] According to Bakhtin, the canonic genres – tragedy, epic, lyric – suppressed this inherently dialogic quality of language in the interests of expressing a unified world-view. These genres, at least before they were 'novelized', are monologic. It was the destiny of the novel as a literary form to do justice to the inherent dialogism of language and culture by means of its discursive polyphony, its subtle and complex interweaving of various types of speech – direct, indirect and doubly-oriented (e.g. parody) – and its carnivalesque irreverence towards all kinds of authoritarian, repressive, monologic ideologies.

Davis is aware of the Bakhtinian defence of the novel, and tries to combat it in his chapter on 'Conversation and dialogue':

conversation is truly 'dialogic,' to use Bakhtin's phrase – that is, including all voices. However, and here I would disagree with Bakhtin, dialogue in novels lacks this crucial and democratic strand – everything that comes from the author is autocratically determined. The very basis of conversation – mutually negotiated turntaking – is replaced by order determined unilaterally by the author.

(pp. 177–8)

This, however, is based on a misunderstanding, or misrepresentation of what Bakhtin means by the dialogic in fiction. The dialogic includes, but is not restricted to, the quoted verbal speech of characters. It also includes the relationship between the characters' discourses and the author's discourse (if represented in the text) and between all these discourses and other discourses outside the text, which are imitated or evoked or alluded to by means of doubly-oriented speech. It is of course true that everything in a novel is put there by the novelist – in this sense the literary text is not, like a real conversation, a totally open system. But it is Bakhtin's point that the variety of discourses in the novel prevents the novelist from imposing a single world-view upon his readers even if he wanted to.

Bakhtin first formulated the idea of the polyphonic novel in his early monograph, *Problems of Dostoevsky's Art*.[12] What then seemed to him to be a unique innovation of Dostoevsky's – the way in which the Russian novelist allowed different characters to articulate different ideological positions in a text without subordinating them to his own authorial speech – he later came to think was inherent in the novel as a literary form. In the revised and much expanded version of the Dostoevsky book, *Problems of Dostoevsky's Poetics* (1963), and in the essays collected in English under the title *The Dialogic Imagination*, he traced its genealogy back to the parodying-travestying genres of classical literature – the satyr play, the Socratic dialogue and the Menippean satire – and to that carnival folk-culture which kept the tradition alive through the Middle Ages and up to the Renaissance.

There is an indissoluble link in Bakhtin's theory between the linguistic variety of prose fiction, which he called heteroglossia, and its cultural function as the continuous critique of all repressive, authoritarian, one-eyed ideologies. As soon as you allow a variety of discourses into a textual space – vulgar discourses as well as polite ones, vernacular as well as literary, oral as well as written – you establish a resistance (to use Davis's word) to the dominance of any one discourse. Even in the classic realist novel and its modern descendants, in which, we are so often told by post-structuralist critics, the author's discourse is privileged and controls the proliferation of meaning by judging and interpreting the discourses of the characters, even there this control is only relative, and largely illusory. 'The possibility of employing on the plane of a single work discourses of various types, with all their expressive capacities intact, without reducing them to a common denominator – this is one of the most characteristic features of prose,' says Bakhtin.[13] To allow characters to speak with their own social, regional and individual accents, whether in quoted direct speech ('dialogue' in the ordinary sense of the term) or by allotting them the task of narrating itself, as in the epistolary novel, the confessional novel, and the colloquial vernacular narrative known to the Russians as *skaz*; or by means of free indirect style, a rhetorical technique discovered by novelists in the late eighteenth century and developed to stunning effect in the nineteenth and twentieth – to do all or any of these things in narrative is to make interpretive closure in the absolute sense impossible.

'The one grand literary form that is for Bakhtin capable of a kind of justice to the inherent polyphonies of life is the "novel" ', says Wayne Booth, introducing the latest translation of *Problems of Dostoevsky's Poetics*, and echoing, consciously or unconsciously, Lawrence's definition of the novel as 'the one bright book of life'.[14] In another essay, called simply 'The Novel', first published in *Reflections on the Death of a Porcupine* (1925), Lawrence wrote:

> You can fool pretty nearly every other medium. You can make a poem pietistic, and still it will be a poem. You can write *Hamlet* in drama: if you wrote him in a novel, he'd be half comic, or a trifle suspicious; a suspicious character, like Dostoevsky's Idiot. Somehow, you sweep the ground a bit too clear in the poem or the drama, and you let the human Word fly a bit too freely. Now in a novel there's always a tom-cat, a black tom-cat that pounces on the white dove of the Word, if the dove doesn't watch it; and there is a banana-skin to trip on; and you know there is a water-closet on the premises. All these things help to keep the balance.[15]

This apologia for the novel was hardly likely to have been known to Bakhtin, yet it anticipates his theory in a remarkable way, especially in the polemical opposition it sets up between the novel and the canonized genres of tragedy and lyric poetry, in its invocation of Dostoevsky, and in the way it relates the novel's treatment of the human Word to its carnivalesque elements – represented here by the black tom-cat, the banana-skin and the water-closet. I have commented elsewhere on the carnivalesque in Lawrence's fiction, especially in *Mr Noon* and *The Lost Girl*, and on Dostoevskyean polyphony in *Women in Love*.[16] But the fact is that Bakhtin's theory of the novel applies equally well to all the other novelists I have mentioned in this essay.

To demonstrate this claim exhaustively here would obviously take too long. But recall that list of set texts I mentioned earlier, chosen to represent recent developments in British fiction, and consider how well they also answer to Bakhtin's theory of the novel: the carnival face-pulling, the parodying and travestying of academic discourse in *Lucky Jim*; the invented polyglossia, the *skaz* energy and vitality, the *Notes from Underground* subversiveness of *A Clockwork Orange*; the disconcerting hybridization of *The French Lieutenant's Woman*, its deliberately unresolved juxtaposition of nineteenth-century discourse with twentieth, and of two antithetical types of fiction categorized by Bakhtin as the existential adventure story and the social-psychological novel of everyday life; the parodying and travestying of literary genres in *Not to Disturb* – the whodunit, the Gothic novel, the Jacobean revenge tragedy; the violent clash of discourses – visionary, parodic, clinical, pornographic, documentary – in *Briefing for a Descent into Hell* and *The White Hotel*; the elaborate exploitation in *The History Man* of the social speech acts Bakhtin studied and classified under the heading of '*causerie*', especially the 'rejoinder' and the 'glance at someone else's word' – a feature of that particular text foregrounded by the author's refusal to make any authoritative judgement or interpretation of his characters, or to make us privy to their thoughts. Finally, *Money* is another *skaz* narrative in the *Notes from Underground* tradition, a demonic carnival, a suicide note from a character who indulges in every excess of the lower body, sexual and gastronomic, that the modern urban culture can provide, a repulsive character in many ways, yet one who retains an undeniable vitality by the sheer punk brilliance of his rhetoric; a hero or anti-hero who not only answers the author back, as Bakhtin said of Dostoevsky's heroes, but actually throws a punch at him.

As for my own contribution to contemporary British fiction, I must leave the Bakhtinian reading of that to others. I will only say that I have found Bakhtin's theory of the novel very useful when challenged to explain how I can write carnivalesque novels about academics while continuing to be one myself.

Chapter 2

Mimesis and diegesis in modern fiction

How does one begin to map a field as vast, as various as modern fiction? It seems a hopeless endeavour, and, in an absolute sense, it *is* hopeless. Even if one could hold all the relevant data in one's head at one time – which one cannot – and could formulate a typology into which they would all fit, some novelist would soon produce a work that eluded all one's categories, because art lives and develops by deviating unpredictably from aesthetic norms. Nevertheless the effort to generalize, to classify, has to be made; for without some conceptual apparatus for grouping and separating literary fictions criticism could hardly claim to be knowledge, but would be merely the accumulation of opinions about one damn novel after another. This is the justification for literary history, particularly that kind of literary history which has a generic or formal bias, looking for common conventions, strategies, techniques, beneath the infinite variety of subject matter. Such literary history breaks up the endless stream of literary production into manageable blocks or bundles, called 'periods' or 'schools' or 'movements' or 'trends' or 'subgenres'.

We are all familiar with a rough division of the fiction of the last 150 years into three phases, that of classic realism, that of modernism and that of post-modernism (though, it hardly needs saying, these phases overlap both chronologically and formally). And we are familiar with various attempts to break down these large, loose groupings into more delicate and discriminating subcategories. In the case of post-modernist fiction, for instance: transfiction, surfiction, metafiction, new journalism, nonfiction novel, faction, fabulation, *nouveau roman, nouveau nouveau roman*, irrealism, magic realism, and so on. Some of those terms are synonyms, or nearly so. Most of them invoke or imply the idea of the new. British writing rarely figures on such maps of post-modern fiction. Our post-modernism, it is widely believed, has consisted in ignoring, rather than trying to go beyond, the experiments of modernism, reviving and perpetuating the mode of classic realism which Joyce, Woolf and Co. thought they had despatched for good.

This kind of map-making usually has an ideological and, in the Popperian sense of the word, historicist motivation. The mode of classic realism, with its concern for coherence and causality in narrative structure, for the autonomy of the individual self in the presentation of character, for a readable homogeneity and urbanity of style, is equated with liberal human- ism, with empiricism, common sense and the presentation of bourgeois culture as a kind of nature. The confusions, distortions and disruptions of the post-modernist text, in contrast, reflect a view of the world as not merely subjectively constructed (as modernist fiction implied) but as absurd, meaningless, radically resistant to totalizing interpretation.

There is a certain truth in this picture, but it is a half-truth, and therefore a misleading one. The classic realist text was never as homogeneous, as consistent as the model requires; nor do post-modern novelists divide as neatly as it implies into complacent neorealist sheep and dynamic antirealist goats. (It hardly needs to be said that the ideology of the post-modernist avant-garde, reversing proverbial wisdom, prefers goats to sheep, John Barth's *Giles Goat-Boy* being one of its canonical texts.) Perhaps I have a personal interest in this issue, since I write as well as read contemporary fiction. I am dissatisfied with maps of contemporary fiction which take into account only the most deviant and marginal kinds of writing, leaving all the rest white space. But equally unsatisfactory is the bland, middlebrow, market-oriented reviewing of novels in newspapers and magazines which not only shies away from boldly experimental writing, but makes what one might call mainstream fiction seem technically less interesting and innov- ative than it often is.

Take, for example, the case of the contemporary British novelist, Fay Weldon. She is a successful and highly respected writer, but her work rarely figures in any discussion of post-modernism in the literary quarterlies. Fay Weldon has been pigeonholed as a feminist novelist, and the criticism of her work is almost exclusively thematic. Now there is no doubt that she *is* a feminist writer, but her handling of narrative is technically very interesting and subtly innovative, and her feminism gets its force precisely from her ability to defamiliarize her material in this way. Typically, her novels follow the fortunes of a heroine, or a group of women, over a longish time span, from childhood in the 1930s and 1940s to the present. The narrator is usually revealed at some point to be the central character, but the narrative discourse mostly uses a third-person reference, typical of traditional author- ial narration, often claiming the privileged insight into the interiority of several characters that belongs to that kind of narration, and not to the confessional autobiographical mode. The tense system is similarly unstable, switching erratically between the narrative preterite and the historical pre- sent. There is very artful use of condensed duration, that is, the summary narration of events which would have occupied a considerable length of time in reality, and which would be sufficiently important to the people involved to be worth lingering over in a more conventional kind of fiction.

This creates a tone of comic despair about the follies and contradictions of human relations, and especially the fate of women. Here is a specimen from Fay Weldon's novel *Female Friends* (1975). Oliver is being promiscuously unfaithful to his wife Chloe and she complains.

'For God's sake,' he says, irritated, 'go out and have a good time yourself. I don't mind.'
He lies in his teeth, but she doesn't know this. She only wants Oliver. It irks him (he says) and cramps his style. He who only wants her to be happy, but whose creativity (he says) demands its nightly dinner of fresh young female flesh.
Gradually the pain abates, or at any rate runs underground. Chloe gets involved in Inigo's school: she helps in the library every Tuesday and escorts learners to the swimming pool on Fridays. She helps at the local birth control clinic and herself attends the fertility sessions, in the hope of increasing her own.
Oh, Oliver! He brings home clap and gives it to Chloe. They are both soon and simply cured. His money buys the most discreet and mirthful doctors; Oliver himself is more shaken than Chloe, and her patience is rewarded: he becomes bored with his nocturnal wanderings and stays home and watches television instead.[1]

The first paragraph of this passage is a familiar kind of combination of direct speech and narrative, deviant only in the use of the present tense for the narrative. The second paragraph exerts the privilege of authorial omniscience somewhat paradoxically, since we know that Chloe is herself narrating the story. It also uses a deviant style of representing speech, apparently quoting Oliver in part, and reporting him in part. The effect of direct quotation arises from the congruence of tense between Oliver's speech and the narrator's speech ('it irks . . . he says'); the effect of reported speech arises from the use of the third-person pronoun ('it irks *him*'). This equivocation between quoted and reported speech allows the narrator to slide in a very loaded paraphrase of Oliver's stated need for young women – it is highly unlikely that he himself used that cannibalistic image, the 'nightly dinner of fresh young female flesh'. The penultimate paragraph uses a summary style of narration that seems quite natural because it is describing routine, habitual actions of little narrative interest. But summary is foregrounded in the last paragraph because applied to events which are full of emotional and psychological pain, embarrassment and recrimination – the sort of thing we are used to having presented scenically in fiction.

One way of describing this mode of writing would be to say that it is a mode of telling rather than showing, or, to use a more venerable terminology, of diegesis rather than mimesis. It seems to me a distinctively postmodern phenomenon in that it deviates from the norms of both classic realism and of modernism, as do, more spectacularly, the writers of the

post-modernist avant-garde in America. Indeed, if we are looking for a
formal, as distinct from an ideological, definition of post-modernism, we
could, I believe, look profitably at its foregrounding of diegesis. The simple
Platonic distinction between mimesis and diegesis, however, is inadequate
to cope with all the varieties and nuances of novelistic discourse. In what
follows I want to combine it – or refine it – with the more complex
discourse typology of the Russian post-formalists (who may have been one
and the same person in some writings) Valentin Volosinov and Mikhail
Bakhtin.

In Book III of *The Republic*, Plato distinguishes between diegesis, the
representation of actions in the poet's own voice, and mimesis, the representation of action in the imitated voices of the character or characters. Pure
diegesis is exemplified by dithyramb, a kind of hymn. (Later poeticians put
lyric poetry into this category – a serious mistake according to Gérard
Genette,[2] but one which need not concern us here.) Pure mimesis is exemplified by drama. Epic is a mixed form, combining both diegesis and mimesis,
that is, combining authorial report, description, summary and commentary
on the one hand, with the quoted direct speech of the characters on the
other. It is important not to confuse 'mimesis' in this sense with the wider
application of the term by Plato (in, for instance, Book X of *The Republic*)
and by Aristotle (in *The Poetics*), to mean imitation as opposed to reality.
In that sense all art is imitation. In Book III Plato is concerned with two
types of discourse by which verbal art imitates reality. To make the distinction clear, Plato (in the person of Socrates) cites the opening scene of *The
Iliad*, where the Trojan priest Chryses asks the Greek leaders Menelaus
and Agamemnon to release his daughter for a ransom.

> You know then, that as far as the lines
>   He prayed the Achaians all,
>   But chiefly the two rulers of the people,
>   Both sons of Atreus,
> the poet himself speaks, he never tries to turn our thoughts from himself
> or to suggest that anyone else is speaking; but after this he speaks as if
> he was himself Chryses, and tries his best to make us think that the
> priest, an old man, is speaking and not Homer.[3]

In other words, the confrontation is introduced diegetically by the authorial
narrator, and then presented mimetically in the speeches of the characters.
To make the point even clearer, Plato rewrites the scene diegetically, trans-
posing direct or quoted speech into indirect or reported speech, for example:

> Agamemnon fell into a rage, telling him [Chryses] to go away now and
> not to come back, or his staff and the wreathings of the god might not
> help him; before he would give her up, he said, she should grow old

with him in Argos; told him to be off and not to provoke him, if he wanted to get home safe.[4]

The original speech in Homer is translated by Rieu as follows:

'Old man' he said, 'do not let me catch you loitering by the hollow ships today, nor coming back again, or you may find the god's staff and chaplet a very poor defence. Far from agreeing to set your daughter free, I intend her to grow old in Argos, in my house, a long way from her own country, working at the loom and sharing my bed. Off with you now, and do not provoke me if you want to save your skin.'[5]

It is evident that, though there is a clear difference between the two passages, the individuality of Agamemnon's speech is not wholly obliterated by the narrator's speech in the Platonic rewriting, and could be obliterated only by some much more drastic summary, such as Gérard Genette suggests in his discussion of this passage: 'Agamemnon angrily refused Chryses' request.'[6] Plato conceived of the epic as a mixed form in the sense that it simply alternated two distinct kinds of discourse – the poet's speech and the characters' speech – and this is in fact true of Homer; but his own example shows the potential within narrative for a much more complex mixing, more like a fusing, of the two modes, in reported speech. This potential was to be elaborately exploited by the novel, which uses reported speech extensively – not only to represent speech, but to represent thoughts and feelings which are not actually uttered aloud. This is where Volosinov and Bakhtin are useful, because they focus on the way the novelistic treatment of reported speech tends towards an intermingling of authorial speech and characters' speech, of diegesis and mimesis.

In *Marxism and the Philosophy of Language* (1930) Volosinov distinguishes between what he calls (borrowing the terms from Wölfflin's art history) the linear style of reporting, and the pictorial style. The linear style preserves a clear boundary between the reported speech and the reporting context (that is, the author's speech) in terms of information or reference, while suppressing the textual individuality of the reported speech by imposing its own linguistic register, or attributing to the characters exactly the same register as the author's. The linear style is characteristic of pre-novelistic narrative, and is associated by Volosinov especially with what he calls authoritarian and rationalistic dogmatism in the medieval and Enlightenment periods. I suggest that *Rasselas* (1759) affords a late example of what Volosinov calls the linear style:

'. . . I sat feasting on intellectual luxury, regardless alike of the examples of the earth and the instructions of the planets. Twenty months are passed. Who shall restore them?'
   These sorrowful meditations fastened upon his mind; he passed four months in resolving to lose no more time in idle resolves, and was

awakened to more vigorous exertion by hearing a maid, who had broken a porcelain cup, remark that what cannot be repaired is not to be regretted.

This was obvious; and Rasselas reproached himself that he had not discovered it – having not known, or not considered, how many useful hints are obtained by chance, and how often the mind, hurried by her own ardour to distant views, neglects the truths that lie open before her. He for a few hours regretted his regret, and from that time bent his whole mind upon the means of escaping from the Valley of Happiness.[7]

In addition to the quoted direct speech of Rasselas at the beginning of the extract, there are two kinds of reported speech here: the reported utterance of the maid, and the reported inner speech, or thoughts, of Rasselas. All are linguistically assimilated to the dominant register of the authorial discourse. The author, Rasselas, and even the maid all seem to speak the same kind of language – balanced, abstract, polite; but the referential contours of the reported speech are very clearly demarcated and judged by the authorial speech. This is typical of Volosinov's linear style and Plato's diegesis: linguistic homogeneity – informational discrimination. It is one of the reasons why we hesitate to describe *Rasselas* as a novel, even though it postdates the development of the English novel. From a novel we expect a more realistic rendering of the individuality and variety of human speech than we get in *Rasselas* – both in direct or quoted speech and in reported speech or thought. (But note that there is a kind of tonal resemblance between the passage from *Rasselas* and the passage from Fay Weldon's *Female Friends* – the cool, confident, detached ironic tone that is generated by the *summary* nature of the narrative discourse – summary being characteristic of diegesis, or what Volosinov calls the linear style.) For Volosinov, naturally influenced by Russian literary history, the rise of the novel virtually coincides with the development of the *pictorial* style of reported speech, in which author's speech and character's speech, diegesis and mimesis interpenetrate. The evolution of the English novel was more gradual.

The rise of the English novel in the eighteenth century began with the discovery of new possibilities of mimesis in prose narrative, through the use of characters as narrators – the pseudo-autobiographers of Defoe, the pseudo-correspondents of Richardson – thus making the narrative discourse a mimesis of an act of diegesis, diegesis at a second remove. These devices brought about a quantum leap in realistic illusion and immediacy, but they tended to confirm Plato's ethical disapproval of mimesis, his fears about the morally debilitating effects of skilful mimesis of imperfect personages. However highminded were the intentions of Defoe (which is doubtful) or of Richardson (which is not) there is no way in which the reader can be prevented from delighting in and even identifying with Moll Flanders or Lovelace in even their wickedest actions. Fielding, his mind trained in a classical school, restored the diegetic balance in his comic-epic-poem-in-prose: the individuality of characters is represented, and relished, in the reproduction of their distinctive speech – Fielding, unlike Johnson in *Rasselas*, does not make all the characters speak in the same register as himself – but the author's speech (and values) are quite clearly distinguished from the characters' speech and values; mimesis and diegesis are never confused. The same is true of Scott, in whose work there is, notoriously, a stark contrast between the polite literary English of the narrator's discourse, and the richly textured colloquial dialect speech of the Scottish characters – a disparity that becomes particularly striking in the shift from direct to reported speech or thought:

> 'He's a gude creature,' said she, 'and a kind – it's a pity he has sae willyard a powny.' And she immediately turned her thoughts to the important journey which she had commenced, reflecting with pleasure, that, according to her habits of life and of undergoing fatigue, she was now amply or even superfluously provided with the means of encountering the expenses of the road, up and down from London, and all other expenses whatever.[8]

The classic nineteenth-century novel followed the example of Fielding and Scott in maintaining a fairly even balance between mimesis and diegesis, showing and telling, scene and summary; but it also broke down the clear distinction between diegesis and mimesis in the representation of thought and feeling, through what Volosinov called the 'pictorial style' of reported speech. In this, the individuality of the reported speech or thought is retained even as the author's speech 'permeates the reported speech with its own intentions – humour, irony, love or hate, enthusiasm or scorn'.[9] Let me illustrate this with a passage from *Middlemarch* (1871–2):

> She was open, ardent, and not in the least self-admiring; indeed, it was pretty to see how her imagination adorned her sister Celia with attractions altogether superior to her own, and if any gentleman appeared to come to the Grange from some other motive than that of seeing Mr Brooke, she concluded that he must be in love with Celia: Sir James Chettam, for example, whom she constantly considered from Celia's point of view, inwardly debating whether it would be good for Celia to accept him. That he should be regarded as a suitor for herself would have seemed to her a ridiculous irrelevance. Dorothea, with all her eagerness to know the truths of life, retained very childlike ideas about marriage. She felt sure that she would have accepted the judicious Hooker, if she had been born in time to save him from that wretched mistake he made in matrimony: or John Milton when his blindness had come on; or any of the other great men whose odd habits it would have been glorious piety to endure; but an amiable handsome baronet, who said 'Exactly' to her remarks even when she expressed uncertainty, – how could he affect her

as a lover? The really delightful marriage must be that where your husband was a sort of father, and could teach you even Hebrew, if you
wished it.[10]

Up to, and including, the sentence 'Dorothea . . . retained very childlike
ideas about marriage', this passage is diegetic: the narrator describes the
character of Dorothea authoritatively, in words that Dorothea could not
use about herself without contradiction (she cannot, for instance, acknowledge that her ideas are childlike without ceasing to hold them). Then the
deixis becomes more problematical. The tag, 'she felt' is an ambiguous
signal to the reader, since it can introduce either an objective report by the
narrator or subjective reflection by the character. Colloquial phrases in the
sequel, such as 'that wretched mistake' and 'when his blindness had come
on' seem to be the words in which Dorothea herself would have articulated
these ideas, though the equally colloquial 'odd habits' does not. Why does
it not? Because, in unexpected collocation with 'great men' ('great men
whose odd habits') it seems too rhetorical an irony for Dorothea – it is a
kind of oxymoron – and so we attribute it to the narrator. But that is not
to imply that Dorothea is incapable of irony. 'Who said "Exactly" to her
remarks even when she expressed uncertainty' – do we not infer that Sir
James's illogicality has been noted by Dorothea herself in just that crisp,
dismissive way? Then what about the immediately succeeding phrase –
'how could he affect her as a lover?' If the immediately preceding phrase
is attributed to Dorothea, as I suggest, then it would be natural to ascribe
this one to her also – but a contradiction then arises. For if Dorothea can
formulate the question 'How can Sir James affect me as a lover?' her
alleged unconsciousness of her own attractions to visiting gentlemen is
compromised. Is the question, then, put by the narrator, appealing directly
to the reader, over the heroine's head, to acknowledge the plausibility of
her behaviour, meaning, 'You do see, gentle reader, why it never crossed
Dorothea's mind that Sir James Chettam was a possible match for her?'
There *is* such an implication, but the reason given – that Sir James said
'Exactly' when Dorothea expressed uncertainty – seems too trivial for the
narrator to draw the conclusion, 'How could he affect her as a lover?' The
fact is that diegesis and mimesis are fused together inextricably here – and
for a good reason: for there is a sense in which Dorothea knows what the
narrator knows – namely, that Sir James is sexually attracted to her – but
is repressing the thought, on account of her determination to marry an
intellectual father figure. When Celia finally compels Dorothea to face the
truth of the matter, the narrator tells us that 'she was not less angry because
certain details asleep in her memory were now awakened to confirm the
unwelcome revelation'. One of these details was surely that very habit of
Sir James of saying 'Exactly' when she expressed uncertainty – a sign of his
admiration, deference and anxiety to please rather than of his stupidity.

Here, then, the character's voice and the author's voice are so tightly interwoven that it is impossible at times to disentangle them; and the author's irony, consequently, is affectionate, filled by a warm regard for Dorothea's individuality – very different from Johnson's judicial irony in the passage from *Rasselas*.

In the next stage of the novel's development, Volosinov observes, the reported speech is not merely allowed to retain a certain measure of autonomous life within the authorial context, but actually itself comes to dominate authorial speech in the discourse as a whole. 'The authorial context loses the greater objectivity it normally commands in comparison with reported speech. It begins to be perceived and even recognizes itself as if it were subjective.' Volosinov notes that this is often associated with the delegation of the authorial task to a narrator who cannot 'bring to bear against [the] subjective position [of the other characters] a more authoritative and objective world'.[11] In the Russian novel, it seems, Dostoevsky initiated this second phase in the development of the pictorial style. In the English novel I think we would point to the work of James and Conrad at the turn of the century: James's use of unreliable first-person narrators (*The Turn of the Screw*) or sustained focalization of the narrative through the perspective of characters whose perceptions are narrowly limited, with minimal authorial comment and interpretation ('In the Cage', *The Ambassadors*); Conrad's use of multiple framing via multiple narrators, none of whom is invested with ultimate interpretative authority (*Lord Jim*, *Nostromo*).

At this point it is useful to switch to Bakhtin's typology of literary discourse. There are three main categories:

1. *The direct speech of the author*. This corresponds to Plato's diegesis.
2. *Represented speech*. This includes Plato's mimesis – i.e. the quoted direct speech of the characters; but also reported speech in the pictorial style.
3. *Doubly-oriented speech*, that is, speech which not only refers to something in the world but refers to another speech act by another addresser.

Bakhtin subdivides this third type of discourse into four categories, stylization, parody, *skaz* (the Russian term for oral narration) and what he calls 'dialogue'. Dialogue means here, not the quoted direct speech of the characters, but discourse which alludes to an *absent* speech act. In stylization, parody and *skaz*, the other speech act is 'reproduced with a new intention'; in 'dialogue' it 'shapes the author's speech while remaining outside its boundaries'. An important type of dialogic discourse in this sense is 'hidden polemic', in which a speaker not only refers to an object in the world but simultaneously replies to, contests, or makes concessions to some other real or anticipated or hypothetical statement about the same object.

These categories all have their subcategories which can be combined and shifted around in the system in a somewhat bewildering way, but the basic distinctions are clear, and I think useful. Let me try and illustrate them with reference to *Ulysses*, a text as encyclopaedic in this respect as in all others.

1. *The direct speech of the author*. This is the narrator who speaks in, for instance, the first lines of the book:

> Stately, plump Buck Mulligan came from the stairhead, bearing a bowl of lather on which a mirror and razor lay crossed.[12]

This is the purely diegetic plane of the text. The sentence describes Mulligan emerging on to the roof of the Martello tower not as Stephen Dedalus sees him (Stephen is below), nor as Mulligan sees himself, but as seen by an objective narrator. Since most narration in *Ulysses* is focalized, and stylistically coloured, by a character's consciousness, or permeated by doubly-oriented speech, such examples are comparatively rare. The author's speech as a distinct medium of communication is scarcely perceptible, in accordance with Joyce's aesthetic of impersonality: 'The artist, like the God of the creation, remains within or behind or beyond or above his handiwork, invisible, refined out of existence, indifferent, paring his fingernails.'[13]

2. *Represented speech*. This includes all the dialogue in the usual sense of that word – the quoted direct speech of the characters, which Joyce preferred to mark with an introductory dash, rather than the usual inverted commas. This category also includes all the passages of interior monologue – mimesis in Plato's terms, but representing thought instead of uttered speech. Molly Bloom's reverie in the last episode, 'Penelope', is perhaps the purest example:

> Yes because he never did a thing like that before as ask to get his breakfast in bed with a couple of eggs since the City Arms hotel when he used to be pretending to be laid up with a sick voice doing his highness to make himself interesting for that old faggot Mrs Riordan that he thought he had a great leg of . . .
>
> (p. 608)

. . . and so on, for twenty thousand uninterrupted words.

The presentation of the thought of Stephen and Leopold Bloom is more varied and complex, combining interior monologue with free indirect speech[14] and focalized narration – in short, a mixture of mimesis and diegesis, in which mimesis dominates. Here, for example, is Bloom in the pork-butcher's shop in 'Calypso':

> A kidney oozed bloodgouts on the willowpatterned dish: the last. He stood by the nextdoor girl at the counter. Would she buy it too, calling the items from a slip in her hand? Chapped: washingsoda. And a pound

and a half of Denny's sausages. His eyes rested on her vigorous hips. Woods his name is. Wonder what he does. Wife is oldish. New blood. No followers allowed. Strong pair of arms. Whacking a carpet on the clothesline. She does whack it, by George. The way her crooked skirt swings at each whack.

(p. 48)

The various kinds of speech in this passage may be classified as follows:
A kidney oozed bloodgouts on the willowpatterned dish: Narrative (focalized through Bloom).
the last. Interior monologue.
He stood by the nextdoor girl at the counter. Narrative (focalized through Bloom).
Would she buy it too, calling the items from a slip in her hand? Free indirect speech.
Chapped: washingsoda. Interior monologue.
And a pound and a half of Denny's sausages. Free direct speech (i.e., the girl's words are quoted but not tagged or marked off typographically from Bloom's).
His eyes rested on her vigorous hips. Narrative (focalized through Bloom).
Woods his name is, etc. (to end of paragraph). Interior monologue.
   3. *Doubly-oriented speech.* In the later episodes of *Ulysses*, the authorial narrator who, however self-effacing, was a stable, consistent and reliable voice in the text, disappears; and his place is taken by various manifestations of Bakhtin's doubly-oriented discourse. 'Stylization' is well exemplified by 'Nausicaa', in which Joyce borrows the discourse of cheap women's magazines and makes it serve his own expressive purpose:

> Gerty was dressed simply but with the instinctive taste of a votary of Dame Fashion for she felt there was just a might that he might be out. A neat blouse of electric blue, self tinted by dolly dyes (because it was expected in the *Lady's Pictorial* that electric blue would be worn) with a smart vee opening down to the division and kerchief pocket (in which she always kept a piece of cottonwool scented with her favourite perfume because the handkerchief spoiled the sit) and a navy three quarter skirt cut to the stride showed off her slim graceful figure to perfection.

(p. 287)

Who speaks here? Clearly it is not the author – he would not use such debased, cliché-ridden language. But we cannot take it, either, to be the author's report of Gerty's thought in free indirect speech. Free indirect speech can always be transposed into plausible direct speech (first person, present tense) and clearly that would be impossible in this case. It is a written, not a spoken style, and a very debased one. It is neither diegesis nor mimesis, nor a blend of the two, but a kind of pseudodiegesis achieved by the mimesis not of a character's speech but of a discourse, the discourse of cheap women's magazines at the turn of the century. (In fact, the style of today's romantic fiction of the Mills & Boon type displays a remarkable consistency and continuity with Gerty's reading. Compare, for example: 'Her dress was white, made from fine Indian cotton. Skimpy little shoulder-straps led to a bodice which was covered with layers of narrow, delicate lace finishing at the waist where it fitted Gina's slender figure to perfection.'[15]) It is essential to the effect of 'Nausicaa' that we should be aware of the style's double reference – to Gerty's experience, and to its own original discursive context. We are not to suppose that Gerty literally thinks in sentences lifted from the *Lady's Pictorial*. But the style of the *Lady's Pictorial* subtly manipulated, heightened, 'objectified' (Bakhtin's word) vividly communicates a sensibility pathetically limited to the concepts and values disseminated by such a medium. The author, like a ventriloquist, is a silent presence in the text, but his very silence is the background against which we appreciate his creative skill.

This is stylization – not the same thing as parody. Parody, as Bakhtin points out, borrows a style and applies it to expressive purposes that are in some sense the reverse of the original purpose, or at least incongruous with it. For example, one of the headlines in 'Aeolus' parodies the style of American tabloid journalism by applying it to an episode in classical antiquity recalled in more appropriate language by Professor MacHugh:

SOPHIST WALLOPS HAUGHTY HELEN
SQUARE ON PROBOSCIS. SPARTANS GNASH
MOLARS. ITHACANS VOW PEN IS CHAMP
– You remind me of Antisthenes, the professor said, a disciple of Georgias, the sophist. It is said of him that none could tell if he were bitterer against others or against himself. He was the son of a noble and a bondwoman. And he wrote a book in which he took away the palm of beauty from Argive Helen and handed it to poor Penelope.

(p. 122)

The anonymous narrator of 'Cyclops' provides an example of Irish *skaz* – the anecdotal chat of pubs and bars:

I was just passing the time of day with old Troy of the D. M. P. at the corner of Arbour Hill there and be damned but a bloody sweep came along and he near drove his gear into my eye. I turned around to let him have the weight of my tongue when who should I see dodging along Stony Batter only Joe Hynes.

– Lo, Joe, says I. How are you blowing? Did you see that bloody chimney-sweep near shove my eye out with his brush?

(p. 240)

We never discover who this narrator is, or to whom he is talking, or in what context. But clearly it is oral narration – *skaz*. There is no perceptible difference, either in syntax or type of vocabulary, between the discourse before and after the dash that in *Ulysses* introduces direct or quoted speech.

Of all the many styles in *Ulysses*, perhaps the most baffling to critical analysis and evaluation has been that of 'Eumaeus', a style which Stuart Gilbert classified as 'Narrative: old'. Rambling, elliptical, cliché-ridden, it is, we are told, meant to reflect the nervous and physical exhaustion of the two protagonists. As with 'Nausicaa', we cannot read the discourse either as author's narration or as representation of Bloom's consciousness, though it does seem expressive of Bloom's character in some respects: his friendliness bordering on servility, his fear of rejection, his reliance on proverbial wisdom. Bakhtin's definition of 'hidden polemic' seems to fit it very well: 'Any speech that is servile or overblown, any speech that is determined beforehand not to be itself, any speech replete with reservations, concessions, loopholes and so on. Such speech seems to cringe in the presence, or at the presentiment of, some other person's statement, reply, objection'.[16]

> *En route* to his taciturn, and, not to put too fine a point on it, not yet perfectly sober companion, Mr Bloom who at all events, was in complete possession of his faculties, never more so, in fact, disgustingly sober, spoke a word of caution re the dangers of nighttown, women of ill fame and swell mobsmen, which, barely permissible once in a while though not as a habitual practice, was of the nature of a regular deathtrap for young fellows of his age particularly if they had acquired drinking habits under the influence of liquor unless you knew a little jiujitsu for every contingency as even a fellow on the broad of his back could administer a nasty kick if you didn't look out.
>
> (p. 502)

Let me return to the simple tripartite historical scheme with which I began – classic realism, modernism, post-modernism – and see what it looks like in the light of the discourse typology of Plato, Volosinov and Bakhtin. The classic realist text, we may say, was characterized by a balanced and harmonized combination of mimesis and diegesis, reported speech and reporting context, authorial speech and represented speech. The modern novel evolved through an increasing dominance of mimesis over diegesis. Narrative was focalized through character with extensive use of 'pictorial' reported speech or delegated to narrators with mimetically objectified styles. Diegesis, to be sure, does not completely disappear from the modernist novel, but it does become increasingly intractable. One can see the strain in those novelists who could least easily do without it: in Hardy, Forster and Lawrence. Hardy hedges his bets, equivocates, qualifies or contradicts his own authorial dicta, uses tortuous formulae to avoid taking responsi-

bility for authorial description and generalization. Forster tries to accommodate diegesis by making a joke of it:

> To Margaret – I hope that it will not set the reader against her – the
> station of King's Cross had always suggested Infinity [. . .] if you think
> this is ridiculous, remember that it is not Margaret who is telling you
> about it.[17]

At other times in *Howards End*, with less success, Forster tries to smuggle
in his authorial comments as if they were his heroine's.

> Margaret greeted her lord with peculiar tenderness on the morrow.
> Mature as he was, she might yet be able to help him to the building of
> the rainbow bridge that should connect the prose in us with the passion.
> Without it we are meaningless fragments, half monks, half beasts, uncon-
> nected arches that have never joined into a man. With it love is born,
> and alights on the highest curve, glowing against the grey, sober against
> the fire.[18]

It is not just the rather purple diction, but the slide from narrative preterite
to 'gnomic present' in the tenses that gives away the author's voice.

Lawrence uses the same technique pervasively – for example in the famous
passage where Lady Chatterley drives through Tevershall. She passes the
school where a singing lesson is in progress:

> Anything more unlike song, spontaneous song, would be impossible to
> imagine; a strange bawling yell that followed the outlines of a tune. It
> was not like savages: savages have subtle rhythms. It was not like animals:
> animals mean something when they yell. It was like nothing on earth
> and it was called singing.[19]

The gnomic present tense – 'savages *have*', 'animals *mean*' – indicates that
this is not just a transcription of Connie Chatterley's thoughts – that the
author is with her, speaking for her, lecturing us over her shoulder.

It has been often enough observed that Lawrence did not always live up
to his own prescription that the novelist should keep his thumb out of the
pan; but the prescription itself is very much in the spirit of modernism.
Impersonality, 'dramatization', 'showing' rather than 'telling', are the cardi-
nal principles of the modernist fictional aesthetic, as variously formulated
and practised by James, Conrad, Ford, Woolf and Joyce. This aesthetic
required either the suppression or the displacement of diegesis: suppression
by the focalization of the narrative through the characters; displacement by
the use of surrogate narrators, whose own discourse is stylized or objectified
– that is, deprived of the author's authority, made itself an object of
interpretation. In James, Conrad, Ford, these narrators are naturalized as
characters with some role to play in the story, but in *Ulysses* they do not
have this validation: as I have tried to show they are conjured out of the

air by the author's ventriloquism. This was the most radically experimental aspect of *Ulysses*, the aspect which even sympathetic friends like Pound and Sylvia Beach found hard to accept. They found it difficult to accept, I suggest, because these elaborate exercises in stylization and parody and dialogic discourse could not be justified, unlike the fragmentary, allusive passages of interior monologue, as a mimesis of character. It is still a common complaint among some readers of *Ulysses* that the introduction of a multiplicity of discourses which have no psychologically mimetic function in such episodes as 'Sirens', 'Cyclops', 'Oxen of the Sun' and 'Ithaca', is mere pedantry and self-indulgence, trivializing the human content of the book. But when we put the enterprise in the perspective of Bakhtin's poetics of fiction we immediately see that in opening up the novel to the play of multiple parodic and stylized discourses Joyce was aiming at a more comprehensive representation of reality than the stylistic decorum of the realist novel allowed; we see how this aim was organically linked to the project of writing a kind of modern epic, or mock epic, a comic inversion of and commentary upon the archetype of Homer. This is Bakhtin in 'Epic and the Novel':

> any and every straightforward genre, any and every direct discourse – epic, tragic, lyric, philosophical – may and indeed must have itself become the object of representation, the object of a parodic, travestying 'mimicry'. It is as if such mimicry rips the word away from its object, disunifies the two, shows that a given straightforward generic word – epic or tragic – is one-sided, bounded, incapable of exhausting the object; the process of parodying forces us to experience those sides of the object that are not otherwise included in a given genre or a given style. Parodic-travestying literature introduces the permanent corrective of laughter, of a critique on the one-sided seriousness of the lofty direct word, the corrective of reality that is always richer, more fundamental and most importantly *too contradictory and heteroglot* to be fitted into a high and straightforward genre.[20]

Bakhtin might have been writing about *Ulysses* in that passage. In fact, he was writing about the fourth play of classical Greek drama, the satyr play, which traditionally followed the tragic trilogy and mocked its grandeur and seriousness. And he notes in passing that 'the figure of the "comic Odysseus", a parodic travesty of his high epic and tragic image, was one of the most popular figures of satyr plays, of ancient Doric farce and pre-Aristophanic comedy, as well as of a whole series of minor comic epics'.[21] Bloom has an ancient genealogy.

The resistance Joyce's readers often feel when they first encounter the later episodes of *Ulysses* is likely to be even greater in the case of *Finnegans Wake*, a book written entirely in doubly-, or rather trebly-, quadruply-, multiply-oriented discourse. Once again, Bakhtin's theory of the novel, and especially his emphasis on the crucial role of Rabelais in assimilating the folk tradition of carnival into literary narrative, seems very relevant. When Bakhtin writes about *Gargantua and Pantagruel*, he might be writing about *Finnegans Wake*:

> we have the first attempt of any consequence to structure the entire picture of the world around the human conceived as a body . . . But it is not the individual human body, trapped in an irreversible life sequence that becomes a character – rather it is the impersonal body, the body of the human race as a whole, being born, living, dying the most varied deaths, being born again, an impersonal body that is manifested in its structure, and in all the processes of its life.[22]

The Rabelaisian body and surely, we must say, the body of HCE, is a body defined by the organs of self-transgression, the bowels and the phallus, mouth and anus, a body perpetually in the process of becoming, eating and defecating, copulating, giving birth and dying at the same time through the displacements and condensations of carnival and dream (for what is dream but the carnival of the unconscious? what is carnival but a licensed communal waking dream?). According to Bakhtin, the two crucial ingredients in the Rabelaisian project, which made the novel possible, were *laughter* – the mockery of any and every type of discourse in the folk-carnival tradition, and what he called 'polyglossia', the 'interanimation of languages', such as obtained between Latin and the vernaculars at the Renaissance. Laughter and the interanimation of languages were also the vital ingredients of *Finnegans Wake*.

For most of his contemporaries, Joyce's greatest achievement was his mimetic rendering of the stream of consciousness within individual subjects, and this is what other novelists, like Woolf and Faulkner, tended to learn from him. 'Let us present the atoms as they fall upon the mind in the order in which they fall, let us trace the pattern, however disconnected and incoherent in appearance, which each sight or incident scores upon the consciousness,'[23] exhorted Virginia Woolf in 1919, when the early episodes of *Ulysses* were first appearing in print. In principle, it was through interior monologue – the unvoiced, fragmentary, associative inner speech of the subject – that this programme could be most completely fulfilled. Yet Virginia Woolf herself never used sustained interior monologue, except in *The Waves*, where it is so artificial as to have very little mimetic force. In her most characteristic work an impersonal but eloquent authorial narrator hovers over the characters and links together their streams of consciousness by a fluid blend of authorial report, free indirect speech and fragments of free direct speech and interior monologue. Joyce himself, as I have already remarked, uses undiluted interior monologue only in 'Penelope', and that to a large extent is what Dorrit Cohn calls a memory monologue[24] – that is, Molly is recalling past events rather than recording the atoms of experience in the order in which they fall upon her mind. *The Sound and the Fury* is also made up of memory monologues. The characters are narrating their stories to themselves, and we, as it were, overhear their narrations. The effect is not in essence very different from an old-fashioned epistolary or journal novel, though of course much more flexible and interiorized. In this way, mimesis turns back into a second-order diegesis – as it can hardly fail to do in narrative.

In pursuing mimetic methods to their limits, modernist fiction discovered that you cannot abolish the author, you can only suppress or displace him. Post-modernism says, in effect: so why not let him back into the text? The reintroduction of the author's speech, the revival of diegesis, has taken many forms. There is a conservative form – a return to something like the balanced combination of mimesis and diegesis of the nineteenth-century novel. The novels of Mauriac and Greene would be examples. 'The exclusion of the author can go too far,' said Greene in his 1945 essay on Mauriac. 'Even the author, poor devil, has a right to exist, and M. Mauriac reaffirms that right.'[25] The note is defensive, however, and Greene's own use of diegesis has been discreet. Very often in this kind of neorealist post-modern fiction the narrator is a character, but with little or no stylization of his discourse in Bakhtin's sense. The distance between the authorial norms and the character's norms is hardly perceptible. The narrator's perspective is limited, but as far as it goes, reliable. C. P. Snow's novels might be cited as an example.

More obviously continuous with modernism are those novels in which the discourse of the characterized narrator is doubly-oriented in Bakhtin's sense: for example, stylized *skaz* in *The Catcher in the Rye*, parodic *skaz* in Mailer's *Why Are We in Vietnam?*, hidden polemic in Nabokov's *Pale Fire*. Some post-modernist novels combine a whole spectrum of stylized, parodic and dialogic narrative discourses – e.g. John Barth's *Letters*, or Gilbert Sorrentino's *Mulligan Stew*.

How, then, does the post-modernist use of narrators differ from the modernist use of narrators? I would suggest that one difference is the emphasis on narration as such in post-modernist fiction. The narrators of modernist novels – e.g. the teacher of languages in Conrad's *Under Western Eyes*, or Dowell in Ford's *The Good Soldier*, must pretend to be *amateur* narrators, disclaiming any literary skill even while they display the most dazzling command of time shift, symbolism, scenic construction, etc. The narrators of post-modernist fiction are more likely to be explicit about the problems and processes involved in the act of narration, and very often the narrators are themselves writers with a close, sometimes incestuous relationship to the author. I find particularly interesting those post-modernist works in which diegesis is foregrounded by the explicit appearance in the text of the author as maker of his own fiction, the fiction we are reading. There is an instance of this towards the end of Margaret Drabble's recent novel *The Middle Ground* which brings out the distinction between modernist and post-modernist writing by reminding us of one of the great exponents of the former, Virginia Woolf:

[. . .] how good that it should end so well, and even as she was thinking this, looking round her family circle, feeling as she sat there a sense of immense calm, strength, centrality, as though she were indeed the centre of a circle, in the most old-fashioned of ways, a moving circle – oh, there is no language left to describe such things, we have called it all so much in question, but imagine a circle even so, a circle and moving spheres, for this is her house and there she sits, she has everything and nothing, I give her everything and nothing [. . .].[26]

Here Margaret Drabble evokes a Woolfian epiphany (the allusion to Mrs Ramsay's dinner party in *To the Lighthouse*, whether conscious or not, is inescapable) but at the same time wryly admits the arbitrariness of its construction. In this she shows herself to be not a neorealist (as she is usually categorized, and as her early work certainly encouraged one to think) but a post-modernist.

About three-quarters of the way through Joseph Heller's novel *Good as Gold*, one of its unnumbered chapters begins:

Once again Gold found himself preparing to lunch with someone – Spotty Weinrock – and the thought arose that he was spending an awful lot of time in this book eating and talking. There was not much else to be done with him. I *was* putting him into bed a lot with Andrea and keeping his wife and children conveniently in the background. For Acapulco, I contemplated fabricating a hectic mixup which would include a sensual Mexican television actress and a daring attempt to escape in the nude through a stuck second-story bedroom window, while a jealous lover crazed on American drugs was beating down the door with his fists and Belle or packs of wild dogs were waiting below. Certainly he would soon meet a schoolteacher with four children with whom he would fall madly in love, and I would shortly hold out to him the tantalising promise of becoming the country's first Jewish Secretary of State, a promise I did not intend to keep.[27]

Up to this point, Heller's novel, though its satirical comedy about Jewish family life and Washington politics is mannered and stylized, has consistently maintained an illusion of referring to the real world – it has, so to speak, challenged us to deny that the real world is as crazy as Heller represents it. But this passage violates the realistic code in two very obvious, and for the reader disconcerting, ways: firstly, by admitting that Gold is a character, in a book, and not a person, in the world; and secondly by emphasizing that this character has no autonomy, but is completely at the disposition of his creator, who is not (or rather once was not) sure what

to do with him. Two simple words have a powerful shock effect in this
passage, because they have been hitherto suppressed in the narrative discourse in the interests of mimesis: *book* (referring to the novel itself) and
I (referring to the novelist himself). The same words occur with similar,
but even more startling, effect in Kurt Vonnegut's novel *Slaughterhouse
Five*.

> An American near Billy wailed that he had excreted everything but his
> brains. Moments later he said, 'There they go, there they go.' He meant
> his brains.
> That was I. That was me. That was the author of this book.[28]

Erving Goffman has designated such gestures 'breaking frame'. The Russian
formalists called it 'exposing the device'. A more recent critical term is
'metafiction'. It is not, of course, a new phenomenon in the history of
fiction. It is to be found in Cervantes, Fielding, Sterne, Thackeray and
Trollope, among others – but not, significantly, in the work of the great
modernist writers. At least, I cannot think offhand of any instance in the
work of James, Conrad, Woolf and Joyce (up to and including *Ulysses*)
where the fictitiousness of the narrative is exposed as blatantly as in my
last few examples. The reason, I believe, is that such exposure foregrounds
the existence of the author, the source of the novel's diegesis, in a way
which ran counter to the modernist pursuit of impersonality and mimesis
of consciousness. Metafictional devices are, however, all-pervasive in post-
modernist fiction. I think for example of John Fowles's play with the
authorial persona in *The French Lieutenant's Woman*, of Malcolm Bradbury's introduction of himself into *The History Man* as a figure cowed and
dispirited by his own character, of B. S. Johnson's sabotage of his own
fictionalizing in *Albert Angelo*. I think of the disconcerting authorial footnotes in Beckett's *Watt*, the flaunting of authorial omniscience in Muriel
Spark, John Barth's obsessive recycling of his own earlier fictions in *Letters*,
and the way the last page of Nabokov's *Ada* spills over on to the book
jacket to become its own blurb. Perhaps, to conclude a list which could be
much longer, I might mention my own novel *How Far Can You Go?* in
which the authorial narrator frequently draws attention to the fictitiousness
of the characters and their actions, while at other times presenting them as
a kind of history, and inviting the sort of moral and emotional response
from the reader that belongs to traditional realistic fiction. For me, and I
think for other British novelists, metafiction has been particularly useful as
a way of continuing to exploit the resources of realism while acknowledging
their conventionality. And need one say that the more nakedly the author
appears to reveal himself in such texts, the more inescapable it becomes,
paradoxically, that the author as a *voice* is only a function of his own
fiction, a rhetorical construct, not a privileged authority but an object of
interpretation?

To conclude: what we see happening in post-modernist fiction is a revival of diegesis: not smoothly dovetailed with mimesis as in the classic realist text, and not subordinated to mimesis as in the modernist text, but foregrounded against mimesis. The stream of consciousness has turned into a stream of narration – which would be one way of summarizing the difference between the greatest modernist novelist, Joyce, and the greatest postmodernist, Beckett. When the Unnamable says to himself, 'You must go on. I can't go on. I'll go on', he means, on one level at least, that he must go on narrating.

Chapter 3

Middlemarch and the idea of the classic realist text

Middlemarch has achieved a unique status as both paradigm and paragon in discussion of the novel as a literary form. Indeed it is scarcely an exaggeration to say that, for many critics, *Middlemarch* is the *only* truly representative, truly great Victorian novel – all other candidates, including the rest of George Eliot's fiction, being either too idiosyncratic or too flawed. Barbara Hardy was surely right when she said in her introduction to *Middlemarch: Critical Approaches to the Novel* (1967) that 'if a poll were held for the greatest English novel there would probably be more votes for *Middlemarch* than for any other work';[1] while one of her contributors, Hilda Hulme, quoted a judgement that 'every novel would be *Middlemarch* if it could'.[2]

That symposium edited by Barbara Hardy probably registered the high-water mark of *Middlemarch*'s modern reputation. More recently criticism has begun to express a more reserved admiration for George Eliot's masterpiece, echoing and amplifying Henry James's suave judgement on reviewing *Middlemarch*: 'It sets a limit, we think, to the development of the old-fashioned English novel.'[3] George Eliot's realism is now regarded not as a kind of timeless truthfulness to human experience (as implied by the tribute, every novel would be *Middlemarch* if it could), but as an historically conditioned, ideologically motivated construction of 'the real'. J. Hillis Miller, for instance, while acknowledging that *Middlemarch* is 'perhaps the masterwork of Victorian realism',[4] is concerned to expose the rhetorical devices by which George Eliot achieves her 'totalizing' effect, and to reveal, beneath her apparently serene mastery of her fictional world, a gnawing epistemological doubt.

A still more radical critique of George Eliot's realism, especially as displayed in *Middlemarch*, is to be found in Colin MacCabe's *James Joyce and the Revolution of the Word* (1979). This important and original study of Joyce incorporates an influential theory of the 'classic realist text', which George Eliot is taken to exemplify, but which seems to me to misrepresent her writing in ways worth detailed examination.

At the time of writing this book, MacCabe was clearly influenced by the post-structuralist phase of criticism in France in the late 1960s and early 1970s, when the purely formal, semiological analysis of literary texts and genres, with which structuralist criticism was originally concerned, was polemicized by the infusion of Roland Barthes's literary historicism, Jacques Lacan's reading of Freud, Louis Althusser's reading of Marx, and Jacques Derrida's deconstruction of the metaphysical basis of western philosophy.[5] In this school of thought, the purely methodological separation made by Saussure between the signifier and the signified in the sign is given ontological status and importance. There is never a perfect fit between language and the world. It is impossible absolutely to say what we mean or mean what we say, since the subject who completes an utterance is no longer exactly the same as the subject who originated it, and the language used by the subject has its own materiality capable of signifying beyond the subject's intention or control. The subject (what George Eliot would have called the individual man or woman) is not a concrete, substantial identity situated outside language, but is produced and continually modified by the entry into language. It is the ideas of language as a kind of 'material' and of consciousness and social relations as a kind of 'production' which perhaps enable proponents of this school of thought to reconcile their rather bleakly anti-humanist semiology with their commitment to revolutionary politics. Certainly they seem closer in spirit to Nietzsche than to Marx, and at times to come perilously near a kind of epistemological abyss of infinitely recessive interpretations of interpretations, rendering all human intellectual effort essentially futile. The underlying message seems to be that, however bleak and frightening this view of man and consciousness may be, it is true; and to deny it can only have the ill effects of all repression – whether in society, the psyche or literature.

Colin MacCabe claims that Joyce's importance resides in the fact that he puts his readers to school in precisely this way, though his critics have misunderstood the lesson and obstinately persist in trying to explain (or 'recuperate') his works, making them conform to a notion of stable 'meaning' such as it was precisely his intention to undermine. In his mature work, Joyce was concerned 'not with representing experience through language, but with experiencing language through a destruction of representation'.[6] To throw into relief Joyce's liberation of language, and destruction of representation, MacCabe contrasts his fiction with 'the classic realist text', as represented by *Middlemarch*, 'which purports to represent experience through language'.

The 'classic realist text' is a term that derives from the criticism of Roland Barthes, especially *S/Z* (1970), and MacCabe is certainly indebted to Barthes in some ways. But his definition of the classic realist text is simpler, and I think less subtle, than Barthes's. According to MacCabe, a novel is a tissue of discourses – the discourses of the characters, as rendered in their speech, and the discourse of the narrator; and it is characteristic of the classic realist text that in it the narrative discourse acts as a 'metalanguage',[7] controlling, interpreting and judging the other discourses, and thus putting the reader in a position of dominance over the characters and their stories. Joyce, in contrast, refuses to privilege one discourse over another in his writing, or to privilege the reader's position *vis-à-vis* the text. Even in his early work, such as the stories of *Dubliners*, superficially consistent with the techniques of classic realism, the narrator's discourse proves ambiguous and enigmatic on close examination; while in, for instance, the 'Cyclops' episode of *Ulysses*, a characteristic specimen of his mature work, the conflicting discourses of the anonymous patron of Barney Kiernan's pub who narrates the main action, the Citizen, Bloom and all the other characters in the bar, are interrupted not by the metalanguage of a reliable authorial narrator but by passages of parodic inflation and hyperbole (sanctioned purely aesthetically by the 'gigantism' theme of the episode) – a counter-text, MacCabe calls it, which 'far from setting up a position of judgement for the reader, merely proliferates the languages available'.[8] Thus the reader of *Ulysses* is never allowed to sink into the comfortable assurance of an interpretation guaranteed by the narrator, but must himself produce the meaning of the text by opening himself fully to the play of its diverse and contradictory discourses.

One symptom of Joyce's rejection of the conventions of reading and representation employed in the classic realist text was his refusal, from his earliest days as a writer, to employ what he called 'perverted commas' in rendering direct speech – using an introductory dash instead. It is the typographical marking off of direct speech from narrative by quotation marks that enforces the authority of the narrator's metalanguage, in Mac-Cabe's view. 'The narrative prose is the meta-language that can state all the truths in the object-language(s) (the marks held in inverted commas) and can also explain the relation of the object-language to the world.'[9]

Let us acknowledge that there is a real difference between the art of George Eliot and the art of James Joyce which MacCabe helps to define. Let us note also that MacCabe himself admits that classic realism is never absolute, and that within George Eliot's novels 'there are always images which counter the flat and univocal process which is the showing forth of the real'.[10] Nevertheless it seems to me that the distortion of George Eliot's practice implied by MacCabe's model of the classic realist text is sufficiently great to be worth contesting, and that this might be a way of extending our understanding of classic realism generally, and of George Eliot's art in particular.

What MacCabe calls a metalanguage (a term borrowed from linguistics and philosophy) will be better known to students of George Eliot as the convention of the omniscient and intrusive narrator, which has a venerable history as a subject of contention in criticism of her work. In the period of her relative eclipse, in the 1920s, 1930s and 1940s, when the Jamesian aesthetic of 'showing' rather than 'telling' was dominant in novel criticism, this feature of her work counted heavily against her. In the 1950s and 1960s several critics such as Wayne Booth, W. J. Harvey and Barbara Hardy instituted a successful defence of the convention and George Eliot's exploitation of it, thus complementing on the aesthetic plane the reinstatement of George Eliot as a great novelist which F. R. Leavis had achieved on the ethical plane.

As Gérard Genette has observed, in his excellent treatise *Narrative Discourse*, the James–Lubbock distinction between 'showing' and 'telling', and the corresponding pair of terms, 'scene' and 'summary', derive from the distinction drawn between mimesis and diegesis in the third book of Plato's *Republic*; and MacCabe's discussion of the matter seems particularly close to Plato's (though it reverses Plato's preferences) because of the importance he gives to the marking off of speech from narration in the classic realist text. Mimesis is narrating by imitating another's speech. Diegesis is narrating in one's own voice.[11] A typology of literary modes (later to evolve into a typology of literary genres)[12] thus emerges: pure diegesis, as exemplified by dithyramb (a kind of hymn), in which the poet speaks exclusively in his own voice; pure mimesis, as exemplified by tragedy and comedy, in which the poet speaks exclusively in imitated voices; and the mixed form of the epic, which combines both modes. Needless to say, Plato greatly distrusted the most mimetic kind of writing, since it is ethically undiscriminating; and he will admit into the Republic only the most austere kind of writing – the purely diegetic, or that which combines diegesis with a little mimesis, but of good personages only.

Realism as a literary quality, or effect, of verisimilitude, is something we think of as very close to, if not quite synonymous with, the classical notion of mimesis or imitation, and we often describe the novel casually as a 'mimetic' literary form. In fact, of course, only drama is a strictly mimetic form, in which words are imitated *in* words, and what is non-verbal – spectacle, gesture, etc. – is imitated non-verbally. Anything that is not dialogue in a novel, if only 'he said' and 'she said', is diegesis, the report of a narrator, 'the poet himself' however impersonal. The only way of getting round this rule is to put the narrating entirely into the hands (or mouths) of a character or characters, as in the pseudo-autobiographical novel or the epistolary novel: then the narrative becomes mimetic of diegesis. But as Genette concludes, 'the truth is that mimesis in words can only be mimesis of words. Other than that, all we have and can have is degrees of diegesis.'[13]

I think there is some advantage to be gained from substituting the Platonic distinction between mimesis and diegesis for MacCabe's distinction between language and metalanguage. Instead of seeing a total break of continuity between the classic realist text and the modern text, we see rather a swing of the pendulum from one end of a continuum of possibilities to the other, a pendulum that has been swinging throughout literary history. Mimesis and diegesis, like metaphor and metonymy, are fundamental, and, on a certain level, all-inclusive categories of representation, and a typology of texts can be established by assessing the dominance of one over the other. We are also better placed to see that the distinction between mimesis and diegesis in George Eliot is by no means as clear-cut as MacCabe implies; and that the diegetic element is much more problematic than he allows.

When Plato refers to the epic as a mixed form, he means that it combines, or alternates between, mimesis and diegesis, the voice of the poet and the voices of the characters he imitates in dialogue. But the classic realist novel 'mixes' the two discourses in a more fundamental sense: it fuses them together, often indistinguishably and inextricably, through the device of free indirect speech by means of which the narrator, without absenting himself entirely from the text, communicates the narrative to us coloured by the thoughts and feelings of a character. The reference to this character in the third-person pronoun, and the use of the past tense, or 'epic preterite', still imply the existence of the author as the source of the narrative; but by deleting the tags which affirm that existence, such as 'he said', 'she wondered', 'she thought to herself', etc., and by using the kind of diction appropriate to the character rather than to the authorial narrator, the latter can allow the sensibility of the character to dominate the discourse, and correspondingly subdue his own voice, his own opinions and evaluations. The device is an extremely flexible one, which allows the narrator to move very freely and fluently between the poles of mimesis and diegesis within a single paragraph, or even a single sentence; and its effect is always to make the reader's task of interpretation more active and problematic. If we are looking for a single formal feature which characterizes the realist novel of the nineteenth century, it is surely not the domination of the characters' discourses by the narrator's discourse (something in fact more characteristic of earlier narrative literature) but the extensive use of free indirect speech, which obscures and complicates the distinction between the two types of discourse.

The work of the Russian literary theorists Mikhail Bakhtin and Valentin Volosinov, which goes back to the 1920s, but has only recently been translated into English, is very relevant here. They (or he – for one may have been a cover for the other) have suggested that it is precisely the dissolution of the boundaries between reported speech and reporting context (i.e. the author's speech) that characterizes the novel as discourse and distinguishes it from earlier types of narrative prose and from lyric verse. Bakhtin characterized the novel as 'polyphonic' and maintained that, 'One of the essential peculiarities of prose fiction is the possibility it allows of using different types of discourse, with their distinct expressiveness intact, on the plane of a single work, without reduction to a single common denominator.'[14] Different types of discourse can be represented in fiction, of course, as the direct speech of characters, without serious disturbance to the authority of the narrator, as in the novels of Fielding or Scott. But once these discourses enter into the narrative discourse itself, in various forms of reported speech, or thought, the interpretative control of the author's voice is inevitably weakened to some degree, and the reader's work increased.

Derek Oldfield, in an essay entitled 'The character of Dorothea', contributed to that symposium on *Middlemarch* edited by Barbara Hardy to which I have already referred, pointed out how George Eliot's narrative method is complicated by this alternation of narrator's and characters' voices, compelling the reader to, in his words, 'zig-zag' his way through the discourse, rather than following a straight, well-marked path.[15] One of the examples he gives is a passage describing Dorothea's naive ideas about marriage, which I have discussed elsewhere (see pp. 31–3). The first part of that passage establishes very clearly the ethical terms in which Dorothea is to be judged: selflessness on the one hand, self-deception on the other. But as the writing proceeds to flesh out this diegetic assessment more mimetically, the reader is progressively more taxed to negotiate the nuances of irony and to resolve the ambiguities of deixis. Exactly how far Dorothea misconceives the nature of the great intellectual figures of the past; whether she is right or wrong in her assessment of Sir James Chettam's intelligence; whether she emerges from the whole passage with more credit than discredit, are questions which the reader must finally decide for himself. There are many other such passages in *Middlemarch*.

It is not, however, only because mimesis often contaminates diegesis in this way that MacCabe's account of the narrator's voice in George Eliot's fiction seems inaccurate.

> The metalanguage within such a text refuses to acknowledge its own status as writing. The text outside the area of inverted commas claims to be the product of no articulation, it claims to be unwritten. This unwritten text can then attempt to staunch the haemorrhage of interpretations threatened by the material of language. Whereas other discourses within the text are considered as materials which are open to reinterpretation, the narrative discourse functions simply as a window on reality. This relationship between discourses can be taken as the defining feature of the classic realist text.[16]

The assertion that the narrator's discourse claims to be 'unwritten' may be puzzling unless one traces it back to Derrida's argument that western culture has always privileged the spoken word over the written, because the spoken word appears to guarantee the 'metaphysics of presence' on which our philosophical tradition is predicated. Speech implies the presence of a speaker, and by inference of an authentic, autonomous self who is the arbiter of his own meanings and able to pass them intact to another. But Derrida argues that this is a fallacy and an illusion. It is the absence of the addresser from the message which allows the materiality of language to generate its own semantic possibilities among which the addressee may romp at will. Writing, in which such absence is obvious, is thus a more reliable model of how language works than speech; and writing which claims truthfulness by trying to disguise itself as speech, as the discourse of a man speaking to men, is in bad faith, or at least deluded.

Now it is true that the narrator's discourse in George Eliot's fiction apostrophizes the reader, and certain that she would have endorsed Wordsworth's description of the writer as a man speaking to men. But in obvious ways, whether consciously or unconsciously, she reminds us that her narration is in fact written. This is particularly true of the more ostentatiously diegetic passages, when she suspends the story to deliver herself of opinions, generalizations, judgements. To call these passages transparent windows on reality seems quite inappropriate. They are in fact often quite obscure, or at least very complicated, and have to be scrutinized several times before we can confidently construe their meaning – a process that is peculiar to reading, and cannot be applied to the spoken word. Consider, for example, this comment on Mr Farebrother, shortly after Lydgate has voted against him in the selection of the hospital chaplaincy.

> But Mr Farebrother met him with the same friendliness as before. The character of the publican and sinner is not always practically incompatible with that of the modern Pharisee, for the majority of us scarcely see more distinctly the faultiness of our own conduct than the faultiness of our own arguments, or the dullness of our own jokes. But the Vicar of St Botolph's had certainly escaped the slightest tincture of the Pharisee, and by dint of admitting to himself that he was too much as other men were, he had become remarkably unlike them in this – that he could excuse others for thinking slightly of him, and could judge impartially of their conduct even when it told against him.[17]

I would defy anyone to take in the exact sense of this passage through the ear alone. There are too many distinctions being juggled, and too many swerves and loops in the movement of the argument: first, we encounter the idea (stated in a double negative, and thus made more difficult to assimilate) that the modern publican and sinner may be combined with the modern Pharisee in the same person, unlike their biblical prototypes. Is Mr Farebrother, who has just been mentioned, such a person, we may wonder, as we begin to negotiate this passage? This would be inconsistent with the previous presentation of his character, but we have to wait for some time to be reassured that this is *not* what the narrator means. Before we come to that point, we have to wrestle with another distinction – between faults of manners (arguments and jokes) and faults of morals (conduct) – a distinction which doesn't correspond exactly to the one between publicans and sinners and Pharisees. The exculpation of Farebrother is highly paradoxical: by admitting that he is too much like other men, he becomes remarkably unlike them: which is to say, that by admitting he is a publican and a sinner, he avoids being a Pharisee as well. So why has the narrator introduced the concept of Pharisee at all? It seems to be floating free, and we puzzle our way through the paragraph, waiting to see to whom it applies. We may be disconcerted to realize that it is applied, explicitly, only to 'the majority of us' ourselves. Perhaps it is also applied implicitly to Lydgate, whose conduct over the election, as he himself is well aware, was not entirely disinterested. On reflection we may decide that the negative comparison between Farebrother and Pharisee is justified by the fact that the Pharisees were a Jewish religious sect and that Phariseeism is an occupational failing of men of religion, but this explanation scarcely leaps off the page.

Mr Farebrother seems to emerge from these complex comparisons with credit. But only a few lines later, after a speech from Mr Farebrother in direct (i.e. mimetic) form –

'The world has been too strong for *me*, I know,' he said one day to Lydgate. 'But then I am not a mighty man – I shall never be a man of renown. The choice of Hercules is a pretty fable; but Prodicus makes it easy work for the hero, as if the first resolves were enough. Another story says that he came to hold the distaff, and at last wore the Nessus shirt. I suppose one good resolve might keep a man right if everybody else's resolve helped him.'

(p. 217)

– we encounter this diegetic comment:

The Vicar's talk was not always inspiriting: he had escaped being a Pharisee, but he had not escaped that low estimate of possibilities which we rather hastily arrive at as an inference from our own failure.

(pp. 217–18)

This seems to check any inclination on the reader's part to overestimate Mr Farebrother's moral stature; and if, in reading the preceding diegetic passage, we mentally defend ourselves against the accusation of Phariseeism by identifying ourselves with Farebrother's candid admission of his faults, we now find ourselves implicated with him in another kind of failing – complacency about one's faults. But if we make *another* adjustment, and take this as a cue to condemn Farebrother, we may be surprised and disconcerted once more, to find ourselves identified with Lydgate – for the passage immediately continues, and ends (as does the whole chapter) with this sentence: 'Lydgate felt that there was a pitiable lack of will in Mr Farebrother.' Since Lydgate has just been portrayed as subordinating his own will to expediency in the matter of the chaplaincy election, he is hardly in a position to throw stones at this particular moral glasshouse, and the sequel will show even greater 'infirmity of will' on his part in the matter of Rosamund.[18] To sum up, the authorial commentary, so far from telling the reader what to think, or putting him in a position of dominance in relation to the discourse of the characters, constantly forces him to think for himself, and constantly implicates him in the moral judgements being formulated.

I like to call this kind of literary effect, the 'Fish effect', because the American critic Stanley Fish has made the study of it so much his own in a series of books and articles written primarily on seventeenth-century poetry and prose, but more lately with a wider range of reference.[19] Basically, his argument is that as we read, lineally, word by word, word group by word group, we form hypotheses and expectations about the meaning that is going to be delivered at the end of the sentence, or paragraph, or text; but, as Fish shows by skilful analyses of particular passages – action-replays of reading in slow motion – very often our expectations are disconfirmed, a different and perhaps entirely opposite meaning from that which we expected is formulated, yet without entirely abolishing the mistakenly projected meaning. In his early work Fish suggested that this effect was contrived by writers who had didactic, usually religious, designs upon their readers, using it to defamiliarize familiar truths; thus Milton reminds us that we are fallen creatures not merely by the fable of *Paradise Lost* but by constantly tripping us up with his syntax. More recently, Fish has argued that the effect is inherent in all discourse, but especially literary discourse, because the meaning of an utterance is determined entirely by its context and the interpretative assumptions that are brought to it – which, in the case of literary utterances, are never simple or fixed. I think both arguments are valid, and both apply to George Eliot's diegetic style, although such deviousness might, superficially, seem incompatible with her chosen stance as narrator: the privileged historian of the moral lives of characters who, it suits her purpose to pretend, are real people in real situations. The opening paragraph of chapter 15 is *à propos*:

A great historian, as he insisted on calling himself, who had the happiness to be dead a hundred and twenty years ago, and so to take his place among the colossi whose huge legs our living pettiness is observed to walk under, glories in his copious remarks and digressions as the least imitable part of his work, and especially in those initial chapters to the successive books of his history, where he seems to bring his arm-chair to the proscenium and chat with us in all the lusty ease of his fine English. But Fielding lived when the days were longer (for time, like money, is measured by our needs), when summer afternoons were spacious, and the clock ticked slowly in the winter evenings. We belated historians must not linger after his example; and if we did so, it is probable that our chat would be thin and eager, as if delivered from a camp-stool in a parrot-house. I at least have so much to do in unravelling certain human lots, and seeing how they were woven and interwoven, that all the light I can command must be concentrated on this particular web, and not dispersed over that tempting range of relevancies called the universe.

(p. 170)

Colin MacCabe's comment on this paragraph is that 'Although at first sight, George Eliot would appear to be questioning her form, the force of the passage is to leave us convinced that we have finally abandoned form to be treated to the simple unravelling of the real.'[20] But this seems a very stubborn refusal to credit George Eliot with ironic selfconsciousness. It is patently obvious by chapter 15 that the narrator of *Middlemarch is* ranging over the tempting range of relevancies called the universe, especially through her famous scientific analogies. And by comparing her own writing to Fielding's, she is implicitly placing it in a tradition of literary fiction, even if this admission is neatly disguised by invoking Fielding's description of himself as a historian. The Fish effect is immediately apparent in the opening of this passage: 'A great historian, as he insisted on calling himself . . .' We don't know, yet, of course, who this historian is, and it is quite a time before we discover his identity, and that he is not a historian at all, but a novelist. '[A]s he insisted on calling himself . . .' might give us a clue that he wasn't a proper historian, but it might equally well be construed as meaning he was a proper historian who insisted on calling himself great. '[W]ho had the happiness to be dead a hundred and twenty years ago . . .' 'Dead' is surely a surprising word in the context. 'Who had the happiness to be alive' would be the more predictable formula, expressing that nostalgia for the good old days which George Eliot so often invokes in her fiction, though in fact seldom quite straightforwardly. The paradox is resolved when we read, 'and so to take his place among the colossi whose huge legs our living pettiness is observed to walk under . . .' Fielding was lucky to have died a hundred and twenty years ago, then, in the sense that he thus became a literary classic – though if he is dead it is hard to see how this brings him any happiness, and the reverence accorded to a classic seems somewhat undercut by the allusion to Shakespeare's Cassius. The narrator, at any rate, takes no responsibility for the analogy. 'Whose huge legs our living pettiness is observed to walk under . . .' Observed by whom? By the makers of such extravagant analogies? '[G]lories in his copious remarks and digressions as the least imitable part of his work.' Was Fielding right in thinking them inimitable, or has George Eliot improved upon them? Of course, she disowns any attempt to compete with him, but then the whole passage is a digression disowning the intention to digress.

Several critics have recently pointed out the presence of paradox and contradiction in George Eliot's superficially smooth, unproblematic narrative style. J. Hillis Miller, for instance, in his article 'Optic and semiotic in *Middlemarch*', identifies three groups of totalizing metaphors or families of metaphors, and comments, 'Each group of metaphors is related to the others, fulfilling them, but at the same time contradicting them, cancelling them out, or undermining their validity'.[21] Thus, for instance, the recurring image of the lives of the characters as a flowing web, an unrolling fabric, objectively there, to which the narrator brings a truthtelling light, is contaminated by other images of the subjectivity of interpretation, the inevitable distortions of perspective. The famous analogy of the candle-flame which confers pattern on the random scratches of the pier-glass, as Miller points out (and Leslie Stephen pointed out before him) applies as well to the narrator's perspective as to that of any character. Steven Marcus, in an interesting, if quirky, article entitled, 'Human nature, social orders and nineteenth-century systems of explanation: starting in with George Eliot', interprets her fondness for setting her novels back in the historical past (a feature of the classic Victorian novel in general) as a defence mechanism designed to control themes that she was both fascinated by and yet feared: sexual passion, class conflict and epistemological scepticism. He notes in her treatment of the past, as early as 'Amos Barton', the first piece of fiction she wrote, the Fish effect, moments when the irony of the narrator's discourse, with which the reader has been feeling a comfortable complicity, suddenly rebounds upon him:

> It is the reader himself who now suddenly discovers that he is being gently but firmly prodded in the ribs, although it is not altogether clear why he should all at once find himself on the wrong end of the stick . . . The effect, however, is momentarily to loosen the reader's grip on the sequence of statements through which he has just worked his way and to cause him to look back, if only for a fraction of an instant, to see if he can ascertain the logical and syntactical course which led him to this uncertainly dislocated and suspended position.[22]

Graham Martin, responding directly to Colin MacCabe's book, has argued that 'we learn as much about *The Mill on the Floss* by looking at discontinuities between the authorial metalanguage and the narrated fiction, as by remarking on their fusion'.[23] All these critics tend to regard the fractures they discern in the smooth surface of George Eliot's narrative method as signs or symptoms of the tremendous stresses and strains she experienced in trying to deal truthfully and yet positively with an increasingly alienated and alienating social reality. But it is not necessary to see them as aesthetic flaws. On the contrary, it is precisely because the narrator's discourse is never entirely unambiguous, predictable, and in total interpretative control of the other discourses in *Middlemarch* that the novel survives, to be read and re-read, without ever being finally closed or exhausted. And this, paradoxically, follows inevitably from the post-Saussurian theories about language and discourse to which Colin MacCabe, and other critics of the same persuasion, subscribe. If it is true that language is a system of differences with no positive terms, that the subject is inevitably split in discourse between the 'I' who speaks and the 'I' who is spoken of, that the relationship between words and things is not natural but cultural, not given but produced, then George Eliot could not write fiction that was a 'transparent window on reality' even if she wanted to. The question, therefore, is whether in trying – or pretending – to do so, she was betrayed into false consciousness and bad art. It has been my purpose to suggest that she was well aware of the indeterminacy that lurks in all efforts at human communication, and frequently reminded her readers of this fact in the very act of apparently denying it through the use of an intrusive 'omniscient' authorial voice.

Chapter 4

Lawrence, Dostoevsky, Bakhtin

The object of this essay is to bring Mikhail Bakhtin's theory and practice to bear on the fiction of D. H. Lawrence – primarily in the hope of enhancing our knowledge and understanding of the kind of literary discourse Lawrence produced; but also to test the usefulness of Bakhtin's concepts and analytical tools. I have tried to show elsewhere the relevance of Bakhtin to the work of James Joyce.[1] If Bakhtin's poetics of fiction proves relevant to another major modern novelist, generally considered antithetical to Joyce in his literary aims and techniques, it would be impressive testimony to the theory's explanatory power. I begin with a brief summary of Bakhtin's key ideas, drawn from the following sources, referred to subsequently by the abbreviations indicated: *Problems of Dostoevsky's Poetics* (*PDP*; 1963), a revised and much expanded version of a book called *Problems of Dostoevsky's Art* first published in 1929; *Marxism and the Philosophy of Language* (*MPL*; 1929), published under the name of Valentin Volosinov, but now thought to be largely the work of Bakhtin; *Rabelais and His World* (*R*; 1965); and four long essays published in English under the title *The Dialogic Imagination* (*DI*; 1981).[2]

Bakhtin, it might be said, rewrote the history of western literature by developing a new typology of literary discourse, which is itself based on a new, post-Saussurean theory of language. Ferdinand de Saussure made modern linguistics possible by his distinction between *langue* (the abstract rules and constraints which allow language to function) and *parole* (the actual utterances which language-users produce). Saussurean linguistics is oriented to *langue*, as is transformational grammar and speech act theory. Recently linguists have become interested in the linguistics of *parole*, or 'discourse' as it is more commonly called, and in this respect they were anticipated by Bakhtin. According to Bakhtin, language is essentially social or *dialogic*. 'The word in living conversation is directly, blatantly oriented towards a future answer word. It provokes an answer, anticipates it and structures itself in the answer's direction' (*DI*, p. 280).

This insight has several interesting entailments. To begin with, it gets us off the hook of deconstructionist scepticism about the possibility of meaning: instead of having desperately to defend the possibility of a fixed or stable meaning in isolated utterances, we can cheerfully accept that meaning exists in the process of intersubjective communication, since no utterance ever is truly isolated. Methodologically, it means that we cannot explain *parole* simply by reference to *langue*: an utterance can only be understood in context, a context that is partly non-verbal and involves the status of and relations between speaker, addressee and the object of reference. Literature provides illuminating representation of how this works in practice – especially prose fiction. For the 'canonized' genres – epic, tragedy and lyric – are what Bakhtin calls 'monologic': they seek to establish a single style, a single voice, with which to express a single world-view. Even if individual characters express distinct and opposing views in such a text, nevertheless an all-pervasive poetic decorum, or the regularities of rhythm and metre, ensure that the total effect is one of stylistic (and ideological) consistency and homogeneity. Prose literature, in contrast, is dialogic or, in an alternative formulation, 'polyphonic' – an orchestration of diverse discourses culled both from writing and oral speech. 'The possibility of employing on the plane of a single work discourses of various types, with all their expressive capacities intact, without reducing them to a common denominator – this is one of the most fundamental characteristic features of prose' (*PDP*, p. 200). The dominance of the novel in the modern era is therefore explained and justified by its capacity to match the rich variety of human speech and to respect the ideological freedom that variety embodies.

There are, however, in Bakhtin's writings two slightly different accounts of how the novel came to fulfil this grand cultural mission. In the first account, Dostoevsky played a crucial role: he *invented* the polyphonic novel, and thus decisively changed the possibilities of the form. Before Dostoevsky, the novel itself was monologic, inasmuch as a dominant authorial discourse – Tolstoy's for example – controlled and judged the discourse of the characters, predetermining the resolution of the issues raised by the novel in the interests of some ideological *parti pris*. This is an argument that runs parallel at many points to the distinction between the classic realist text and the modern text put forward by some post-structuralist critics.[3] In Dostoevsky, in contrast, the authorial voice is never dominant, the characters are free to 'answer back', and the reader is confronted with the challenging, disconcerting, ultimately unresolved interaction of diverse discourses representing diverse attitudes and values, sometimes within the same speaking or thinking subject.

Later, it would seem, Bakhtin came to see the pre-Dostoevskian novel as already a dialogic type of literary discourse, and to trace its roots back to the 'serio-comic' genres of classical literature – Menippean satire, the Socratic dialogue and the satyr play. In feudal times this tradition of parodic, travestying, multivocal discourse was perpetuated in the unofficial culture of carnival. At the Renaissance its energies were released into the mainstream of literature by, pre-eminently, Rabelais and Cervantes, and in this fashion the novel was born, and flourished in all its variety – the picaresque, the confessional, the epistolary, the sentimental, the Shandean, the Gothic, the historical and so on. In the nineteenth century the novel achieved a kind of stability, a formal synthesis, and established its dominance over all other literary forms through the unparalleled richness and subtlety of its discursive texture, in which the interplay of narrator's speech and characters' speech, made possible by development of free indirect style, was particularly important. (The voice of the narrator in chapter 1 of *Middlemarch*, for instance, ironically, teasingly, affectionately playing off the language of Dorothea's naive idealism against the language of the philistine community and both against the values of the implied author, is already dialogic in Bakhtin's terms.) What Dostoevsky did was to loosen the grip of the authorial discourse and allow the other discourses in the text to interact in more dramatic and complicated ways than the classic nineteenth-century novel allowed. He was an important but by no means unique innovator in this respect.

Bakhtin perhaps never quite managed to reconcile these two accounts of the evolution of the dialogic or polyphonic novel. There are obvious reasons for preferring the later, more gradualist version, since a scheme of European literary history which depends crucially on the work of a single author in a single literary tradition would seem to be inherently flawed. But of all Bakhtin's works it is his study of Dostoevsky that is most illuminating in connection with D. H. Lawrence. Before we proceed to the main topic of this essay, however, it may be useful to recapitulate Bakhtin's typology of fictional discourse.

There are three principal categories:

1. *The direct speech of the author*. This means the author as encoded in the text, in an 'objective', reliable, narrative voice.
2. *The represented speech of the characters*. This may be represented by direct speech ('dialogue' in the non-Bakhtinian sense): or by the convention of soliloquy or interior monologue: or in those elements of reported speech which belong to the language of the character rather than the narrator in free indirect style.
3. *Doubly-oriented or doubly-voiced speech*. This category was Bakhtin's most original and valuable contribution to stylistic analysis. It includes all speech which not only refers to something in the world but also refers to another speech act by another addresser. It is divided into several subcategories, of which the most important are stylization, *skaz*, parody and hidden polemic. *Stylization* occurs when the writer borrows another's discourse and uses it for his own purposes – with the same general intention as the original, but in the process casting 'a slight shadow of objectification over it' (*PDP*, p. 189). This objectification may

be used to establish a distance between the narrator and the implied author, especially when the narrator is an individualized character, perhaps narrating his own story. When such narration has the characteristics of oral discourse it is designated *skaz* in the Russian critical tradition, though Bakhtin argues that the 'oral' quality is less important than the adoption of another's discourse for one's own aesthetic and expressive purposes. Stylization is to be distinguished from *parody*, when another's discourse is borrowed but turned to a purpose opposite to or incongruous with the intention of the original. In both stylization and parody, the original discourse is lexically or grammatically evoked in the text. But there is another kind of doubly-oriented discourse which refers to, answers, or otherwise takes into account another speech act never articulated in the text: *hidden polemic* is Bakhtin's suggestive name for one of the most common forms of doubly-oriented discourse.

Monologic literature is, of course, characterized by the dominance of category 1 in Bakhtin's typology of discourse. In most pre-novelistic narrative (e.g. chivalric romance, moral fable) the authorial narrator does not merely impose his own interpretative frame on the tale, but makes the characters speak the same kind of language as himself. The eighteenth- and nineteenth-century novel allowed the individuality of characters' voices to be heard through such devices as the epistolary novel or free indirect style, and even admitted doubly-oriented speech to a limited degree (Bakhtin himself gives some good examples from *Little Dorrit*: *DI*, pp. 303–7). But clearly the fully dialogic novel is a comparatively modern phenomenon, marked by the attenuation of the first of Bakhtin's discourse categories and an increasingly subtle and complex deployment of types 2 and 3. Dostoevsky's *Notes from Underground*, for instance, one of his most original and distinctively 'modern' texts, is something of a virtuoso performance in the deployment of doubly-oriented speech, as Bakhtin ably demonstrates (*PDP*, pp. 227–34).

There is nothing like *Notes from Underground* to be found in Lawrence's *oeuvre*. For one thing, he very rarely employed the technique Bakhtin calls *Ich-Erzählung*, narration by an 'I' figure. (The only texts of this kind I can think of are his first novel, *The White Peacock*, and the late story, 'None of that', not one of his best, which has two such narrators, one framed within the other.) Lawrence's fiction is remarkably consistent and homogeneous in narrative method, invariably using an authorial narrator to frame and mediate the scenic or interiorized presentation of the action to the reader. This narrative voice is generally thought to be the dominant discourse in his fiction, and a formal characteristic that sets him somewhat apart from the modernist movement. I have myself written on another occasion:

> [Lawrence's] narrative voice, however much it varies in tone, from the shrewdly down-to-earth to the lyrically rhapsodic, and whatever charac-

ter's consciousness it is rendering, is always basically the same, unmistakably Lawrentian. Not for him the mimicry, the pastiche, the rapid shifts of voice and linguistic register, that we encounter in Joyce or [T. S.] Eliot.[4]

This, it must be admitted, sounds more like a description of monologic than of dialogic discourse, and not an encouraging basis for a Bakhtinian reading of Lawrence. However, I think I exaggerated the homogeneity of Lawrence's narrative style, and in any case a variety of linguistic styles and registers is not in itself either a necessary or a sufficient criterion for the polyphonic novel. Bakhtin himself observes that in Dostoevsky's novels there is considerably less 'language differentiation, that is, fewer language styles, territorial and social dialects, professional jargons and so forth', than in, for example, the work of the more monologic Tolstoy; that Dostoevsky has been accused by many critics (including Tolstoy himself) of a 'monotony of language'; but that what makes a novel polyphonic is not the mere presence of different styles and dialects, but 'the dialogic angle at which these styles are juxtaposed and counterposed in the work' (*PDP*, p. 182). In other words, whereas in Tolstoy the variety of characters' speech is always contained and controlled by the author's speech, in Dostoevsky the characters' speech, though formally less differentiated and individualized, is freer in the way it generates and sustains a continuous struggle between competing interests and ideas. I should like to suggest that the same is true of Lawrence's most impressive mature fiction, and especially *Women in Love*. His development from *Sons and Lovers*, through *The Rainbow*, to *Women in Love*, was in fact a steady progression towards a kind of fiction which Bakhtin had already described in his study of Dostoevsky. There is irony in such an assertion, since Lawrence's recorded remarks about Dostoevsky are generally derogatory, and he expressed a strong preference for Tolstoy,[5] but there may have been some 'anxiety of influence' behind those comments. Consider how exactly Bakhtin's description of *Crime and Punishment* applies to *Women in Love*:

> Everything in this novel – the fates of people, their experience and ideas – is pushed to its boundaries, everything is prepared, as it were, to pass over into its opposite . . . everything is taken to extremes, to its uttermost limit. There is nothing in the novel that could become stabilised, nothing that could relax within itself, enter the ordinary flow of biographical time and develop in it . . . everything requires change and rebirth. Everything is shown in a moment of unfinalised transition.
>
> (*PDP*, p. 167)

Behind this observation there is another seminal distinction drawn by Bakhtin between the adventure novel and the social-psychological novel of everyday life. In the latter, the plot is articulated through family and class relationships, unfolded in historical or biographical time (such as the classic nineteenth-century novel of, say, Tolstoy or George Eliot) – there is, says Bakhtin 'no place for contingency here'. The plot of the adventure novel, in contrast, 'does not rely on already available and stable positions – family, social, biographical: it develops in spite of them . . . All social and cultural institutions, establishments, social states and classes, family relationships, are no more than positions in which a person can be eternally equal to himself' (*PDP*, pp. 103–4). What Dostoevsky did, according to Bakhtin, was to put the adventure plot 'at the service of the idea' – in other words, to make it the vehicle for exploring profound spiritual and metaphysical problems, crossing it with apparently incongruous genres such as the confession and the saint's life. *Women in Love*, too, is a kind of philosophical adventure story whose chief characters are questing, with religious fervour, for some new, ultimately satisfying way of life, at a moment of crisis for civilization. One of the most striking and 'experimental' features of this novel is its foregrounding of debates, arguments and moments of spiritual or erotic crisis and illumination, by relegating or deleting the kind of detail that we expect from the 'social-psychological novel of everyday life.'

This tendency is already observable in the later stages of *The Rainbow*, but in *Women in Love* it is taken much further, to a degree that breaks the mould of the traditional novel. The fine, tough mesh of social and kinship relationships and economic factors which conditions the actions of the protagonists in *The Rainbow* (and still more in *Sons and Lovers*) seems to melt away in *Women in Love*. Ursula's and Gudrun's parents, for instance, Will and Anna Brangwen, such powerful presences in *The Rainbow*, are diminished figures in the sequel, who scarcely impinge on the lives or consciousness of their daughters, even though the latter are still living at home. Little attention is given to the practical problems of life in *Women in Love*. The plot is arranged so as to leave the protagonists free to choose their fates – a small private income allows Birkin to give up his job, and his offer of marriage allows Ursula to give up hers. Gudrun agrees to become governess to Winifred Crich not out of economic necessity or self-interest, but as a stage in her relationship with Gerald: 'Gudrun knew it was a critical thing for her to go to Shortlands. She knew it was equivalent to accepting Gerald Crich as a lover.'[6]

'Plot in Dostoevsky,' says Bakhtin, 'is absolutely devoid of any sort of finalising foundations. Its goal is to place a person in various situations that expose and provoke him, to bring people together and make them collide and conflict – in such a way, however, that they do not remain within this area of plot-related contact but exceed its bounds' (*PDP*, pp. 276–7). Just so in *Women in Love*: the exiguous plot – essentially a double love story – exists merely to bring the protagonists into contact and conflict, and the issues thus raised are neither resolved nor contained within the history of their relationships.

We can appreciate the point more clearly by invoking Frank Kermode's useful comparison between *Women in Love* and that classic nineteenth-century novel of two interlinked couples, *Middlemarch.*[7] The fortunes of the Victorian quartet are traced, in a scrupulously recreated historical context, through 'biographical time', determined at every point by social, familial and economic factors. There is no place for contingency here. *Women in Love*, in contrast, is set in a deliberately ambiguous period which has elements of both pre-war and post-war England, and the reader has little sense of the precise duration of the story. The most memorable events of this story are, precisely, contingent: the drowning of Diana Crich at the water party, for instance, Gerald's brutal control of his terrified horse at the level crossing, the release of the rabbit Adolf from his hutch, or Birkin throwing stones at the reflection of the moon. These events do not seem to belong to any pattern of cause and effect – they simply happen, arbitrarily, randomly or spontaneously, and are invested with meaning by the reactions of those who are involved as actors or as spectators. Even when the action does seem to be conventionally motivated, the enactment is usually highly unconventional. Hermione, for instance, strikes Birkin with the paper-weight out of anger, frustration and jealousy, but her murderous attack seems in excess of the provocation, just as Birkin's reaction seems remarkably free from the sense of outrage that would be 'normal' after such an experience.

This is not the place to attempt to say what *Women in Love* 'means'. There have been enough attempts already, and there is some danger that, in the process of trying to extract a coherent body of thought from the novel, one will 'monologize' it, as Bakhtin accuses some of Dostoevsky's critics of doing to the Russian novelist's work. 'The catharsis that finalises Dostoevsky's novels might be ... expressed in this way,' says Bakhtin: '*nothing* conclusive has yet taken place in the world, the ultimate word of the world and about the world has not yet been spoken, the world is open and free, everything is still in the future and will always be in the future' (*PDP*, p. 166). This describes very well the ending of *Women in Love*:

> 'You can't have two kinds of love. Why should you!'
> 'It seems as if I can't' he said. 'Yet I wanted it.'
> 'You can't have it, because it's false, impossible,' she said.
> 'I don't believe that,' he answered.

Thus the novel literally ends, the dialogue between the hero and heroine still continuing. It began with a dialogue, between Ursula and Gudrun, about the pros and cons of marriage. In between, there are scores of similar scenes, where couples, trios, quartets and larger groups of people conduct debates on issues that are general and abstract and yet of vital importance to the chief characters. Although Rupert Birkin is the principal spokesman for Lawrence's own ideas in the novel, and a kind of self-portrait, he is not allowed to win these arguments. There are no winners. *Women in Love* is not a *roman à thèse*. It has not got a single *thèse*, but several, of which Lawrence's treatment is remarkably even-handed.

We may take as representative of the novel in this respect, chapter 3, 'Class-room', in which first Birkin and then Hermione visit Ursula's school, where she is conducting a botany lesson. It is typical of this novel that there is no attempt to evoke the physical specificity of the classroom, or the individual or collective character of the children; they are the thinnest pretext for mounting the debate, and are soon dismissed. Hermione questions the value of education – 'When we have knowledge, don't we lose everything but knowledge?' Birkin questions her good faith – 'You have no sensuality. You have only your will and your conceit of consciousness, and your lust for power, to *know*.' And Ursula questions the value of Birkin's 'sensuality, the great dark knowledge you can't have in your head' (pp. 45–7). We know from other, nonfictional texts, that Lawrence himself believed in the value of such dark knowledge, but Birkin is not allowed to triumph in this scene – indeed, he is often made to look slightly ridiculous (e.g. 'There was silence in the room. Both women were hostile and resentful. He sounded as if he were addressing a meeting'; p. 48). The advantage is constantly circulating between the three participants in the debate, partly because the latter has a subtext of emotional relationships. Hermione is trying to ingratiate herself with Birkin and to 'upstage' Ursula, whom she recognizes as a potential rival: but Hermione's sentiments strike Birkin as a kind of caricature of his own. Exasperated by this, and driven by a desire to break away from Hermione's influence, he attacks her with brutal scorn. Ursula, for her part, is puzzled and disturbed by Birkin's behaviour and opinions, and yet irresistibly, almost unconsciously, attracted by him. When both the others have gone, she weeps, 'but whether for misery, or joy, she never knew' (p. 49).

What makes this scene dialogic in the ideological as well as the purely formal or compositional sense (i.e. containing a lot of direct speech), is that the narrator never delivers a finalizing judgemental word on the debate or its protagonists. The narrator also 'circulates' between them. The narrator seldom speaks in a clearly distinct voice of his own, from a plane of knowledge above the characters: rather, he rapidly shifts his perspective on their level, and shows us now what Ursula is thinking of Birkin, now what Birkin is thinking of Ursula, now what Hermione is thinking of both of them, and they of her. This fluid, flexible handling of point of view was always characteristic of Lawrence's writing, but it was not always so impartial. In the first part of *Sons and Lovers*, for instance, Walter Morel is represented much more objectively, externally, than Mrs Morel. He is evoked for us by description of his dress, behaviour, etc., often in summary fashion. We seldom get the actual movement of his thought represented in free indirect style. He is allowed to speak only in direct speech that is rendered alien and uncouth-seeming by its dialect features. The conscious-ness of Mrs Morel, on the other hand, like that of her son Paul, is often represented in free indirect speech that borrows its eloquence and well-formed grammar in part from the authorial narrator. Thus, although the narrator *tells* us that Mr Morel was as much a victim of the tensions within the family as any of the other members, we do not as readers *feel* this on our pulses. Mr Morel is made to seem the villain, the Other, by the mobilization of the most powerful discourses in the text against him.

At the other end of his career, Lawrence was apt to forsake the dialogic principle in a more blatant way. In the 'leadership' novels, and to some extent in *Lady Chatterley's Lover*, we do feel that Lawrence is writing the *roman à thèse*, that he has predetermined the outcome of the struggle he has set in motion, fixed the game and rigged the pack. In *Women in Love*, in contrast, the reader is bounced, bewilderingly, exhilaratingly, from one subject position to another, and made to feel the force of each. Of course, the relationship between Ursula and Birkin is meant to seem more positive and hopeful than the doomed, mutually destructive passion of Gudrun and Gerald; but the latter pair have their own nobility and eloquence, and the quality of their carnal knowledge does not seem so very different from some of the 'darker' passages of lovemaking between Birkin and Ursula. As Frank Kermode has observed, 'in this version of Lawrence's apocalypse, it is necessary for those on the side of life to comply with dissolution in such a way that it is hard to distinguish them from the party of death'.[8] Or, in Bakhtin's words, quoted earlier, about *Crime and Punishment*, 'everything is prepared, as it were, to pass over into its opposite'.

Ursula says to Hermione, of Birkin, 'He says he wants me to accept him non-emotionally, and finally – I really don't know *what* he means. He says he wants the demon part of himself to be mated – physically – not the human being. You see, he says one thing one day, and another the next – and he always contradicts himself – ' (p. 330). Here the contradictions and instability of Birkin's (and Lawrence's) views are brought out by the quintessentially dialogic method of having them quoted by the baffled Ursula to an interested third party. The effect is ironic, almost comic. And, as we have seen, Ursula is left free to defend her own idea of love at the end of the novel. But in *The Plumed Serpent* or *The Woman Who Rode Away*, or *Lady Chatterley's Lover*, there is one privileged ideological pos-ition for the heroine to occupy, and towards which a dominant authorial discourse inexorably guides her.

So far, I have been describing the dialogic quality of Lawrence's fiction mainly in terms of the relationship between categories 1 and 2 of Bakhtin's typology of literary discourse – essentially, the dominance of the second type over the first, allowing a variety of subject positions to be articulated in the text without any obvious determination in favour of any one of them. But what about Bakhtin's third category, doubly-voiced or doubly-oriented discourse? It seems to me that we might usefully categorize some of the more heightened and rhapsodic passages describing erotic experience in *Women in Love* as 'stylization' in Bakhtin's terms. Consider, for example, this passage:

> 'You are mine, my love, aren't you?' she cried, straining him close.
>
> 'Yes,' he said softly.
>
> His voice was so soft and final, she went very still, as if under a fate which had taken her. Yes, she acquiesced – but it was accomplished without her acquiescence. He was kissing her quietly, repeatedly, with a soft, still happiness that almost made her heart stop beating. 'My love' she cried, lifting her face and looking with the frightened gentle wonder of bliss. Was it all real? But his eyes were beautiful and soft and immune from stress or excitement, beautiful and smiling lightly to her, smiling with her. She hid her face on his shoulder, hiding before him, because he could see her so completely. She knew he loved her, and she was afraid, she was in a strange element, a new heaven round about her.
>
> (p. 350)

This passage represents Ursula's sensations by borrowing words and phrases, syntax and rhythms, characteristic of the genre known today (somewhat anomalously) as 'romance' – i.e. the heroine-centred love story. I believe many readers, confronted with the passage out of context, would attribute it to a Mills and Boon author, or an earlier exponent of the same genre. It is not, admittedly, stylized or objectified to the extent of say, the 'Nausicaa' episode of *Ulysses*, but it is certainly comparable to the consciously Decadent prose in which Stephen Dedalus's sexual initiation is described in *A Portrait of the Artist as a Young Man*:

> It was too much for him. He closed his eyes, surrendering himself to her, body and mind, conscious of nothing in the world but the dark pressure of her softly parting lips. They pressed upon his brain as upon his lips as though they were the vehicle of a vague speech: and between them he felt an unknown and timid pressure, darker than the swoon of sin, softer than sound or odour.[9]

In each case, the echo of another discourse, a somewhat suspect written discourse, puts the reader on his guard against identifying too readily and deeply with the emotion of the character that is being described, against confusing sincerity with truth. Ursula's 'bliss' is genuine, and the moment is an authentic threshold to a new and more meaningful relationship with Birkin, but it is only a beginning. She still perceives this relationship in the unregenerate terms of sentimental 'love', and the language warns us of this. For her full initiation into the dark knowledge and power that Birkin offers her, Lawrence turns to a different kind of stylized discourse, borrowed from religious and quasi-religious sources – biblical, gnostic, occult:

He stood before her, glimmering, so awfully real, that her heart almost stopped beating. He stood there in his strange, whole body that had its marvellous fountains, like the bodies of the sons of God who were in the beginning. There were strange fountains of his body, more mysterious and potent than any she had imagined or known, more satisfying, ah, finally, mystically-physically satisfying. She had thought there was no source deeper than the phallic source. And now, behold, from the smitten rock of the man's body, from the strange marvellous flanks and thighs, deeper, further in mystery than the phallic source, came the floods of ineffable darkness and ineffable riches.

(p. 354)

Such passages are often deplored and ridiculed by readers hostile to Lawrence, and treated with embarrassed shiftiness by his admirers. Obviously it is a very risky technique, and there will always be disagreement as to how successful it is in gesturing towards a reality on the other side of language ('she knew, as well as he knew, that words themselves do not convey meaning, that they are a gesture we make, a dumb show like any other'; p. 209). But it would be absurd to suppose that Lawrence did not know what risks he was taking – that he was trying to write in a monologically referential style, and somehow failed to observe the normative stylistic criteria of elegance, precision and good taste. As Bakhtin says, 'If we . . . perceive stylization or parody in the same way ordinary speech is perceived, that is as speech directed only at its referential object, then we will not grasp these phenomena in their essence: stylisation will be taken for style, parody simply for a poor work of art' (*PDP*, p. 185).

A story which illustrates this point very clearly is the late story by Lawrence called 'Things', a cruel but amusing portrait of his friends, Earl and Aschah Brewster.[10] Technically it is a very interesting piece, being in Bakhtin's terms a kind of stylized *skaz*. It begins:

They were true idealists, from New England. But that is some time ago: before the war. Several years before the war, they met and married: he a tall, keen-eyed young man from Connecticut, she a smallish, demure, Puritan-looking young woman from Massachusetts. They both had a little money. Not much, however. Even added together, it didn't make three thousand dollars a year. Still – they were free. Free!

Ah! Freedom! To be free to live one's own life! To be twenty-five and twenty-seven, a pair of true idealists with a mutual love of beauty, and an inclination towards 'Indian thought' – meaning, alas, Mrs. Besant – and an income a little under three thousand dollars a year! But what is money? All one wishes to do is to live a full and beautiful life. In Europe, of course, right at the fountain-head of tradition. It might possibly be done in America: in New England, for example. But at a forfeiture of a certain amount of 'beauty'. True beauty takes a long time to mature.

(p. 208)

The rhythm and syntax of this prose – its short, staccato sentences, moodless exclamations ('Ah! Freedom!'), its frequent qualifications and reservations, signalled by the words, 'but', 'however', 'still' – all create the impression of an oral narrator, of someone speaking his thoughts as they come to him, without the logical ordering, sifting and polishing one expects from writing. More interesting still is the way that the diction seems to be borrowed from the character to whom it refers. It is not only the words 'Indian thought' and 'beauty' that are quoted from the speech of Valerie and Erasmus, though they alone are enclosed in inverted commas. 'But what is money? All one wishes to do is to live a full and beautiful life. In Europe, of course, right at the fountain-head of tradition.' This is also a kind of quotation: it articulates the motivation of the couple in their own slightly precious language of idealistic connoisseurship. The implied author lets us hear his own accent and his own opinion in the parenthesis, 'meaning, alas, Mrs. Besant': but for most of the story he reveals the superficiality of the couple's pursuit of the good, the true and the beautiful by describing it in their own kind of language. The style of the story is a kind of condensation of thousands of remarks, rhetorical questions and reflections the characters might be imagined as having uttered or formulated mentally to themselves during the years covered by the story. And this discourse is *itself* a kind of doubly-oriented discourse, since it always seems to be anxiously aware of some other discourse – pragmatic, rational, sceptical – against which it is defending itself.

> They explored Paris *thoroughly*. And they learned French till they almost felt like French people, they could speak it so glibly.
>   Still, you know, you never talk French with your *soul*. It can't be done. And though it's very thrilling, at first, talking French to clever Frenchmen – they seem *so* much cleverer than oneself, still, in the long run, it is not satisfying. The endlessly clever *materialism* of the French leaves you cold, in the end, gives a sense of barrenness and incompatibility with true New England depths. So our two idealists felt.
>
> (p. 210)

Here Lawrence tells us how his two characters 'felt', in the kind of language they would have used, perhaps actually did use, to explain and justify to themselves, to each other, and to an Other, their decision to leave France. In the next few lines the Other (an anonymous spokesman for common sense) is allowed to speak directly in the text, and dialogic discourse becomes overt dialogue:

> They turned away from France – but ever so gently. France had disappointed them. 'We've loved it, and we've got a great deal out of it. But after a while, after a considerable while, several years, in fact, Paris leaves

one feeling disappointed. It hasn't quite got what one wants.' 'But Paris isn't France.' 'No, perhaps not. France is quite different from Paris. And France is lovely – quite lovely. But *to us*, though we love it, it doesn't say a great deal.'

So when the war came, the idealists moved to Italy.

(p. 210)

But Italy also disappoints them, and this disappointment is again represented in a tissue of putative quotation from the speech and thought of Erasmus and Valerie, in free indirect style:

And though they had had a very wonderful time in Europe, and though they still loved Italy – dear Italy! – yet: they were disappointed. They had got a lot out of it: oh, a very great deal indeed! Still, it hadn't given them quite, not *quite*, what they had expected. Europe was lovely, but it was dead. Living in Europe, you were living on the past. And Europeans, with their superficial charm, were not *really* charming. They were materialistic, they had no *real* soul.

(p. 212)

'Things' is an ironic quest-story. Disillusioned with Europe, the couple return to America, only to find that they cannot afford a house big enough to accommodate the beautiful 'things' they have acquired in exile. They put the 'things' in store, and experiment with the simple life in a log-cabin in the West, but that is a disaster. They return to Europe, but that is 'a complete failure'.

[Erasmus] found he couldn't stand Europe. It irritated every nerve in his body. He hated America too. But America at least was a darn sight better than this miserable, dirt-eating continent: which was by no means cheap any more, either.

(pp. 218–19)

We catch here a significant, new linguistic register in the discourse – homely, sardonic, distinctively American – which signals the couple's reluctant coming-to-terms with their real problem: the fact, intimated in the first paragraph of the story, but never faced by them till now, that their income is insufficient to support their ideals. (The economic dependence of ideals upon money is of course an ironic comment on the former.) They are compelled to the conclusion that Erasmus must work for a living, as a teacher at a midwestern university. This decision is in some sense a defeat, especially for Erasmus, yet it is also a relief. ('He was a changed man, quieter, much less irritable. A load off him. He was inside the cage.') The couple's acceptance of a way of life antithetical to everything they had previously aspired to is represented by the change in their speech, from the refined, cultured, 'European' cadences and constructions of the earlier part of the story, to a native American idiom characterized by a kind of crass, cracker-barrel folk-wisdom. The story ends like this:

'Europe's the mayonnaise all right, but America supplies the good old lobster – what?' 'Every time!' she said, with satisfaction. And he peered at her. He was in the cage: but it was safe inside. And she, evidently, was her real self at last. She had got the goods. Yet round his nose was a queer, evil, scholastic look, of pure scepticism. But he liked lobster.

(p. 220)

In 'Things', Lawrence puts his characters in a double bind, allowing them a choice only between equally inauthentic ways of life, and mocking them with the inauthenticity of the language in which they articulate and defend these choices. The frequency with which the words 'but' or 'yet' or 'still' occur in the text epitomizes the hopelessness of the couple's quest, their restless oscillation between alternatives doomed to be unsatisfying. Thus, in spite of its elaborate use of doubly-voiced discourse, the story is hardly 'polyphonic' in Bakhtin's sense. Though the characters are allowed to 'answer back', their self-defence is undermined by the inherent contradictions of their quest. The story is, however, in its cruel way, comic.

This brings me, finally, to the question of whether it makes any sense to place D. H. Lawrence in the tradition of the serio-comic, or carnivalesque, writing which Bakhtin came to see as crucial to the evolution of the novel as a literary form. At first sight it seems an unpromising speculation, for though there is incidental comedy in much of Lawrence's fiction, it is generally very much dominated by a basically 'serious' tone and pushed to the margins of narratives that are essentially tragic or romantic in structure, leading to climaxes of death and/or rebirth. Bakhtin himself faced much the same problem in relation to Dostoevsky, who was central to the original formation of the 'polyphonic' novel, but who, at first sight, seems to have little in common with the ribald comedy of the carnivalesque tradition. Bakhtin met this difficulty with the concept of 'reduced laughter', the idea that the carnivalesque subversion of orthodox hierarchies can be achieved without overt comedy:

Under certain conditions and in certain genres . . . laughter can be reduced. It continues to determine the structure of the image, but it itself is muffled down to the minimum: we see, as it were, the track left by laughter in the structure of represented reality, but the laughter itself we do not hear . . . In Dostoevsky's great novels, laughter is reduced almost to the minimum (especially in *Crime and Punishment*). In all his novels, however, we find a trace of that ambivalent laughter, absorbed by Dostoevsky together with the generic carnivalization, performing its work of artistically organizing and illuminating the world . . . the more important – one could say, the decisive – expression of reduced laughter is to be found in the ultimate position of the author . . . this position excludes all one-sided or dogmatic seriousness, and does not permit any single point of view, any single polar extreme of life or thought, to be absolutized . . . We speak here of Dostoevsky the artist. Dostoevsky the journalist was by no means a stranger to cramped and one-sided seriousness, to dogmatism, even to eschatology. But these ideas of the journalist, once introduced into the novel, become then merely one of the embodied voices of an unfinalized and open dialogue . . . Reduced laughter in carnivalized literature by no means excludes the possibility of somber colours within a work. For this reason the somber coloration of Dostoevsky's works should not confuse us: it is not their final word.

(*PDP*, pp. 164–6)

I have quoted this passage at length because of its suggestive relevance to D. H. Lawrence – in particular, the distinction between the artist and the journalist, which one might usefully apply to the relationship between the ideas expounded by Lawrence in nonfictional texts like *The Crown*, and their appearance in fictional texts like *Women in Love* or *England, My England*. If a suspicion remains that the concept of 'reduced laughter' is a rather convenient 'loophole' (to use another of Bakhtin's own terms) through which writers not obviously recognizable as carnivalesque, such as Dostoevsky and Lawrence, can nevertheless be accommodated with that tradition, it is worth noting that a work has recently been added to the Lawrence canon which may be called carnivalesque without apology or qualification – that indeed can hardly be read without some such generic frame of reference. I refer, of course, to *Mr Noon*.

Mr Noon is an unfinished, but substantial novel, written by Lawrence in 1920–1, of which only the first part (included in *A Modern Lover*, 1934, and *Phoenix II*, 1968) was known until the manuscript of the second, longer part came to light quite recently. The whole of the extant work was published in the Cambridge edition of Lawrence's works in 1984.[11] The first part is about a schoolteacher, Gilbert Noon (closely based on a Nottinghamshire friend of Lawrence's, George Henry Neville), who gets into a sexual scrape with another young schoolteacher, and is forced to resign his job in consequence. The second part is set in Germany, where Gilbert (now much more like Lawrence himself) meets and falls in love with Johanna Keighley, the sister of his German professor, married to an Englishman (and a transparent portrait of Frieda Weekley). The remainder of the novel chronicles Johanna's desertion of her husband for Gilbert and their symbolic journey across the Alps on foot, a story based closely on the elopement of Frieda with Lawrence, and its immediate sequel.

As it stands, the two parts of *Mr Noon* do not cohere on the level of either character or narrative, and this was probably one reason why Lawrence abandoned it. The two parts are, however, linked thematically, and there is a character called Patty Goddard, an unfulfilled married friend of Gilbert's, a 'soft, full, strange, unmated Aphrodite of forty', in Part I, who was evidently designed to provide the hero with a truly rewarding sexual relationship – a role that, in the event, Lawrence transferred on to the more glamorous, exotic and fact-based character of Johanna. In short, *Mr Noon* deals with a theme (the sexual relationship) and draws on experience (Lawrence's own relationship with Frieda) that were crucially important to him, and about which he had written many times before. But what was unusual about this book was that Lawrence conceived it from the beginning as a comedy, and started it because he was blocked on the rather tiresomely 'monologic' *Aaron's Rod*. 'I . . . can't end it,' he wrote to a correspondent at the time, 'so I began a comedy.'[12] The comedy in *Mr Noon* is generated partly by situation (there are, for instance, several amusing scenes in which the lovers are surprised *in flagrante delicto*, or in post-coital *déshabille*) and partly by the narrator's voice, which is intrusive but not monologic – on the contrary, it is very varied in tone: teasing, hectoring, facetious, ironic, rhapsodic and prophetic by turns. The two sources of comedy are piquantly combined in chapter 15, when the authorial narrator prevents the reader, as it were, from disturbing the lovers' privacy. The scene occurs early in the relationship between Gilbert and Johanna, and describes their second sexual encounter, snatched in a brief interlude before dinner is served in the flat of Johanna's brother-in-law. It begins with a powerfully erotic image and a hymn to sexual desire:

> Johanna was hovering in the doorway of her room as he went down the passage. A bright, roused look was on her face. She lifted her eyelids with a strange flare of invitation, like a bird lifting its wings. And for the first time the passion broke like lightning out of Gilbert's blood: for the first time in his life. He went into her room with her and shut the door. The sultriness and lethargy of his soul had broken into a storm of desire for her, a storm which shook and swept him at varying intervals all his life.
>
> Oh wonderful desire: violent, genuine desire! Oh magnificence of stormy elemental desire, which is at once so elemental and so intensely individual! Oh storms of acute sex passion, which shatter the soul, and re-make it, as summer is made up out of the débâcle of thunder! . . . The cyclone of actual desire – not mere titillation and functional gratification – or any other -ation – broke now for the first time upon Gilbert, and flung him down the wind. Not, dear moralist, to break against the buttresses of some christian cathedral which rose in his path. Not at all. It flung him smack through the cathedrals like a long-shotted shell. Heaven knows where it did not fling him. I'll tell you later on.
>
> But for the moment, I insist on apostrophising desire, intense individual desire, in order to give my hero time. O thunder-god, who sends the

white passion of pure, sensual desire upon us, breaking through the sultry
rottenness of our old blood like jagged lightning, and switching us into
a new, dynamic reaction, hail!

(pp. 136–7)

Here Lawrence apostrophizes desire in a kind of portentous language akin
to the more rhapsodic erotic passages of *The Rainbow* and *Women in Love*,
but pretends to be doing so only to give his lovers time to consummate
their passion. This Shandean joke is saucily entertaining in its own right
and also protects the paean to desire from any ironic scepticism on the
reader's part. The reader, indeed, soon finds himself on the sharp end of
the narrator's irony:

> Oh thunder-god, god of the dangerous bolts – ! – No, gentle reader,
> please don't interrupt, I am *not* going to open the door of Johanna's
> room, not until Mr Noon opens it himself. I've been caught that way
> before. I have opened the door for you, and the moment you gave your
> first squeal in rushed the private detective you had kept in the back-
> ground. Thank you, gentle reader, you can open your own doors. I
> am busy apostrophising Jupiter Tonans, Zeus of the Thunder-bolt, the
> almighty Father of passion and sheer desire. I'm not talking about *your*
> messy little feelings and licentiousness, either. I'm talking about desire.
> So don't interrupt. Am *I* writing this book, or are you?

(p. 137)

The narrator of *Mr Noon* frequently addresses the reader directly in this
way, drawing attention to the fictionality of the text by reference to its
conventions, and to the 'real author' behind it (a D. H. Lawrence persecuted
by censors and hostile critics). This metafictional strain in the text, which the
Russian formalists called 'baring the device' and Erving Goffman 'breaking
frame', is characteristic of Bakhtin's serio-comic, carnivalesque literary tradition, as are other features of *Mr Noon*: passages of parodic, travestying,
tongue-in-cheek writing, earthy humour centring on backsides and
excretion, farcical incidents in which the pretensions of polite society are
subverted or overturned. Cumulatively, these features have a very positive
effect on Lawrence's treatment of the relationship between Gilbert and
Johanna. Without in any way undermining the authenticity and credibility
of their passion for each other, or diminishing the joy it brings them,
Lawrence also avoids sentimentalizing or idealizing the lovers, and achieves
a remarkable balance and objectivity in dealing with extremely intimate
personal experience. Although its narrative structure is irreparably broken-
backed, and the jocularity of the narrative voice is overdone at times, one
cannot but regret that Lawrence abandoned *Mr Noon*, and never resumed
the experiment of writing in an overtly carnivalesque mode.

For the only novel in his *oeuvre* which at all resembles *Mr Noon* is *The*

Lost Girl (1920), which Lawrence wrote not long before, and which he described, while it was in progress, as 'a rather comic novel'.[13] Both novels begin in a similar vein, treating thinly disguised Eastwood personages with high-spirited humour, and have an elopement to Italy as their narrative climax. There are a few mildly metafictional asides by the authorial narrator of *The Lost Girl* (e.g. 'Surely enough books have been written about heroines in similar circumstances. There is no need to go into the details of Alvina's six months in Islington'; p. 32), though nothing like the radically disruptive apostrophizing of the reader in *Mr Noon*. Nor is there much explicit ribaldry in *The Lost Girl*, since, as John Worthen shows in his introduction, Lawrence was consciously trying to write a book that would not be 'at all improper: quite fit for Mudie's' (p. xxx). However, in Alvina's sudden, spontaneous choice of midwifery as a profession, which so shocks her bourgeois family (because of its association with what Bakhtin terms 'the lower body') and for which she trains in an atmosphere of bawdy humour and sexual harassment (see pp. 32–9); and in the spectacularly physical Red Indian act of the Natcha-Kee-Tawara troupe, through whom Alvina ultimately finds sexual and personal liberation, we may see displaced manifestations of carnivalesque behaviour.

If the Rabelaisian vein of *Mr Noon* was rather regrettably attenuated in Lawrence's subsequent novels, the best of them nevertheless respond well to a Bakhtinian critical approach, as I have tried to suggest in commenting on *Women in Love*. The compatibility is more than merely formal: there is obviously an interesting parallel to be drawn between the socio-political implications of Bakhtin's theories and D. H. Lawrence's 'metaphysic' – between Bakhtin's view that carnival behaviour was progressively suppressed, outlawed and marginalized in the era of bourgeois capitalism,[14] and Lawrence's view that man's (and woman's) instinctual life had been denied and repressed by the same social forces. But to pursue that parallel further is beyond the scope of this essay.

Chapter 5

Dialogue in the modern novel

In my first book of criticism, entitled *Language of Fiction*, I wrote that

> If we are right to regard the art of poetry as an art of language, then so
> is the art of the novel; and . . . the critic of the novel has no special
> dispensation from that close and sensitive engagement with language we
> naturally expect from the art of poetry.[1]

I do not withdraw that assertion, but I should want, now, to add an
important rider: that the signifying system of the novel cannot be limited
to the surface structure of the text, the 'words on the page', the object of
'close reading' or 'practical criticism' in its classic form. Novels are narrative
discourse, and narrative is a kind of language in itself that transcends the
boundaries of natural languages within which stylistic criticism operates
most confidently and competently. It was my neglect of this simple and
obvious truth in *Language of Fiction* – my attempt to reduce all questions
of meaning and value in novels to questions of specific verbal usage – that
now seems to me a fatal flaw in its theoretical argument, and a limitation
(perhaps not quite so fatal) of its critical power.

Another aspect of the art of the novel neglected in that book is dialogue,
both in the ordinary literary-critical sense of the word – the representation
of direct speech in prose fiction – and in the more comprehensive sense to
be learned from the writings of Mikhail Bakhtin. Indeed everything I have
to say here could take as its epigraph these two, closely adjacent passages
from Bakhtin's *Problems of Dostoevsky's Poetics*:

> The possibility of employing on the plane of a single work discourses of
> various types, with all their expressive capacities intact, without reducing
> them to a single common denominator – this is one of the most fundamen-
> tal characteristics of prose. Herein lies the profound distinction between
> prose style and poetic style . . . For the prose artist the world is full of
> other people's words, among which he must orient himself and whose
> speech characteristics he must be able to perceive with a very keen ear.
> He must introduce them into the plane of his own discourse, but in such

a way that this plane is not destroyed. He works with a very rich verbal palette.[2]

The truth of this description of the novelist's art is immediately apparent to me from my experience of writing as well as reading prose fiction. Yet it is a truth to which criticism of the novel has hardly done justice. This is because poetics, the explicit or implicit theoretical base of criticism, has always privileged poetry. As Bakhtin says, a literary stylistics derived from the practice of the canonized poetic genres – epic, lyric, tragedy – is not appropriate to prose fiction. These genres are what he calls 'monologic' – they employ a single style, and express a single world-view. Even if different speakers are represented in such a text, nevertheless an all-pervasive poetic decorum ensures that the total effect is one of stylistic (and, Bakhtin would add, ideological) consistency and uniformity. The novel, in contrast, is inherently 'dialogic' or, in an alternative formulation, 'polyphonic' – an orchestration of diverse discourses culled from both writing and oral speech. If poetic exceptions to this rule immediately spring to mind, I think that most of them will come either from the modern period, when the novel was the dominant form, and the other genres became, in Bakhtin's term, 'novelized': or, if earlier, they were influenced by what he calls the unofficial discourse of carnival, and the serio-comic genres of antiquity that prepared the way for the novel.

Now of course the ability of the great novelists to represent different types of speech has not been entirely ignored by criticism, but it has been treated mainly as a means of expressing character, or as an aspect of the novel's realism considered as an end in itself – the reproduction, in a pointed and entertaining form, of behaviour that we recognize from life. Fielding's Squire Western, Jane Austen's Miss Bates, Dickens's Mrs Gamp are cases that spring to mind along with a hundred others. The limitation of such an approach is that it underestimates the extent to which the total meaning of a given novel is mediated through a plurality of voices, some, on occasion all, of which cannot be treated as the author's. When, for the purposes of practical criticism of the novel, we take what is deemed to be a representative passage from a novel by Dickens, or George Eliot, or Thomas Hardy, or D. H. Lawrence, we invariably choose a passage of narrative description that is either authorial, or focalized through a character with whom the implied author is in sympathy. In other words we look for something like the equivalent of the lyric voice in poetry – some unified and homogeneous verbal expression of the author's personal vision of the world. Most of the passages singled out for close analysis in *Language of Fiction* are of this kind. But of course the unique quality of an individual writer's vision of the world and experience may be conveyed just as effectively through the reproduction and manipulation of voices other than his own. Evelyn Waugh's *A Handful of Dust*, for instance, begins thus:

'Was anyone hurt?'

'No one, I am thankful to say,' said Mrs. Beaver, 'except two house-maids who lost their heads and jumped through a glass roof into the paved court. They were in no danger. The fire never reached the bedrooms, I am afraid. Still, they are bound to need doing up, everything black with smoke and drenched in water and luckily they had that old-fashioned sort of extinguisher that ruins *everything*. One really cannot complain. The chief rooms were *completely* gutted and everything was insured. Sylvia Newport knows the people. I must get on to them this morning before that ghoul Mrs Shutter snaps them up.'

Mrs. Beaver stood with her back to the fire, eating her morning yogh-ourt. She held the carton close under her chin and gobbled with a spoon.

'Heavens, how nasty this stuff is. I wish you'd take to it, John. You're looking so tired lately. I don't know how I should get through the day without it.'

'But, mumsy, I haven't as much to do as you have.'

'That's true, my son.'[3]

The pleasure this passage yields, and its force as a comment on a particular form of modern decadence, is produced by the reader's work of inference. Our inference of the event being narrated – a domestic fire – proceeds *pari passu* with an appalled recognition of the selfish and commercial motives of the narrator, Mrs Beaver. The passage is funny as well as shocking because the very same features that express the character's callousness also function to delay the reader's full understanding of that callousness; thus the passage is full of little surprises, disconfirmations of expectations, which heighten to a comic degree the gap between moral norms and Mrs Beaver's attitudes and values. To demonstrate this it is necessary to replay the passage in slow-motion:

'Was anyone hurt?'

'No one, I am thankful to say,' said Mrs Beaver, 'except two housemaids . . .'

'Except two housemaids' is a pretty substantial qualification of 'no one' – indeed a logical contradiction. That the speaker evidently does not see it as such tells us a lot about the arrogance of her character and her social class, and makes us revise our original assessment of the apparently benevolent sentiment, 'I am thankful to say'. The unexpectedness of the qualification, 'except two housemaids', is delayed, and thus heightened, by the phrase, 'I am thankful to say', and also by the interpolated speech tag, 'said Mrs. Beaver'. The impact of this sentence would be much weakened if the order of clauses were rearranged to read: 'No one, except two housemaids, I am thankful to say, said Mrs. Beaver.' But we don't perceive the full enormity of her attitude to the housemaids until we complete the sentence, 'two housemaids, who lost their heads and jumped through a glass roof into the paved court'. We infer that not only were they *hurt* – they must have been very severely injured, perhaps fatally. So far from dwelling sympathetically on their misfortune, however, the speaker proceeds to blame them for the impetuousness of their action: 'They were in no danger.' The next sentence, 'The fire never reached the bedrooms', which seems to be a logical expansion of the proposition that the maids were in no danger, is followed by the disconcerting tag 'I am afraid'. The first-time reader experiences a kind of moral vertigo at this point. Why would anyone regret that the maids were in no danger? As the next sentence begins 'Still, they are bound to need', it is possible that the 'they' refers back to the housemaids, and it is only as we come to '[bound to need] doing up' that we realize that Mrs Beaver is more interested in the rooms than in their occupants – because, we infer, she is an interior decorator, and hopes to get the contract to repair the damage. 'Luckily they had that old-fashioned sort of extinguisher that ruins *everything*. One really cannot complain.' Banal, everyday language, full of cliché and lazy hyperbole – there is absolutely nothing here for a stylistics based on poetic criteria of excellence to get a grip on; yet an extraordinary intensity and richness of meaning is generated by the contrast between what the words should, according to ethical norms, signify, and what they do in fact signify in this context: a consistent inversion of the moral and natural orders, which is sustained through the succeeding lines in Mrs Beaver's relation to her son.

Context is, of course, the key. The fact that the meaning of an utterance is always determined by a context that is partly non-verbal is the reason why semantics is the most difficult area of linguistic research. Meaning in actual speech can never be analysed in purely linguistic terms, because the relations between addresser, addressee and topic are not contained within the linguistic data. Bakhtin, writing, as he often did, under the name of his friend Volosinov, gives an example of two people sitting in a room and one of them uttering the word 'Well!'[4] On its own, this word is unintelligible. Postulate that the room is in Russia, that the month is May, and that both people have observed that it is snowing outside, and the word becomes charged with meaning: surprise, annoyance, solidarity between the two people sharing this disappointing delay of spring. As Bakhtin says, much would be conveyed in a real-life speech situation by the intonation with which the word 'Well!' is pronounced – intonation in speech having a quasi-metaphorical function. 'If this potential were realised,' he says, 'then the word "well" would unfold into something like the following metaphorical expression: "How *stubborn* the winter is, it won't give way, even though it is high time." '

Now the literary text cannot reproduce intonation with any exactness or delicacy of discrimination (though much may be done by the use of italics, by punctuation or the omission of it, by the placing of words and clauses in relation to each other). But what the literary text *can* do is to provide a verbal description of what in real life would be the non-verbal or non-verbalized contexts of a given utterance – even an utterance like 'Humph!', the meaning of which is entirely determined by intonation and context. The example I am thinking of occurs in chapter 17 of book II of Sterne's *Tristram Shandy*, where Mr Shandy, Uncle Toby and Dr Slop, the Roman Catholic obstetrician, are listening to Corporal Trim reading a sermon that has been discovered in an old book. Dr Slop makes a reference to the sacraments, of which there are, of course, seven in the Roman Catholic Church but only two recognized in the articles of the Church of England:

> – Pray, how many have you in all, said my Uncle Toby, for I always forget? – Seven, answered Dr. Slop. – Humph! said my Uncle Toby; though not accented as a note of acquiescence, – but as an interjection of that particular species of surprise, when a man in looking into a drawer, finds more of a thing than he expected. – Humph! replied my Uncle Toby. Dr. Slop, who had an ear, understood my Uncle Toby as well as if he had wrote a whole volume against the seven sacraments – Humph! replied Dr. Slop (stating my Uncle Toby's argument over again to him) – Why, sir, are there not seven cardinal virtues? Seven mortal sins? Seven golden candlesticks? Seven heavens? – 'Tis more than I know, replied my Uncle Toby.[5]

Here, Sterne realizes what Bakhtin calls the metaphorical potential of intonation, precisely by finding a metaphorical translation of Uncle Toby's grunt – the analogy of a man looking into a drawer and finding more of a thing than he expected.

Evelyn Waugh does not do this in the opening passage of *A Handful of Dust*. He gives some indication of Mrs Beaver's intonation by italicizing 'everything' and 'completely' ('that old-fashioned sort of extinguisher that ruins *everything* . . . the rooms were *completely* gutted') but he provides no contextual information, and we have to infer what the speaker is referring to, and work out for ourselves the implications of her tone. He is not always so self-denying in this novel, but some of the most effective passages in it, and in Waugh's other early novels, consist of dialogue with a minimum of narrative description and authorial commentary. Perhaps that is why he was one of the first novelists to exploit the possibilities of the telephone in fiction, telephonic communication being the kind of speech that most closely approximates to the state of *absence* that Derrida[6] has taught us is characteristic of written discourse, but without the compensatory communicative power of literary rhetoric. In telephonic communication, the interlocutors are absent from each other's physical space, unable to employ or react to body language, and even the metaphorical potential of intonation is restricted by the flattening, thinning acoustics of the telephone receiver. Telephonic conversation in fiction thus lends itself readily to effects of comic confusion of meanings and intentions (in one of my own novels, a crossed line leads to the storming of the British Museum Reading Room by the London Fire Brigade);[7] it also lends itself to ironic effects of alienation and loss. Chapter XI of Waugh's *Vile Bodies* consists entirely of the following dialogue between hero and heroine (Ginger is Adam's friend):

> Adam rang up Nina.
> 'Darling, I've been so happy about your telegram. Is it really true?'
> 'No, I'm afraid not.'
> 'The Major *is* bogus?'
> 'Yes.'
> 'You haven't got any money?'
> 'No.'
> 'We aren't going to be married today?'
> 'No.'
> 'I see.'
> 'Well?'
> 'I said, I see.'
> 'Is that all?'
> 'Yes, that's all, Adam.'
> 'I'm sorry.'
> 'I'm sorry, too. Good-bye.'
> 'Good-bye, Nina.'
> Later Nina rang up Adam.
> 'Darling, is that you? I've got something rather awful to tell you.'
> 'Yes?'
> 'You'll be furious.'
> 'Well?'
> 'I'm engaged to be married.'
> 'Who to?'
> 'I hardly think I can tell you.'
> 'Who?'
> 'Adam, you won't be beastly about it, will you?'
> 'Who is it?'
> 'Ginger.'
> 'I don't believe it.'
> 'Well, I am. That's all there is to it.'
> 'You're going to marry Ginger?'
> 'Yes.'
> 'I see.'
> 'Well?'
> 'I said, I see.'
> 'Is that all?'
> 'Yes, that's all, Nina.'

'When shall I see you?'
'I don't want ever to see you again.'
'I see.'
'Well?'
'I said, I see.'
'Well, good-bye.'
'Good-bye . . . I'm sorry, Adam.'[8]

One of the ironies of this beautifully written exchange is the frequency of the tag 'I see' – precisely what the two interlocutors cannot do as regards each other.

Evelyn Waugh belonged to what may be called the first post-modernist generation of English novelists – the first, that is, who had to define their work against the achievement of the great modernists such as James, Conrad, Joyce, Virginia Woolf. Every new generation of writers must do the same – take the work of their immediate predecessors into account, but do something different. In Freudian, or Harold Bloomian terms, it is an Oedipal struggle of sons against their literary fathers, but the novelists of the 1930s faced a particularly daunting set of precursors. Several of them besides Waugh chose to foreground dialogue in their fiction – one thinks, for example, of Henry Green, Christopher Isherwood and Ivy Compton-Burnett. Whereas the modernist novel was characteristically a novel of consciousness, of the subconscious and the unconscious, of memory, reverie, introspection and dream, the thirties novel is characteristically about social and verbal interaction, presented objectively and externally. The stream of consciousness gives way to a stream of talk, but it is talk without the reassuring gloss of the classic novel's authorial voice, without a privileged access to the thoughts and motivations of characters, so that the 'modern' note of disillusion, fragmentation and solipsism persists. The very title of A Handful of Dust asserts this continuity of theme with the modernist movement, though formally it could hardly be more different from Eliot's mythopoeic montage in The Waste Land.

I said just now that something of the intonational level of speech could be conveyed in written discourse by punctuation or the omission of punctuation. This is because punctuation can only indicate pauses in speech, not intonational pitch, and in printed texts, especially after the eighteenth century, is highly conventional, bearing little relation to the way people break up their utterances in actual speech. For example, if a person is apostrophized by name in a line of printed dialogue, it is customary to put a comma immediately after the preceding phrase. Thus, in the passage from A Handful of Dust, we find 'I wish you'd take to it, John' though it is likely that Mrs Beaver would say 'I wish you'd take to it John', with no perceptible pause between 'it' and 'John'. An interesting example of the power of the convention is afforded by the title of Ring Lardner's first

book *You Know Me Al* (1916), which is invariably punctuated in standard
reference books as *You Know Me, Al*, although there is no comma in the
original title. The book consists of letters written home, to an old buddy
called Al, by a brash and barely literate baseball rookie, who writes as he
talks. Ring Lardner was, of course, a master of the narrative style known
in Russian poetics as *skaz* – the oral vernacular; and the title *You Know
Me Al* epitomizes his skill. The absence of the comma that would be
conventional in the printed title after *Me* compels the reader to punctuate
the phrase himself in order to interpret it, and this compels him to pronounce it silently to himself, recreating its rhythm and intonation, recognizing and relishing its rhetorical function – at once phatic and self-con-
gratulatory.

Henry Green used the same technique to great effect on upper-class
English speech in those late novels of his that consist almost entirely of
dialogue. Here is a typical passage from *Nothing* (1951), a comedy about
the generation gap. The middle-aged Jane Weatherby is having lunch at the
Ritz with her rather stolid admirer, Richard Abbot.

> 'Richard,' she said at last, having dabbed her red mouth with a napkin,
> 'I'm worried to death about my Philip!'
>
> 'What's the lad up to now?'
>
> 'Oh my dear he so needs a father's influence. The dread time has come
> I'm afraid! I'm fussed dear Richard.'
>
> 'If I'm to help I must know more you know.'
>
> 'I almost can't find the way to tell you it's all so confusing but there's
> Philip's whole attitude to women.'
>
> 'Playing fast and loose?'
>
> 'Oh no I rather wish he would though I fear he is far too much of a
> snob for that, no no, worse, it's the other, oh dear if I go on like this I
> shall never explain, oh but Richard what has one done to deserve things?
> Sometimes I almost wonder if he knows the facts of life even. You see
> he respects girls so!'
>
> Mrs Weatherby made her eyes very round and large to give Dick
> Abbot an adorable long glance of woe.
>
> 'Good God,' he replied with caution.[9]

Like Lardner, Henry Green compels the reader to produce the intonational
quality of his characters' speech by eliminating purely conventional punctuation. The commas that do occur have a definite rhetorical function – they
cluster around that part of Jane's speech where it becomes most flustered
and disorganized ('no no [comma] worse [comma] it's the other [comma]').
The general sparseness of pointing elsewhere also slows down the pace of
reading, makes us aware of the way speech is constructed, its evasions,
gaps, shortcuts, defences: in short, it is a foregrounding device which makes
the language not merely a vehicle of communication, as it is for the two

interlocutors within the realistic conventions of the novel, but an object of aesthetic interest and value. It exemplifies Roman Jakobson's definition of the poetic function of language, 'the set towards the message for its own sake'.[10]

The humour of the unexpected adverbial qualifier at the end of the passage (' "Good God," he replied *with caution*') is something that Green learned from Waugh, I fancy. One is reminded of Paul Pennyfeather's ejaculation in *Decline and Fall* when he is unjustly sent down from Oxford: ' "God damn and blast them all to hell," said Paul Pennyfeather meekly to himself as he drove to the station.'[11] We do not find this kind of adverbial description of the way speech is uttered in Ivy Compton-Burnett. She confines herself strictly to the bare, neutral speech tags, 'he said', 'she said', and frequently dispenses with even those. Nor is she interested in creating the illusion of actual speech. Her characters talk in short, well-formed declarative or interrogative sentences of almost uniform structure. The effect is highly artificial, but not monotonous because the characters are apt to speak with alarming candour, and to deconstruct each other's remarks by their rejoinders. Here, for instance, is a dialogue from *A God and His Gifts* (1963), between Hereward, whose father has just died, and his mother, the widow, who comes into the room. The rather Jeeves-like butler Galleon is in attendance:

'Mamma, this is brave and wise. The first steps have to be taken. It is like you to know it.'
    'It is like most of us. How can we help knowing?'
    'At the moment you wish you had no more to take.'
    'No, I wish both your father and I had more.'
    'I know what it is to you to be here without him.'
    'Well, it is the alternative to being nowhere.'
    'You are feeling he is the more fortunate?'
    'No, I suppose I am. But it is not the word.'
    'We all have to die in our time. There is no escape.'
    'When we have had to be alive. And when the two things are so different. We ought not to have to do both.'
    'It is true, my lady, if I may interpose,' said Galleon. 'The one does not help with the other. It seems to render it unnatural.'[12]

The reversal of the stream of consciousness novel could hardly go further than it does in Ivy Compton-Burnett. Everything that is thought is spoken aloud, or rather, nothing that is not spoken aloud can be known. It is arguable, I think, that her novels, and the novels of Waugh and Henry Green, have been somewhat undervalued by academic criticism because their foregrounding of dialogue made them resistant to a method of analysis biased in favour of lyric expressiveness in literary language.

One of the most venerable distinctions in literary criticism is that drawn by Plato in Book III of *The Republic*, between diegesis and mimesis, the two ways of representing action in literary discourse: either the poet describes it in his own voice – diegesis – or he imitates the voices of the personages involved – mimesis. Epic is a mixed form, combining and alternating the two modes of presentation, author's speech and characters' speech.

This distinction will serve well enough to analyse the work of novelists who modelled their narratives very closely on classical epic – Henry Fielding, say, or Sir Walter Scott, and even the post-modernist novelists I have just mentioned, in whom the boundaries between author's voice and characters' voices are very clear, though the balance is shifted radically in favour of the latter. But the Platonic distinction is not adequate to describe novelistic discourse in general, for two reasons. Firstly, the relationship between mimesis and diegesis in the novel is much more subtle and complicated than in the classical epic; and, secondly, we encounter in the novel a third kind of discourse which cannot be classified according to a simple binary opposition – what Bakhtin calls doubly-voiced or doubly-oriented discourse.

The classic nineteenth-century novel is often defined in terms of the dominance of the authorial discourse over the other discourses in the text, and this is true inasmuch as the authorial narrator of a novel like *Emma*, or *Middlemarch*, seems to be the most direct vehicle of the implied author's values. But through the technique of free indirect style the character's voice and the character's autonomy are never entirely suppressed by the authorial narrator. Rather we have a subtle interplay between the two. Consider, for example, this passage from *Middlemarch*:

> It had now entered Dorothea's mind that Mr. Casaubon might wish to make her his wife, and the idea that he would do so touched her with a sort of reverential gratitude. How good of him – nay, it would be almost as if a winged messenger had suddenly stood beside her path and held out his hand towards her! For a long while she had been oppressed by the indefiniteness which hung in her mind like a thick summer haze, over all her desire to make her life greatly effective. What could she do, what ought she to do?[13]

There is irony here, to be sure, at the expense of Dorothea's reverential attitude to Casaubon, her innocent equation of a potential spouse with a sexless angel, but there is also sympathy and compassion; and through the fragments of free indirect speech embedded in the authorial narrator's more measured prose – 'How good of him . . . what could she do, what ought she to do?' – we hear the authentic note of Dorothea's genuine humility and longing for a meaningful life.

There is, however, another passage about Dorothea's marriage prospects, a little earlier in the novel, which cannot be analysed simply as an interweaving of author's voice and character's voice:

And how should Dorothea not marry? – a girl so handsome and with such prospects?

This is a rhetorical question, inviting agreement that Dorothea is bound to marry. But where does the question come from? Who speaks it? Clearly it is not Dorothea's own thought, rendered in free indirect speech. Equally clearly, it is not the authorial narrator speaking directly, since we already know that this narrator has no more respect than Dorothea for marriage-ability as determined by purely material factors such as fortune and good looks. No, it is the voice of Middlemarch that is evoked here by the narrator, the voice of provincial bourgeois wisdom which the narrator mimics, with an ironic intention of her own quite opposite from the inten-tion of those who utter such sentiments in the drawing rooms of Middle-march. This is what Bakhtin means by doubly-oriented or doubly-voiced discourse: discourse which refers not only to something in the world (in this case, Dorothea's marriage prospects), but at the same time refers to another speech act. According to Bakhtin, it is an effect especially character-istic of prose fiction, and the one that most strikingly manifests the differ-ence between the novel and the monologic genres privileged by traditional poetics.

In the eighteenth century, doubly-voiced discourse is mainly apparent in the relatively obvious form of 'I-narrators', as in Defoe's pseudo-autobio-graphical narratives, or Richardson's epistolary novels. In any text where the reader is conscious that the author is not addressing him directly, but through the represented discourse of some persona or character, or in the accents of some recognizable literary style, we have the phenomenon of doubly-voiced discourse. (And in the gap between the silence of the author and the speech of the narrator or narrators, an interpretative problem is apt to arise.) Bakhtin distinguishes between what he calls stylization, in which the author adapts and heightens a given style with the same expressive intentions as the original, and parody, where the style is used for purposes opposite to or incongruous with the intentions of the original. *Huckleberry Finn* or *The Catcher in the Rye* would be examples of stylization – or more precisely, stylized *skaz*; Fielding's *Jonathan Wild* would be an example of parody, parody of heroic biography. Bakhtin was particularly interested in the type of doubly-voiced discourse which he called 'hidden polemic', which refers to or anticipates another speech act without actually evoking it verbally in the text in the manner of stylization and parody. Something of a virtuoso performance in this mode is Nabokov's *Pale Fire*, in which the entire discourse is structured in response to another discourse which is never heard in the text (except in the poem by John Shade), but which must be inferred by the reader if the book is to be intelligible: the discourse of sanity, the rational, common-sense account of the events which Kinbote is narrating in terms of paranoid fantasy. Stylization, parody, *skaz* and hidden polemic are all to be found in rich profusion in the later episodes of James Joyce's *Ulysses*, which is a kind of thesaurus of Bakhtinian discourse types.

Bakhtin's own favourite source of examples was Dostoevsky. Indeed, Bakhtin originally hailed Dostoevsky as the inventor of the 'polyphonic novel', the novel in which a variety of conflicting ideological positions are given a voice and set in play both between and within individual speaking subjects, without being placed and judged by an authoritative authorial voice. Later, Bakhtin came to think that the novel was always an inherently polyphonic form, and that Dostoevsky made a crucial, but not unique, contribution to its development. His second thoughts were surely better. Even in the so-called classic realist text, and still more obviously in modern fiction in the realist tradition, we find, on close inspection, an amazing variety of discursive texture, and a surprising degree of interpretative freedom for the reader.

In Bakhtin's theory, 'polyphonic' is virtually synonymous with 'dialogic'. For him, any discourse in which more than one accent or tone is brought into play makes apparent the essentially dialogic nature of language itself, a fact that the monologic genres try to suppress. 'The word in living conversation,' says Bakhtin, 'is directly, blatantly oriented towards a future answer word. It provokes an answer, anticipates it, and structures itself in the answer's direction.'[14] The novel, supremely among the literary forms, demonstrates this process in action, and is one important ground for valuing it.

The import of Bakhtin's concept of dialogism goes, I think, even further. Instead of trying desperately to defend the notion that individual utterances, or texts, have a fixed, original meaning which it is the business of criticism to recover, we can locate meaning in the dialogic process of interaction between speaking subjects, between texts and readers, between texts themselves. If it is true, as Bakhtin asserts, that no utterance stands absolutely alone, that every utterance must be understood in relation to that which provoked it, and shapes itself in anticipation of a future response, that is also true of literary texts. As Bakhtin himself suggests in a brief but pregnant passage in *Problems of Dostoevsky's Poetics*, every literary discourse contains a hidden polemic. It 'senses its own listener, reader, critic, and reflects in itself their anticipated objections, evaluations, points of view. In addition, it senses alongside itself another discourse, another style'[15] – the style of peers, rivals and precursors, which it rejects, competes with, seeks to supplant. No one who has tried to write, or teach the reading of literary texts, can doubt the truth of this assertion, which applies of course as much to the genres Bakhtin calls monologic as to the dialogic writing he favoured.

Chapter 6

After Bakhtin

One of the landmarks in modern scholarly debate about the relation between literary and linguistic studies was a famous 'Conference on style' held at the University of Indiana in 1958. That conference, and its proceedings (published under the title of *Style in Language* in 1960)[1] is especially associated with the name of Roman Jakobson, whose 'Closing statement: linguistics and poetics', is, of all the contributed papers, certainly the most frequently reprinted and referred to. In fact, it was hardly representative of that conference, being based on a tradition of poetics and linguistics, deriving from the Russian formalists and the Prague Linguistic Circle, little known to most of the other participants. The main aim of the conference was to effect some *rapprochement* between the empirical–intuitive methods of the Anglo-American New Criticism, epitomized in the venerable presence of I. A. Richards, and the inductive, experimental methods of applied linguistics (exemplified by, for example, a statistical analysis of stylistic deviations in suicide notes – surely the psycholinguistic equivalent of dissecting cadavers in pathology labs).[2]

No, Jakobson's paper at that conference was not a closing statement, it was an opening statement. It opened many people's eyes to the existence of a structuralist poetics based on a Saussurean theory of language very different from what was known as 'structural linguistics' in Britain and America at that time; and it opened a phase in recent intellectual history in which European structuralism began to have a powerful impact on the humanities – at first in France, later in Britain and America – especially in linguistics and literary criticism. We are all familiar with the story, and with its sequel, when the Saussurean model of the linguistic sign, and the serene, deductive logic of the structuralist enterprise which it supported, began to be undermined or deconstructed by the critiques of the two Jacques, Lacan and Derrida. Thus was ushered in the era of post-structuralism, which we now inhabit, a noisy and crowded bazaar in which many different, competing voices are to be heard, peddling their wares. Most of them, however, feel obliged to take into account both the formalist–structuralist critique of the subjectivity of traditional literary criticism, and the deconstructionist uncovering of an unacknowledged subjectivity, a 'transcendental signified', at the heart of classical structuralism itself. The emphasis has shifted in recent years from the structuralist attempt to analyse discourses, including literary texts, in terms of the signifying systems of which they are manifestations, to the problem of reading, of interpretation. But this new hermeneutics is permeated by a fundamental scepticism about the possibility of recuperating a fixed or stable meaning from discourse. The nature of language is such, the deconstructionists tell us, that any text is bound to undermine its own claim to a determinate meaning.[3] The only control over the infinite proliferation of meanings, Stanley Fish tells us, is that exercised by an interpretive community, such as academic literary critics.[4] The effect of structuralism and post-structuralism on traditional literary studies might be compared to that of an earthquake followed by a tidal wave, for both undermined the idea, central to such studies, of the author as a substantial, historic entity, the unique and authenticating origin of the text, whose communicative intention, conscious or unconscious, intrinsic or extrinsic to the text itself, it was the business of the critic to elucidate. It was on this scene of crisis and contention in literary studies that Mikhail Bakhtin made his entrance – or his work did, for he was dead before many of us had heard of him.

We are 'after Bakhtin' in a special sense, for reasons that are well known. Although his first major work, *Problems of Dostoevsky's Art*, was published in Russia in 1929, it was hardly known inside or outside that country until it was reissued in a revised and much expanded form in 1963 under the title *Problems of Dostoevsky's Poetics*. In the intervening Stalinist years, Bakhtin was prevented from publishing under his own name. Towards the end of his life he was to some extent rehabilitated and allowed to publish, but much of his work, written over several decades, has only became available since his death in 1975. The drama of Bakhtin's life, the belatedness with which his extraordinarily original work has been received, has contributed to his appeal and perhaps encouraged the growth of a somewhat uncritical cult around his name, as Paul de Man warned in an article in *Poetics Today* in 1983.[5] It has also rendered his work assimilable by a number of different – and mutually opposed – critical ideologies. Bakhtin himself began writing in opposition to – or, as he would say, in dialogue with – the Russian formalists, and was obliged to give his arguments a Marxist gloss by collaborating with or publishing under the names of his more conformist friends, Volosinov and Medvedev in the 1920s and 1930s. In consequence he has been eagerly enlisted by latterday Marxist critics who want to attack the alleged idealism of Saussurean linguistics and classical structuralism without succumbing to the nihilistic scepticism of deconstruction. There is some misrepresentation involved here. Bakhtin was no materialist, and his theories were not wholly incompatible with classical structuralism (let us not forget that Jakobson admired Bakhtin and personally helped to secure his rehabilitation). However, Bakhtin's thought is so many-sided and fertile that he is inevitably open to colonization by others.

I should admit my own interest. As a critic I have always been concerned with the construction of a poetics of fiction, and the development of a literary history of the novel grounded in such a poetics rather than in content or context. As a practising novelist I find the post-structuralist attack on the idea of the author and on the communicative function of language unappealing, to say the least. I have found the work of Bakhtin both useful and inspiring on all these counts, and like many other readers have been awestruck by the discovery that he was thinking his way, with the minimum of intellectual and material support, through the questions which preoccupy us, decades before we even thought of them. There is certainly a temptation to regard Bakhtin as some kind of prophet providenti-ally sent to deliver us from our critical discontents, and his work as some kind of theoretical panacea. But the temptation must be resisted. There are problems, contradictions and loose ends in Bakhtin's thought, and grappling ith them is part of being 'after Bakhtin'.

Bakhtin's thinking about language and literature is essentially binary; that is to say, he works with pairs of terms – monologic/dialogic, poetry/prose, canonical/carnivalesque, and so on. This habit of thought is of course characteristic of the whole structuralist tradition from Saussure onwards. One thinks of Saussure's *langue/parole*, Jakobson's metaphor/metonymy, Barthes's *lisible/scriptible*, and so on. However, there is a tendency for binary oppositions to become hierarchies, one term being privileged over the other. Sometimes this is a quite overt tactic, adopted for polemical purposes, as in the case of Barthes. But to the extent that a binary opposition becomes a hierarchy, its explanatory power in application to the totality of its subject matter is weakened. *S/Z* succeeds because it subverts its own hierarchy, by demonstrating how a *lisible* text can become *scriptible* in the hands of a clever critic. Jakobson frequently drew attention to the built-in bias of poetics and literary criticism towards metaphor rather than meton-ymy, a bias reflected in the relative neglect of realistic fiction by poetics and literary stylistics until recently. Bakhtin himself, one might say, began by questioning the privileging of *langue* over *parole* in Saussurean linguistics.

Saussure's linguistics is focused on *langue*, on the abstract system of rules and differences that enables language to signify. Only the system is stable, repeatable and therefore describable in grammatical terms – the manifes-tations of the system being infinitely variable. Bakhtin in contrast called for a linguistics of *parole*, of language in *use*, recognizing that this entailed taking into account the non-linguistic components of any speech act, and thus abandoning the hope of a scientifically precise total description of language. In this respect he anticipated the interest of linguistics many decades later in what is sometimes called discourse analysis. To Saussure the word was a two-sided sign, signifier and signified. To Bakhtin it was a 'two-sided *act* . . . It is determined equally by whose word it is and for whom it is meant . . . A word is territory *shared* by both addresser and addressee, by the speaker and his interlocutor.'[6]

'Every decoding is another encoding', another modern authority has asserted.[7] Bakhtin teaches us that this need not be a reason for denying the possibility of communicating meaning in discourse. To mean is precisely to take this condition, that every decoding is another encoding, into account when we speak. 'The word in living conversation is directly, blatantly, oriented towards a future answer word: it provokes an answer, anticipates it and structures itself in the answer's direction.'[8]

Here, however, at the very heart of Bakhtin's thinking about language, we encounter a puzzle or paradox, with which I shall concern myself in the rest of this essay. If language is innately dialogic, how can there be monologic discourse?[9] Bakhtin's literary theory, especially his theory of the novel, depends heavily on the distinction between monologic discourse on the one hand, and dialogic or (in an alternative formulation) polyphonic discourse on the other. The genres canonized by traditional poetics – tragedy, epic, lyric – are monologic: they employ a single style and express a single world-view. The discourse of the novel, in contrast, is an orchestration of diverse discourses culled from heterogeneous sources, oral and written, conveying different ideological positions which are put in play without ever being subjected to totalizing judgement or interpretation. Originally Bakhtin attributed the discovery of this discursive polyphony to Dostoevsky. Later he came to think that it was inherent in the novel as a literary form, and he traced it back historically to the comic and satiric writing of the classical period that parodied and travestied the state-approved solemnities of tragedy and epic, and to the carnival tradition in popular culture that sustained an unofficial resistance to the monologic discourses of medieval christendom. (In passing it is important to note that Bakhtin did not believe that Christianity itself was essentially or originally a totalizing, monologic ideology. In his view the New Testament is essentially dialogic, and, in such episodes as Christ's entry into Jerusalem on an ass and the crowning with thorns, distinctly carnivalesque. It was later commentators who tried to reduce the Socratic ambiguities and obliquities of Christ's teaching to a monologic system.)

Bakhtin's literary theory is attractive to me personally as both critic and novelist in putting the novel at the centre instead of at the margins of poetics, and approaching it via the typology of discourse rather than via the Aristotelian categories of plot and character, or the Romantic concept of 'style as the man'. If classical poetics privileged tragedy, modern poetics has tended to privilege the lyric poem, but, as Bakhtin himself pointed out, a stylistics which takes lyric poetry as the literary norm is quite inadequate to cope with the language of the novel.[10] That was the point I started from in my first work of criticism, called *Language of Fiction* (1966), a book written in complete ignorance of Bakhtin (and, for that matter, of Russian formalism and structuralism). In omitting the definite article before the word *Language* in my title (it is, more often than not, restored in bibliographies) I was perhaps groping towards Bakhtin's perception that 'it makes no sense to describe "*the* language of the novel" because the very object of such a description, the novel's unitary language, does not exist'.[11] But in trying to bring a New-Critical attentiveness to verbal texture to bear on a number of nineteenth- and twentieth-century novels, I still tended to select passages for analysis which were either authorial description or were focalized through characters with whom the implied author was in sympathy, and I never took a passage that consisted mainly of direct speech. In other words, I was looking almost unconsciously for the most direct linguistic expression of the implied author's attitudes, values and world-view, and thus treating the novel by analogy with the lyric poem. But as Bakhtin reminds us, a novel is made up of more than one kind of language:

> Herein lies the profound distinction between prose style and poetic style . . . for the prose artist the world is full of other people's words, among which he must orient himself and whose speech characteristics he must be able to perceive with a very keen ear. He must introduce them into the plane of his own discourse, but in such a way that this plane is not destroyed. He works with a very rich verbal palette.[12]

As an example of what this means in practice, let me cite the opening passage of a short story by Katherine Mansfield, 'The fly', which I discussed briefly in *Language of Fiction*, because it had been the subject of an interesting article in *Essays in Criticism* in 1962 by F. W. Bateson and B. Shahevitch, endeavouring to show (as I was) that 'close reading' was just as much 'in order for realistic fiction as for a poem', though the formal features to be analysed were different.[13]

> 'Y'are very snug in here,' piped old Mr Woodifield, and he peered out of the great, green-leather armchair by his friend the boss's desk as a baby peers out of its pram. His talk was over; it was time for him to be off. But he did not want to go. Since he had retired, since his . . . stroke, the wife and girls kept him boxed up in the house every day of the week except Tuesday. On Tuesday he was dressed and brushed and allowed to cut back to the City for the day. Though what he did there the wife and girls couldn't imagine. Made a nuisance of himself to his friends, they supposed . . . Well, perhaps so. All the same, we cling to our last pleasures as the tree clings to its last leaves. So there sat old Woodifield, smoking a cigar and staring almost greedily at the boss, who rolled in his office chair, stout, rosy, five years older than he, and still going strong, still at the helm. It did one good to see him.[14]

This is not the place to attempt a detailed and exhaustive analysis of the passage. I wish merely to draw attention to the way in which the authorial narrator's discourse – most clearly identifiable, perhaps, in the similes, cast in the 'gnomic' present tense, 'as a baby peers out of its pram' and 'as the tree clings to its last leaves' – is crossed by and intermingled with the discourses of the characters – Woodifield, whose repression of the idea of death, a repression that, in the person of the boss, proves to be the central theme of the story, is betrayed by the aposiopesis in the phrase 'since his . . . stroke', and Woodifield's womenfolk, whose impatient, patronizing chatter is evoked in, 'Though what he did there the wife and girls couldn't imagine. Made a nuisance of himself to his friends, they supposed . . .' The familiarly possessive definite article here, '*the* wife and girls' suggests that Woodifield has heard or overheard their talk – that it is an indirect quote within an indirect quote. Or is it the narrator quoting the earlier occurrence of the same phrase ('the wife and girls') in a sentence that is clearly Woodifield's indirect speech? The deixis of the passage is ambiguous and often undecidable. For instance: 'On Tuesday he was dressed and brushed and allowed to cut back to the City for the day.' The passive constructions, 'dressed and brushed', recalling the ironic simile of the baby peering out of the pram, may encourage us to begin reading this sentence as authorial, but the idiomatic 'cut' seems to belong to Woodifield's discourse, suggesting that he is well aware of the indignities of second childhood. The authorial narrator's 'Well, perhaps so', seems disapproving of the women's dismissive attitude to Woodifield's weekly outing; and the rather poetic simile of the tree clinging to its leaves reproves the reader who may have taken the earlier simile of the baby in the pram as an invitation to patronize the old man. The reader, in short, instead of being told at the outset what the story is to be about, and whose story it is, and what position he should adopt towards the various characters in it, is listening, as it were, to a babble of different discourses, each with its own values, prejudices, ironies, and is obliged to construct and continuously revise his own hypothesis about the story's import.

To give Bateson and Shahevitch their due, they observed that 'This mixing of direct statement with indirect or concealed dialogue is used all through the story . . . The result is that we have very little regular narrative. Instead, in a frame of thin lines of this quasi-narrative, which could almost be spoken by a chorus, we have the effect of drama.'[15] A very Bakhtinian remark, I think, the full implications of which the authors themselves did not perhaps appreciate. Certainly I did not when I first read it. To Bakhtin this fusion of author's discourse and characters' discourses through free indirect speech and what he called doubly-oriented speech was constitutive of the novel as a literary form. Characters, and the persona of the authorial narrator herself, are constituted not simply by their own linguistic registers or idiolects, but by the discourses they quote and allude to.

A corollary of Bakhtin's insight is that language which in itself is flat, banal, clichéd and generally automatized can become vividly expressive when mimicked, heightened, stylized, parodied and played off against other kinds of language in the polyphonic discourse of the novel. That is why a novelist, as Bakhtin says, must have a very keen ear for other people's words (not an essential qualification for the lyric poet) and why he cannot afford to cut himself off from low, vulgar, debased language; why nothing linguistic is alien to him, from theological treatises to the backs of cornflakes packets, from the language of the barrack room to the language of, say, academic conferences.

Perhaps here, in relation to our own professional discourse, is the place to confront the question I posed earlier: if language is inherently dialogic, how can there be monologic discourse, on the postulated existence of which Bakhtin's literary theory depends? One answer might be that in writing, as distinct from oral speech, the physical absence of the addressee from the context of the speech act makes it possible for the addresser to ignore or suppress the dialogic dimension of language, and thus create the illusion of monologic discourse. It was after all in 'living conversation', not in writing, that Bakhtin said the word is 'directly, blatantly oriented towards a future answer word', in the passage I quoted earlier.

Consider the typical scholarly article or book in the fields of literary criticism and literary theory. Such discourses may take issue with the arguments and interpretations of other scholars (hence the ritual citation of other treatments of the subject at the outset) but they don't do so by directly engaging with these opponents in a dialogue. The professional scholar typically states his opinions as if they were facts, and avoids the pronouns 'I' and 'you', preferring the consensual terms 'we' and 'the reader', which bind together both addresser and addressee in a fiction of solidarity and agreement. The only literary critic I can think of who consistently employs an 'I – you' form of address is D. H. Lawrence. This is interesting, because in *Women in Love*, Lawrence wrote what is probably the nearest thing to a Dostoevskian novel, in Bakhtin's terms, to be found in English literature.[16] As critic, notably in *Studies in Classic American Literature*, he harangues, exhorts, questions and teases his readers somewhat in the style of Dostoevsky's Underground Man. More idiosyncratically still, he harangues, exhorts, questions and teases the writers he is discussing – Whitman, for instance:

'And of these one and all I weave the song of myself – '
Do you? Well then, it just shows you haven't *got* any self. It's a mush, not a woven thing. A hotch-potch, not a tissue. Your self.
Oh Walter, Walter, what have you done with it? What have you done with yourself? With your own individual self? For it sounds as if it had all leaked out of you, leaked out into the universe.[17]

The shock of encountering this style of critical discussion throws into relief the superficial monologism of most scholarly discourse.

I say 'superficial' because scholarly discourse is in fact saturated in the kind of dialogic rhetoric that Bakhtin named 'hidden polemic', when an utterance not only refers to a given topic, but engages with, or anticipates or seeks to discredit another actual or hypothetical speech act about the same topic. Our articles and monographs will make little sense to a reader who is outside the ongoing 'conversation' to which they belong, and who is unable to identify the echoes of, allusions to, sly digs at, flattering appeals to, other writers on the same subjects. But scholarly discourse aspires to the condition of monologue inasmuch as it tries to say the last word on a given subject, to affirm its mastery over all previous words on that subject.

In Bakhtin's perspective it is not possible to say 'the last word' about anything in the human sphere, whatever may be the case in the physical sciences, and he venerated Dostoevsky for founding his art of fiction upon this principle: at the end of Dostoevsky's novels, says Bakhtin, '*nothing conclusive has yet taken place in the world, the ultimate word of the world and about the world has not yet been spoken, the world is open and free, everything is still in the future and always will be in the future*'.[18] The pretence of literary and linguistic scholarship to say the last word about its subject therefore always entails a certain measure of self-deception or bad faith which manifests itself in various discursive symptoms. For instance it has been observed – I think it was in an article in *PMLA* some years ago – that the Prefaces and Forewords to academic books are always much milder and more tentative than the discourses they introduce: full of quali-fications, disclaimers, professions of humility, effusive thanks to friends, colleagues and spouses – all propitiative and ingratiating gestures. It is as if the authors, rather dismayed by the monologic arrogance of the discourses they have produced, are seeking, at the last minute, a dialogue with their potential readers over the heads of these discourses.

From the same source comes the curious mixture of boredom, irritation and embarrassment with which one reads reviews of one's own books – I speak personally, but perhaps for others too. A review should be, in prin-ciple, a dialogic rejoinder to one's own discourse, but that discourse did not want or expect a rejoinder, it pretended to render all further discussion of the matter superfluous, to leave the reader in a state of dumb admiration. Hence, if your reviewer agrees with you, he seems to be stating the obvious, which is boring, or he agrees with you for the wrong reasons, which is embarrassing, and if he disagrees with you, it is because he has missed the point, or is airing a view of his own, which is irritating. He may, of course, have discovered some genuine flaw in your argument, which is most disconcerting of all, since it raises the awful prospect of having to try and revise or modify an argument that was not designed for revision and modification.

Some people, especially women, might say that I am describing or carica-
turing a specifically male model of scholarly discourse, based on power and
domination, and perhaps I am. I am not suggesting that academic critical
discourse has to be like that, only that, by and large, it *is*. Even Bakhtin
himself follows the model in the early chapters of his Dostoevsky book. In
his theoretical work, however, he avoided the trap and managed to write a
genuinely dialogic kind of criticism in which the key propositions are
continuously open to self-questioning, modification and revision.

To define monologic discourse as a kind of illusion or fiction that is
facilitated by writing rather than speaking does not, however, entirely solve
the problem raised by Bakhtin's privileging of dialogic discourse. What
about the poetic genres classified by Bakhtin as monologic – lyric, epic,
tragedy? Are they to be regarded as inherently less interesting and less
valuable than the novel? It has to be admitted that the spectre of a critical
dualism hovers over Bakhtin's work, and that it could easily encourage a
limiting division of writers into sheep and goats such as the school of Leavis
and *Scrutiny* encouraged in this country not long ago. There is a tendency
in Bakhtin to assimilate everything that is progressive, life-enhancing and
liberating in writing to the concept of the novel. As Clark and Holquist
observe, 'Bakhtin assigns the term "novel" to whatever form of expression
within a given literary system reveals the limits of that system as inadequate,
imposed or arbitrary. The canonical genres are then associated with whatever is fixed, rigid, authoritarian.'[19] The very notion of genre is defined by
the repeatability of its rules and conventions. The novel, Bakhtin asserted,
is an anti-generic genre: 'It is plasticity itself. It is a genre that is ever
questing, ever examining itself and subjecting its established forms to
review.'[20] This, of course, is absolutely true, and Bakhtin is not the only
critic to have said it. But the question remains: must we therefore relegate
the monologic genres to an inferior status?

In the evolution of the novel itself, Bakhtin saw a continual struggle
between monologic and dialogic tendencies: between, on the one hand, a
kind of prose fiction that was written in a single homogeneous style – Greek
romance, Renaissance pastoral romance, the eighteenth-century novel of
sentimental pathos (and, I would be inclined to add, the Gothic novel); on
the other hand, the kind of prose fiction that rejoiced in and exploited the
multiplicity of languages and dialects in a given historical epoch – the
Menippean satires of the classical world, the great works of Rabelais and
Cervantes in the Renaissance, the English comic novel of the eighteenth
century. Clark and Holquist call these two traditions the 'monoglot' and
the 'heteroglot', and summarize Bakhtin's theory of the novel thus:

> The two lines, heteroglot and monoglot, come together and merge at the
> beginning of the nineteenth century. Although the major representatives
> of the novel are from that point on mixed, features of the heteroglot line

tend to dominate. Because the heteroglot line is more open to difference, it could more easily absorb the increasing tide of self-consciousness. In other words, the heteroglot novel was able to accommodate more of the self because it is more sensitive to otherness.[21]

This historicist, almost messianic view of the novel as a literary form helps to explain why it has dominated the modern era, and why the monoglot fiction of the past seems to the modern reader either quaint or tedious – why, for instance, we tend to prefer Nashe's heteroglot *The Unfortunate Traveller*, never reprinted in the seventeenth century, to the monoglot *Arcadia* of Sir Philip Sidney, immensely popular and frequently reprinted in the same period. But, the sceptical reader is likely to ask, what about the great writers who, either before or after the full flowering of the novel, chose to write in the medium of poetry – what about, to take a few names at random, Chaucer, Shakespeare, Milton, Keats, Browning, Eliot, Yeats?

Some of these writers can easily be accommodated in Bakhtin's literary-historical scheme by his concept of novelization, that is, the infiltration and fertilization of the canonic poetic genres by the heteroglot, carnivalesque discourse of the novel conceived in its broadest sense. Bakhtin never claimed that *verse* as a medium was necessarily monologic. One of his favourite sources of examples of dialogic discourse was Pushkin's verse novel, *Eugene Onegin*. I am not sure that he knew the work of Chaucer, but it would not be difficult to argue that the qualities in the *Canterbury Tales* which have made it seem, in comparison to most other Middle English texts, so startlingly modern and accessible to modern readers, are precisely those qualities which Bakhtin characterizes as novelistic. Bakhtin did know Shakespeare, and apparently lectured on him, though I have not encountered any substantial discussion of Shakespeare in Bakhtin's published writings. However, it would not be difficult to construct a Bakhtinian reading of Shakespearean drama, which is manifestly polyphonic in comparison to classical or neoclassical drama, and to relate this to the evolution of Elizabethan theatre from the carnivalesque tradition of the mystery plays, with their parodic-travestying subplots and refusal of stylistic decorum. The history of nineteenth- and twentieth-century poetry, especially the popularity of the dramatic monologue in this period, gives ample evidence of the novelization of the lyric impulse as the novel became the dominant literary form. Browning and T. S. Eliot would be obvious examples. Indeed, *The Waste Land*, which originally bore the Bakhtinian epigraph, 'He do the police in different voices', could be seen as the apotheosis of Bakhtin's poetic, since it is a work constructed wholly out of what Bakhtin called heteroglossia and polyglossia – fragments of speech and writing in different languages and different registers that interact and resonate without the restraints of narrative logic.

But still the nagging doubts persist: what about Milton, Keats, Yeats and many other ostensibly monologic poets? If they are all redeemable through the loophole of novelization, then the loophole would seem to be bigger than the surrounding wall. There is some evidence that Bakhtin himself was troubled by this built-in bias of his literary theory. In order to bring out the special qualities and formal characteristics of novelistic discourse, he perhaps exaggerated its difference from the poetic genres. Thus, in the essay, 'Discourse in the novel' probably written in 1934–5, we find him making a sharply defined distinction between the dialogism of prose and the polysemy of poetry:

> no matter how one understands the interrelationship of meanings in a poetic symbol . . . this interrelationship is never of the dialogic sort; it is impossible . . . to imagine a trope (say, a metaphor) being unfolded into two exchanges of a dialogue . . . The polysemy of the poetic symbol presupposes the unity of a voice with which it is identical, and it presupposes that such a voice is completely alone within its own discourse. As soon as another's voice, another's accent, the possibility of another's point of view breaks through this play of the symbol, the poetic plane is destroyed and the symbol is translated on to the plane of prose.[22]

If this were so, one would have to say that a poem like Yeats's 'Among schoolchildren' is a masterpiece of prose, since its primary symbols – swan, girl, scarecrow – are mediated through a wide spectrum of linguistic registers, from the homely to the hieratic, and the persona of the poet is present to us both as the 60-year-old smiling public man seen by the nuns and their pupils, and the inner self racked by nostalgia, frustration and desire.

Can there, in fact, be such a thing as an *absolutely* monologic literary text? Bakhtin himself came to doubt it. In a remarkable passage, in an article written in 1959–61, and first published in 1976, quoted in Tzvetan Todorov's excellent monograph, *Mikhail Bakhtin: The Dialogic Principle*, Bakhtin says, or rather asks (for the passage is characteristically a dialogue with himself):

> To what extent is a discourse purely single-voiced and without any objectal character, possible in literature? Can a discourse in which the author does not hear the author's voice, in which there is no one but the author and all of the author, can such a discourse become the raw material of a literary work? Isn't a certain degree of objectal character a necessary condition for any style? Doesn't the author always find himself *outside* of language in its capacity as the material of the literary work? Isn't every writer (even the purest lyric poet) always a 'playwright' insofar as he distributes all the discourses among alien voices, including that of the 'image of the author' (as well as the author's other *personae*)? It may be that every single-voiced and nonobjectal discourse is naive and inappropriate to authentic creation. The authentically creative voice can

only be a *second* voice in the discourse. Only the second voice – *pure relation*, can remain nonobjectal to the end and cast no substantial and phenomenal shadow. The writer is a person who knows how to work language while remaining outside of it; he has the gift of indirect speech.[23]

Does this remarkable passage, which seems to collapse the distinction between dialogic and monologic discourse, render all Bakhtin's previous literary theory invalid? I think not. But it encourages us to apply the distinction in terms of dominance or 'set' rather than as two mutually exclusive categories – in the same way as one applies Jakobson's distinction between metaphor and metonymy, or Plato's distinction between diegesis and mimesis (from which Bakhtin's distinction ultimately derives). One could develop a typology of genres or modes of writing according to whether they exploit and celebrate the inherently dialogic nature of language in living speech, or suppress and limit it for specific literary effects. Performed with the kind of detachment and self-consciousness Bakhtin describes in the passage I have just read, monologism need not be naive or repressive. There is a prose monologism of the avant-garde. In the later fiction of Samuel Beckett, for instance, a post-modernist sense of solipsism, alienation and the absurd, is eloquently expressed by a monologic discourse that seems weirdly independent of any other source of speech, that proceeds by self-cancellation rather than interaction: 'a voice alone within its own discourse', to use Bakhtin's phrase for the lyric poet. The concluding sentence of the passage from Bakhtin I just quoted seems to me particularly worth pondering: 'The writer is a person who knows how to work language while remaining outside of it; he has the gift of indirect speech.' Bakhtin joins hands here with the speech act theorists who have defined literary discourse in terms of the peculiarity of its illocutionary force: a literary text is not a real speech act, but an imitation of a speech act. It is uttered and received at a second remove. Normal criteria of 'felicity' are therefore not always relevant.[24] Bakhtin's statement also engages with one of the most radical and controversial planks in post-structuralist literary theory, namely the disenfranchisement of the author. If we go back to Roland Barthes's seminal 1968 essay, 'The death of the author', we find him beginning thus:

In his story *Sarrasine* Balzac, describing a castrato disguised as a woman, writes the following sentence: '*This was woman herself, with her sudden fears, her irrational whims, her instinctive worries, her impetuous boldness, her fussings, and her delicious sensibility.*' Who is speaking thus? Is it the hero of the story bent on remaining ignorant of the castrato hidden beneath the woman? Is it Balzac the individual, furnished by his personal experience with a philosophy of Woman? Is it Balzac the author professing 'literary' ideas on femininity? Is it universal wisdom? Romantic psychology? We shall never know, for the good reason that writing is the destruction of every voice, of every point of origin. Writing is that neutral, composite, oblique space where our subject slips away, the negative where all identity is lost, starting with the very identity of the body writing.[25]

This is both very similar to Bakhtin and antithetical to him. Because the sentence from *Sarrasine* cannot with confidence be attributed to any single voice, Barthes argues that we must abandon the whole idea of writing having an origin. Bakhtin would say that this fusion of several different voices, by which the excitement of the focalizing character is expressed and simultaneously ironized by the evocation of other, stereotyped social discourses about women – that this effect is constitutive of the novel as a literary form, and that it in no way prohibits us from inferring the existence of a creative mind that produces it by a kind of literary ventriloquism. In the late passage I quoted, he came to the realization that this is true of all literary discourse, whether or not the surface structure of the text betrays the fact. Barthes says: because the author does not coincide with the language of the text, he does not exist. Bakhtin says, it is precisely because he does not so coincide that we must posit his existence.

Chapter 7

Crowds and power in the early Victorian novel

In the most memorable episode of Mrs Gaskell's novel *North and South* (1855), the heroine, Margaret Hale, gets involved in a violent demonstration. Circumstances have brought her, a genteel southerner, to live in the northern industrial city of Milton, a thinly disguised version of Manchester. There she meets a mill-owner, John Thornton, whose harsh style of management, based on a dogmatic faith in market forces, she finds repellent, though she is impressed by his energy and integrity. Thornton's employees strike when he refuses to consider their claim for an increase in wages. At this juncture Margaret calls on the Thornton house to fetch a water bed for her ailing mother, and, preoccupied with her errand, hardly notices the ominous mood of the crowd gathering around Thornton's mill, which is next to his house. Only when she reaches the door, 'She looked round and heard the first long far-off roll of the tempest; saw the first slow-surging wave of the dark crowd come, with its threatening crest, tumble over and retreat, at the far end of the street.'[1]

Once inside the house, Margaret learns that the striking workers are furious because Thornton has imported cheap Irish labour in their place. Margaret finds herself, willy-nilly, in a siege situation with Thornton and his womenfolk, who manifest varying degrees of courage and panic as they watch, from an upper window, the crowd breaking through the gates of the mill, evidently intent on doing injury to the imported Irish workers. Thornton reveals that he has sent for the military. Margaret, appalled at the prospect of violence, whether by the strikers towards the Irish, or by the military towards the strikers, urges Thornton to go out into the courtyard and appeal to the crowd to desist. 'If you have any courage or noble quality in you, go out and speak to them, man to man!' (p. 232). Unable to refuse this challenge to his honour and virility, Thornton goes out into the courtyard and confronts the crowd, watched by Margaret from an open ground-floor window. Her impressions of the crowd are conveyed in such phrases as, 'a thousand angry eyes', 'the savage satisfaction of the rolling angry murmur', 'cruel and thoughtless' and 'mad for prey'. Thornton is unable to make himself heard. Seeing some of the demonstrators preparing to throw clogs and stones, Margaret fears that 'in another instant the stormy passions would have passed their bounds, and swept away all barriers of reason' (p. 233). Impulsively she dashes out into the courtyard and interposes herself between Thornton and the 'angry sea of men'. 'Oh, do not use violence', she cries to them. 'Do not damage your cause by this violence' (pp. 234–5). Feeling responsible for Thornton's dangerous situation, 'She only thought how she could save him. She threw her arms around him. She made her body into a shield from the fierce people beyond.' Someone throws a stone at Thornton which hits Margaret a glancing blow on the head, drawing blood and rendering her half-unconscious. Appalled and ashamed at this deed, the crowd suddenly loses heart, and rapidly disperses.

As Martin Dodsworth points out in his Introduction to *North and South*, this action is highly charged with sexual significance. To say that 'the whole riot is replete with associations of orgasm' (p. 19) is perhaps overstating the case, but there is no doubt that Margaret's protective gesture is not simply heroic – it also reveals her unacknowledged attraction to Thornton, licensing an intimate physical contact, indistinguishable from an embrace, which would in normal circumstances be unthinkable. Indeed, Margaret is deeply compromised by her public gesture and feels obliged, subsequently, to reject Thornton as a lover in order to demonstrate the purity of her motives. Thus the incident neatly serves a double narrative function – it both reveals the mutual erotic attraction of hero and heroine and retards their union.

To read this episode exclusively in emotional and sexual terms is, however, to diminish and misrepresent *North and South*, which is on one level a novel about industrial relations, about the rights and duties of capital and labour. Margaret belongs by class and emotional allegiance to the side of capital, but she has friends among Mr Thornton's employees, and her position in Milton as a stranger from the genteel South, with a professional and agrarian background, makes her critical and questioning about the supply-and-demand principles upon which Thornton conducts his business. Her gesture of placing herself between Thornton and the workers epitomizes her mediating role in the novel, aiming to neutralize the violence inherent in a conflict-model of industrial relations. Thornton is blamed for provoking his employees at a time of economic depression and great suffering. The corresponding figure on the workers' side is his employee, Nicholas Higgins, an honest and upright man, but stubbornly convinced that only a highly disciplined union will wring concessions from masters like Thornton.

One of Higgins's workmates is a man of much weaker moral fibre called Boucher. With a sick wife and a large family of hungry children, Boucher cannot afford to strike, but obeys the Union out of fear. 'Yo' may be kind hearts, each separate,' he says bitterly to Higgins, 'But once banded together, yo've no more pity for a man than a wild hunger-maddened wolf' (p. 207). When the strike shows no sign of succeeding, the desperate Boucher becomes one of the ringleaders of the riot at Thornton's mill. He is the only one of the rioters Margaret identifies by name. She observes his face in the crowd, 'forlornly desperate and livid with rage' (p. 233). After her intervention and wounding, 'even the most desperate – Boucher himself – drew back, faltered away, scowled and finally went off, muttering curses on the master' (p. 235). Higgins deplores the riot, which brings the strike into disrepute and causes it to collapse, and reproaches Boucher for his part in it. Boucher is arrested, but Thornton does not press charges, on the grounds that his unemployability will be punishment enough, which indeed proves to be the case. Boucher tries unsuccessfully to get work from a mill-owner notorious for refusing to employ union members. Rejected by the masters as a troublemaker and by his workmates as a class traitor, Boucher commits suicide. Margaret blames Higgins for this tragedy. 'Don't you see how you've made Boucher what he is, by driving him into the Union against his will – without his heart going with it?' Higgins seems to accept the reproach to the extent of dedicating himself to the support of Boucher's widow and children.

Mrs Gaskell's anti-union bias is very clear in all this. In spite of her respect for working-class leaders like Higgins, and sympathy for the sufferings of the workers in times of economic recession, she fears the consequences of their collective action. The spontaneous combination of individuals into a threatening and lawless crowd is causally connected through the Higgins–Boucher subplot to the organized 'combination' of the trades union. Boucher personifies the mindless anarchy and violence that may be released, and cannot be controlled, by working-class militancy. In this respect *North and South* is typical of a group of early Victorian novels which Raymond Williams called 'industrial novels', and which in their own day were sometimes called 'condition of England' novels. The ones Williams discussed in *Culture and Society* were, in addition to *North and South*, Mrs Gaskell's earlier novel, *Mary Barton* (1848), Disraeli's *Sybil* (1845), Dickens's *Hard Times* (1854), Charles Kingsley's *Alton Locke* (1850) and George Eliot's *Felix Holt* (1866).[2] As Williams noted, the authors' fear of violence, especially violent collective action, dominated their treatment of social and political issues and often warped the narrative and emotional logic of their stories. A turning-point in the plots of four of these novels is a riot in which the principal characters are involved in some way. Both Kingsley's and George Eliot's eponymous heroes are implicated in riots which they are trying to control or prevent, and sent to prison in consequence. The climax of *Sybil* finds the heroine caught up in a violent and destructive rebellion of disaffected workers. The two novels which do not have a riot in them are *Mary Barton*, which has an ideologically motivated murder instead, and *Hard Times*. The reason *Hard Times* contains no violent collective action is, I think, because it was partly based on Dickens's journalistic reporting of a prolonged strike of cotton workers in Preston in 1855.

According to Humphrey House, Dickens went to Preston 'expecting to find discontent, disorder, and even rioting', and was surprised to find 'that everything was so quiet and the men so well-behaved'.[3] Perhaps he was not only surprised but secretly disappointed, for he betrayed in other novels a kind of horrified fascination with mob violence, notably in the riot scenes of *Barnaby Rudge* (1841), generally taken by modern critics to be his response to the Chartist agitation of the late 1830s, and in his novel about the French Revolution, *A Tale of Two Cities* (1859). Another historical novel with a topical subtext was Charlotte Brontë's *Shirley* (1849), set in the period of the Napoleonic wars but clearly reflecting, in its treatment of Luddite activity, more recent working-class militancy. In a climactic scene the two heroines of the novel watch the assault of an armed mob on the mill of Robert Moore, whose machines they are intent on wrecking. Moore is a hero in the same mould as Mrs Gaskell's Thornton, convinced that the market must control the economy even if it means operatives starving and their masters going bankrupt. Like Thornton, he is converted to a more flexible and humane model of industrial relations by the end of the novel. (Moore's enlightenment comes as a result of visiting the Midlands: 'While I was in Birmingham,' he tells Caroline Helstone, 'I looked a little into reality, considered closely, and at their source, the causes of the present troubles of this country.'[4])

I want to come back to that minor character in *North and South* called Boucher. Pronounced 'Bowcher' in Lancashire, it is not such an exotic name for a mill-hand as one might suppose, but it is foregrounded against the name of the other worker who plays a significant part in the story, Higgins. There are 289 Higginses in the 1987 telephone directory for South Manchester, but only 20 Bouchers. Proper names in fiction are of course never neutral: they always signify, if it is only ordinariness. The commonplace 'Higgins' is appropriate to a representative Lancashire workman. The surnames of the hero and heroine, Thornton and Hale, are also perfectly ordinary English names, but they carry fairly obvious symbolic connotations (toughness and prickliness, health and energy) appropriate to the characters. Boucher, however, is neither a common regional name, reinforcing the realistic code in which the novel is written, nor (as long as we pronounce it 'Bowcher') an obviously symbolic one. But as soon as we recognize the derivation of the name from *boucher*, French for 'butcher', and note this character's crucial role in the riot at Thornton's mill, the symbolic force of the name becomes evident, whether Mrs Gaskell consciously intended it or not. It is like a riddle in a Freudian dream-analysis. Butcher – France – riot: the chain of association is short and leads us straight to the French Revolution, the guillotine and the Terror.

What I hope to show in the remainder of this essay is that the fear of working-class militancy manifested in early and mid-Victorian 'condition of England' novels, most intensely in their treatment of crowd behaviour, was fuelled and informed by memories and myths of the French Revolution. I say 'memories and myths' because in one sense these novelists were responding to real history and in another they were influenced by and contributing to a highly imaginative, quasi-fictional interpretation of that history.

The French Revolution ushered in the modern political era. It was notable for being a popular uprising which had permanent political effects. Though led for the most part by bourgeois intellectuals, it was driven by the energies of the common people, especially the *sansculottes* of Paris, who took the political initiative at crucial moments – notably the storming of the Bastille in July 1789 which started the Revolution, the march on Versailles in October of the same year which compelled the king to move his court to Paris, and the sack of the Tuileries palace in August 1792 which led to the suspension of the monarchy. Henceforward there was a completely new relationship between crowds and political power in Europe.

I have borrowed the phrase 'crowds and power' from the title of a sociological-cum-anthropological treatise by Elias Canetti,[5] better known perhaps as a novelist, the author of *Auto-da-Fé*. At the beginning of his book, Canetti expounds an interesting typology of crowds, distinguishing first between the closed crowd and the open crowd. The closed crowd assembles by arrangement in a defined space which limits its numbers – a political rally or religious celebration would be examples. The open crowd appears to gather spontaneously, and seeks voraciously to grow in numbers. It is constituted by a 'discharge' of energy, 'the moment when all who belong to the crowd get rid of their differences and feel equal' (p. 17). The open crowd's tendency to destructiveness, especially of property, is an instinctive rejection of barriers and boundaries, anything which affirms and creates distance between human beings. A closed crowd can become an open crowd – this Canetti designates as an 'eruption', observing that 'since the French Revolution these eruptions have taken on a form which we feel to be modern', (p. 22). There are five emotional types of crowd, classified according to whether their primary motivation is baiting, flight, prohibition, reversal or feasting. The revolutionary crowd is a reversal crowd – indeed Canetti cites the storming of the Bastille as the classic example of this type. A crowd of striking workers is a prohibition crowd – but as *North and South* demonstrates, not to mention more recent political controversy in Britain over flying pickets, it has always been seen as potentially a reversal crowd.

Obviously there were reversal crowds in history before the French Revolution. Earlier in the eighteenth century, to look no further, there were food riots in France and England in which crowds would compel greedy merchants in times of shortage to sell their produce at low prices. The violent actions of the London mob in the Gordon riots, and in support of

Wilkes, aimed to 'reverse' legislation and judicial verdicts. The London mob was, however, to a large extent inspired and manipulated by politicians higher up the social scale, while the food riots were genuinely popular manifestations, but short-lived in their effects. What was unprecedented about the French Revolutionary crowd was that it developed an autonomous will of its own and effected permanent political change.

It also, of course, spilled a great deal of blood. One of the most horrifying episodes of the French Revolution, the September Massacres of 1792, was a manifestation of crowd power, and the support of the *sansculottes* was essential to Robespierre's Reign of Terror. The degeneration of the Revolution of liberty, equality and fraternity into a bloodbath destroyed its own leaders, alienated sympathetic foreign observers and bequeathed to posterity the conviction or nagging fear that revolution inevitably produces a tyranny worse than the one it overthrows. The conclusion drawn by thoughtful, more or less progressive and liberal-minded Victorians, such as the authors of the novels I have mentioned, was that a Revolution in England must be avoided by removing the conditions which might provoke it. By representing Chartism and militant industrial action in terms that consciously or unconsciously alluded to the more violent episodes of the French Revolution, they aimed to dissuade the working class from organized political protest, and to frighten their own class into doing something about the condition of England. This rhetorical strategy, and the idea of the French Revolution which it exploited, derived very largely from the work of Thomas Carlyle.

To give some idea of the authority of Carlyle in the early Victorian period, and the impact of his monumental history of the French Revolution, first published in 1837, a year before the birth of the Chartist movement, one might quote the testimony of Charles Kingsley's autodidact hero, Alton Locke: 'I know no book, always excepting Milton, which at once so quickened and exalted my poetical view of man and his history, as that great prose poem, the single epic of modern days, Thomas Carlyle's *French Revolution*.'[6] The comparison with epic poetry is a conventional literary tribute. *The French Revolution* is in fact much more like a novel, what we would call today a 'non-fiction novel' or the 'new journalism', that is to say, a narrative which claims to be historically true, but uses techniques developed in prose fiction to tell its story in a vivid and exciting way: scenic construction, shifting points of view, free indirect speech, present tense narration, polyphonic discourse, prolepsis, iterative symbolism and so on. There is, in fact, no device listed by Tom Wolfe as characteristic of the new journalism in his anthology of that name published in 1973, which cannot be found in Carlyle's *French Revolution*. No wonder it excited and enthused novelists like Kingsley and Charles Dickens – who, according to Carlyle's biographer Froude, carried the book around with him everywhere on its first appearance.[7] Dickens of course acknowledged his debt to Carlyle in the Preface to *A Tale of Two Cities*, but the historian's influence is almost as palpable in *Barnaby Rudge*.

Carlyle was particularly good at crowd scenes. His description of the storming of the Bastille, the march on Versailles, the storming of the Tuileries, the September Massacres, are wonderfully vivid and exciting. Hilaire Belloc, who took a very different, much more partisan view of the French Revolution, commended Carlyle for comprehending 'one chief fact of the Revolution: the mob. Alone of all European peoples, the French are able to organize themselves from below in large masses, and Paris, which wrought the Revolution, can do it better than the rest of France.'[8] As Belloc observes, Carlyle was the last person one would have expected to acknowledge this fact, because of his own proto-fascist belief in the necessity for strong leaders, but in the writing of *The French Revolution*, mimesis triumphed over ideology:

> so thoroughly has he got inside his subject, so vitally has he raised it up and made it move of its own life, that in his book you see the French mob doing precisely what he would have told you, had you asked him, no mob could do . . . when he stops to comment on them . . . he is often wrong, but when the description begins he becomes right again by a pure instinct for visualising and for making men act in harmony and in consort in his book.[9]

'The French Revolution,' says Carlyle early in his book, 'means here the open violent rebellion, and Victory, of disimprisoned Anarchy against corrupt worn-out Authority.'[10] It is 'surely a great Phenomenon: nay, it is a *transcendental* one, overstepping all rules and experience, the crowning phenomenon of our Modern Time'. It is 'the Death–Birth of a world' (I, 171). Carlyle's treatment of the Revolution is, then, frankly apocalyptic, and his message to the ruling class of early Victorian England was: if you want to avoid apocalypse on this side of the English Channel, you'd better get your act together. As he drew towards the close of his long narrative he spelled it out in his own prophetic style:

> 'if the gods of this lower world will sit on their glittering thrones, indolent as Epicurus' gods, with the living Chaos of Ignorance and Hunger weltering uncared-for at their feet, and smooth Parasites preaching, Peace, peace, when there is no peace,' then the dark Chaos, it would seem, will rise; – has risen, and O Heavens! has it not tanned their skins into breeches for itself? [This is a reference to one of the more horrifying atrocities of the Revolution, eerily proleptic of modern horrors, of a tannery at Meudon where the corpses of the guillotined were flayed to make leather.] That there be no second Sansculottism in our earth for a thousand years, let us understand well what the first was; and let Rich and Poor of us go and do *otherwise*.
>
> (II, 382)

The power of the revolutionary mob is very much part of Carlyle's apocalyptic vision:

> Perhaps few terrestrial Appearances are better worth considering than mobs. Your mob is a genuine outburst of Nature . . . Shudder at it; or even shriek over it, if thou must; nevertheless consider it. Such a complex of human Forces and Individualities hurled forth, in their transcendental mood, to act and react, on circumstances and on one another.
>
> (I, 201)

The mob is both admired and feared here: admired for its energy, feared because of its destructive potential. It is 'a genuine outburst of Nature' – hence by implication opposed to Culture, which normally regulates human behaviour.

Canetti lists nine common symbols for the crowd, and all but one of them are drawn from the natural world: fire, the sea, rain, rivers, forest, corn, wind, sand and the heap. In Carlyle and the Victorian novelists the favourite metaphor is the sea. Fire is also frequently invoked, but its metaphoric force is somewhat weakened by the fact that there is also a metonymic or causal connection between crowds and fire: crowds often set fire to things. The overturning of the culture/nature distinction in crowd behaviour, and the mob's compulsion, noted by Canetti, to break down all barriers and boundaries that normally create distance between human beings, are therefore more strikingly conveyed in metaphors of inundation. The mob that surrounds the palace of Versailles, for instance, is described by Carlyle as a 'living deluge' (I, 223). He invites the reader to 'glance now, for a moment, from the royal windows! A roaring sea of human heads, inundating both courts, billowing against all passages: Menadic women, infuriated men, mad with revenge, with love of mischief, love of plunder!' (I, 226). There is a strain of similar imagery in Mrs Gaskell's account, cited earlier, of the rioting strikers in *North and South*: 'the slow-surging wave of the dark crowd', 'the angry sea of men', their 'rolling angry murmur'. The narrator of *Barnaby Rudge* observes that 'a mob is usually a creature of very mysterious existence, particularly in a large city . . . it is as difficult to follow to its various sources as the sea itself, nor does the parallel stop here, for the ocean is not more fickle and uncertain, more terrible when roused, more unreasonable or more cruel'.[11] The description of the storming of the Bastille in *A Tale of Two Cities* is particularly notable for its elaborate use of sea-imagery. For example:

> 'Come then!' cried Defarge, in a resounding voice. 'Patriots and friends, we are ready! The Bastille!'
> With a roar that sounded as if all the breath in France had been shaped into the detested word, the living sea rose, wave on wave, depth on

depth, and overflowed the city to that point. Alarm-bells ringing, drums beating, the sea raging and thundering on its new beach, the attack begun . . . So resistless was the force of the ocean bearing [Defarge] on, that even to draw his breath or turn his head was as impracticable as if he had been struggling with the surf at the South Sea, until he was landed in the outer court-yard of the Bastille.[12]

The sea of black and threatening waters, and of destructive upheaving of wave against wave, whose depths were yet unfathomed and whose forces were yet unknown. The remorseless sea of turbulently swaying shapes, voices of vengeance, and faces hardened in the furnaces of suffering until the touch of pity could make no mark on them.

But, in the ocean of faces where every fierce and furious expression was in vivid life, there were two groups of faces – each seven in number – so fixedly contrasting with the rest, that never did sea roll which bore more memorable wrecks with it. Seven faces of prisoners, suddenly released by the storm that had burst their tomb, were carried high overhead.

(p. 249)

When Carlyle's *French Revolution* was first published it was subtitled, 'A History of Sansculottism'[13] – an indication that Carlyle saw the new relationship between crowds and power as the key to understanding his subject. It is in this respect that Carlyle differs from that other great British critic of the Revolution, Edmund Burke. In his *Reflections on the Revolution in France* (1790) Burke had written indignantly of the 'band of cruel ruffians and assassins' who burst into Marie Antionette's bedchamber at Versailles, and of the 'horrid yells, and shrilling screams and frantic dances, and infamous contumelies, and all the unutterable abominations of the furies of hell, in the abused shape of the vilest of women', that accompanied the royal couple on their forced march to Paris.[14] But these are virtually the only remarks Burke makes about the Revolutionary crowd; they are asides in an argument that is essentially abstract – constitutional, moral, philosophical – and aimed at the bourgeois professional and intellectual class who were directing the Revolution and sitting in the National Assembly. (He was of course writing before the onset of the Terror.) It was Carlyle who put the crowd, the *sansculottes*, and their behaviour, at the very centre of the Revolutionary phenomenon, to a powerful emotive effect that novelists subsequently harnessed for their own purposes.

Indeed, Carlyle uses the word 'sansculottism' as more or less synonymous with Revolution throughout his work, and it is very much part of his apocalyptic vision: 'on a sudden, the Earth yawns asunder, and amid Tartarean smoke, and glare of fierce brightness, rises SANSCULOTTISM, many headed, fire-breathing, and asks: What think you of *me*?' (I, 171). The word *sansculottes* means literally 'without knee-breeches', and was originally a derogatory epithet applied by royalists to the working-class radicals, who wore trousers. But Carlyle does not explain this and sometimes seems to invite a literal rather than a metonymic interpretation of the term, especially by using the rather arch variation, 'sansunmentionables'. That is to say, there is in the word *sansculottes* a suggestion of bared buttocks, one of the oldest and most universal human gestures of insult and contempt, which Carlyle seems to invite, or at least does nothing to suppress. Furthermore, in actual fact many of the *sansculottes* did not wear trousers, but skirts. Women played a part of unprecedented importance in the crowds of the French Revolution, notably in the great march on Versailles which was instigated and largely carried through by women.

Carlyle shows himself to be both fascinated and disturbed by this episode in the section of his book that deals with it, entitled 'The insurrection of women'. He tries to dismiss it with ridicule and irony: 'how unfrightful it must have been; ludico-terrific, and most unmanageable' (I, 203). He applies mock-heroic epithets to the women – they are 'Menads', 'Amazons', 'Judiths'. He seizes gleefully on the fact that the march on Versailles took place in pouring rain, and summons up an image of the Esplanade 'covered with groups of squalid dripping women' (I, 211). He compares their alternative National Assembly to Erasmus' ape imitating his master shaving. But he cannot deny the effectiveness of the women's intervention, or the fact that it was a turning-point in the Revolution.

Dickens was also disturbed by the role of women in the Revolution, and unlike Carlyle did not try to laugh it off. The most ruthless and cruel revolutionaries in *A Tale of Two Cities* are women – Madame Defarge, always ominously knitting, like one of the Fates, and the anonymous blood-thirsty harridan known as 'the Vengeance'. In one of the few episodes in the novel he took directly from Carlyle, the summary execution of the wretched old extortionist Foulon, who had once recommended the hungry people to eat grass, Dickens emphasizes the participation of women, not mentioned by Carlyle:

> The men were terrible ... but the women were a sight to chill the boldest ... Give us the blood of Foulon, Give us the heart of Foulon, Give us the body and soul of Foulon, Rend Foulon to pieces, and dig him into the ground, that grass may grow from him. With these cries, numbers of the women, lashed into blind frenzy, whirled about, striking and tearing at their own friends until they dropped into a passionate swoon, and were only saved by the men belonging to them from being trampled underfoot.
>
> (p. 252)

This passage is heavily suggestive of pagan myth and ritual, especially the cult of Dionysus, whose priestesses, the Bacchae or Maenads, would work themselves up into a similar kind of frenzy. The same connotations are carried over to Dickens's description, later in the novel, of the Carmagnole, the wild chanting dance performed in the streets of Paris by *sansculottes* of both sexes at the height of the Revolution:

> They advanced, retreated, struck at one another's hands, clutched at one another's heads, spun round alone, caught one another and spun round in pairs, until many of them dropped . . . No fight could have been half so terrible as this dance. It was so emphatically a fallen sport – a something, once innocent, delivered over to devilry.
>
> (p. 307)

The key to these passages from Carlyle and Dickens is the idea of transgression. The transgression of traditional power relations between the classes inherent in Revolution is associated with transgression of traditional gender roles and codes of social behaviour. It is as if Revolution is a kind of return of the repressed. The orgiastic energy of pagan ritual, partly repressed by Catholic Christianity, but allowed a licensed expression in the tradition of Carnival, further repressed by Protestantism, capitalism and the Enlightenment[15] seems to erupt in a new and deadly serious form in the Revolutionary mob. The carnival crowd is, in Canetti's typology, primarily a feasting crowd; but it is also a kind of reversal crowd. As Mikhail Bakhtin, the great theorist of carnival, observed:

> The feast was a temporary suspension of the entire official system with all its prohibitions and hierarchic barriers. For a short time life came out of its usual, legalized and consecrated furrows and entered the sphere of utopian freedom.[16]

That quotation comes from Bakhtin's *Rabelais and His World*, in which Bakhtin's theory of the carnivalesque is most elaborately developed, and it is interesting to note that according to Bakhtin, 'At the time of the French Revolution Rabelais enjoyed a tremendous prestige in the eyes of its leaders. He was even made out to be a prophet of the Revolution. His home-town, Chinon, was renamed Chinon-Rabelais.'[17] According to Bakhtin, 'the primary carnivalistic act is the mock crowning and subsequent discrowning of the carnival king',[18] a phrase that seems grimly appropriate to the fate of Louis XVI in the course of the Revolution – at first invited to preside over it, subsequently executed by it. The Revolution in Dickens often seems like a demonic carnival. It is perhaps significant that in *Hard Times* he put forward a tamed and sentimentalized version of carnival, a 'closed' rather than an 'open' crowd – Mr Sleary's circus – as a rather inadequate answer to the alienation of modern industrialized society.

It is a critical commonplace that there is a contradiction between the values Dickens's novels explicitly affirm – love, peace, domesticity, sociability – and the investment of his most powerful imaginative energies in the presentation of evil, anarchy and the grotesque. Though he deplored the Gordon riots, he described them in *Barnaby Rudge* with a verve and gusto that came near to identification with the mob, as he half-jokingly acknowledged to Forster when he was writing these scenes: 'I have let all the prisoners out of Newgate, burnt down Lord Mansfield's and played the very devil . . . I feel quite smoky when I am at work.'[19]

The description of the attack on Newgate in *Barnaby Rudge* was clearly inspired by the storming of the Bastille, and the destruction of the country house called the Warren earlier in the novel corresponds loosely to the sack of the Tuileries. To both actions Dickens imparts a demonic, orgiastic character.

Men who had been into the cellars, and had staved the casks, rushed to and fro stark mad, setting fire to all they saw – often to the dresses of their own friends – and kindling the building in so many parts that some had no time to escape, and were seen, with drooping hands and blackened faces, hanging senseless on the window-sills to which they had crawled, until they were sucked and drawn into the burning gulf. The more the fire crackled and raged, the wilder and more cruel the men grew; as though moving in that element they became fiends, and changed their earthly nature for qualities that give delight in hell.

(pp. 506–7)

Now, now the door was down. Now they came rushing through the jail, calling to each other in the vaulted passages . . . whooping and yelling without a moment's rest; and running through the heat and flames as if they were cased in metal. By their legs, their arms, the hair upon their heads, they dragged the prisoners out. Some threw themselves upon the captives as they got towards the door, and tried to file away their irons; some danced about them with a frenzied joy, and rent their clothes, and were ready, as it seemed to tear them limb from limb.

(p. 586)

These descriptions have a nightmarish quality that is peculiar to Dickens. But the storming of the Bastille, the march on Versailles and the sack of the Tuileries haunted the imaginations of other Victorian novelists, and lie behind such scenes as the attack on Thornton's mill in *North and South* and the assault on Robert Moore's mill in *Shirley*. Perhaps the most blatant representation of English industrial unrest in terms of the French Revolution occurs at the climax of Disraeli's *Sybil*.

The story of this novel concerns an idealistic young Conservative politician, Egremont, who takes an enlightened interest in social problems, especially after meeting Sybil, the beautiful daughter of a Chartist called Walter Gerard. After Parliament's refusal to consider the Chartist petition of 1839 and subsequent civil disturbances ('Terrible news from Birm-

ingham,' one of the characters reports, 'they are encamped in the Bull Ring
amid smoking ruins, and breathe nothing but havoc'[20]), Gerard throws in
his lot with the violent or 'physical force' wing of the Chartist movement,
much to Sybil's dismay, and is charged with conspiracy. When he returns
home to a triumphant welcome, Sybil is somewhat reassured by the peace-
ful, orderly demonstration. But certain individuals in the movement are
intent on provoking a violent uprising, partly for selfish personal motives.
A general strike turns violent when the Hell-cats of Wodgate, who seem to
be Black Country metal workers, led by an ignorant demagogue nicknamed
'Bishop Hatton', join the miners of Lancashire:

> The march of Bishop Hatton at the head of the Hell-cats into the mining
> districts was perhaps the most striking popular movement since the Pil-
> grimage of Grace. Mounted on a white mule, wall-eyed and of hideous
> form, the Bishop brandished a huge hammer with which he had
> announced that he would destroy the enemies of the people.
>
> (pp. 357–8)

Whereas the miners demonstrate peacefully,

> The Hell-cats and their followers were of a different temper . . . They
> destroyed and ravaged; sacked and gutted houses; plundered cellars; . . .
> burst open doors, broke windows . . . in short, they robbed and rioted.
>
> (p. 359)

Sybil, who happens to be travelling through the country at the time of
these disturbances, is offered the protection of the de Mowbray family of
Mowbray castle. This is an imitation-Norman castle built by a Whig peer
of ignoble pedigree – just the kind of pseudo-aristocracy Disraeli's Young
England group in the Conservative Party most despised. Lady de Mowbray,
however, is a genuine aristocrat, who becomes a kind of Marie Antoinette
figure when the castle is besieged by the Hell-cats.

> When they perceived the castle, this dreadful band gave a ferocious shout.
> Lady de Mowbray showed blood; she was composed and courageous.
> She observed the mob from the window, and reassuring her daughter
> and Sybil, she said she would go down and speak to them.
>
> (p. 387)

There is a resemblance here to the scene in *North and South* with which I
began. Both scenes have perhaps a common origin in Carlyle's description
of the invasion of the palace of Versailles, and his injunction to the reader
to 'glance now, for a moment, from the royal windows'. In such scenes the
heroine, and vicariously the reader, is placed in the besieged building, and
thus inevitably identifies with the occupants and owners, threatened by the
mob.

The Hell-cats invade the castle, break into the cellars, get drunk and vandalize the luxurious apartments:

> bands were parading the gorgeous salons and gazing with wonderment on their decorations and furniture. Some grimy ruffians had thrown themselves with disdainful delight on the satin couches and the state beds: others rifled the cabinets with an idea that they must be full of money, and finding little in their way, had strewn their contents – papers and books, and works of art – over the floors of the apartments: some-times a band who had escaped from below with booty, came up to consummate their orgies in the magnificence of the dwelling-rooms.
>
> (p. 392)

Compare Carlyle's description of

> How deluges of frantic Sansculottism roared through all passages of this Tuileries, ruthless in vengeance; how the valets were butchered, hewed down . . . how in the cellars wine bottles were broken, wine-butts were staved-in and drunk; and upwards to the very garrets, all windows tum-bled out their precious royal furnitures: and with gold mirrors, velvet curtains, down of ript feather beds, and dead bodies of men, the Tuileries was like no Garden of the Earth.
>
> (II, 125)

Eventually, the Hell-cats set fire to the castle, and their leader perishes in the flames:

> the flame that, rising from the keep of Mowbray, announced to the startled country that in a short hour the splendid mimicry of Norman rule would cease to exist, told also the pitiless fate of the ruthless savage, who, with analogous pretension, had presumed to style himself the Liber-ator of the People.
>
> (pp. 396–7)

Sybil is rescued from a fate worse than death by Egremont, and conveniently turns out to be an heiress, so that he can marry her without disturbance to the class system. The love story of *Sybil* is its least convincing element. As a socio-political novel of ideas, however, it is lively, thought-provoking and well-informed. Disraeli drew cleverly on his political experience and on documentary sources such as Parliamentary Blue Books to make his panor-amic picture of England convincing. But the climax of his novel, as far as I know, had no factual source or analogue in England. The sack and destruction of Mowbray castle is a fiction which projects certain well-established images of the French Revolution on to the social and political unrest of England in the late 1830s and early 1840s.

There is one classic English novel which describes the action of a reversal crowd as disciplined, orderly and responsible, uncontaminated by criminal and antisocial elements, and that was published some years before Carlyle's *French Revolution*. I refer to the account of the Porteus riots in Sir Walter Scott's *The Heart of Midlothian* (1818). In 1736, a popular smuggler called Wilson was hanged in Edinburgh before a sympathetic crowd. The officer in charge of the execution, Captain Porteus, overreacted to the crowd's behaviour and ordered his men to fire on them, killing several innocent people. Porteus was tried and convicted of murder, but at the last moment was granted a royal reprieve from London, to the great indignation of the populace. That night a highly disciplined mob, its ringleaders disguised in women's dress, broke into the Tolbooth, the old prison of Edinburgh, abducted Porteus and publicly hanged him. Nobody else was harmed, and so punctilious were the ringleaders that they left payment at the ropemaker's shop from which they took the rope to hang their victim. Their work completed, they melted away, and no one was ever successfully convicted for the action.

Scott's narration of this sequence of events is brilliant, and scrupulously fair. By telling the story partly from the point of view of a Scottish minister who is pressganged into acting as chaplain to the condemned man, and vigorously protests against the lawlessness of the action, Scott makes clear that he does not approve it; but at the same time he makes us understand the provocation and gives the perpetrators full credit for their determination and self-discipline, which contrast favourably with the muddle and panic of the official custodians of law and order. It is a very good example of Georg Lukács's perceptive insight into Scott's work, that it was ideologically much more progressive than his actual politics. 'It was the French Revolution, the revolutionary wars and the rise and fall of Napoleon,' says Lukacs, 'which for the first time made history a *mass experience*.'[21] Through his recreation of episodes of Scottish history Scott intuitively expressed the new self-consciousness and self-assertiveness of the common people in the Revolutionary period, even though he himself was a romantic Tory with aristocratic aspirations.

The Victorian novelists were unable or unwilling to achieve that degree of disinterestedness. The idea of mass experience, mass consciousness, mass behaviour, frightened them, and their fictional representation of crowds in action is invariably negative. The crowd attracts lawless and violent elements in society, and gives them an opportunity to indulge their evil inclinations; it also releases the evil and destructive potential inherent in all of us. The crowd is cruel, fickle and irrational, liable to be overcome by a collective madness. Of course one finds such a view of the crowd in literature before the Revolutionary period – in the plays of Shakespeare, for instance.[22] But the French Revolution, especially as represented by Carlyle, had given the idea of the power of the crowd a new and nightmarish dimension which, as I have tried to show, powerfully affected the treatment of the condition of England in the early Victorian novel.

Chapter 8

Composition, distribution, arrangement
Form and structure in Jane Austen's novels

Each of Jane Austen's novels has its own distinctive identity, but they also have a strong family resemblance, one to another. What kind of fiction did she write, and what was special about it? The short answer is that she fused together the sentimental novel and the comedy of manners with an unprecedented effect of realism. A longer answer will entail a description of these categories and qualities in terms of narrative form and structure.

By the 'sentimental novel', in this context, I mean the didactic, heroine-centred love story of which the prototype was Samuel Richardson's *Pamela; or Virtue Rewarded* (1740–1) and which survives today in the popular women's fiction generally known as 'romance'. This latter designation is somewhat ironic since Samuel Richardson prided himself on writing a kind of prose fiction that eschewed the characteristic devices and implausibilities of traditional romance and would be morally improving precisely because it was 'true to life'. The eponymous heroine of *Pamela* is a young maid-servant in a great house who, at the death of her mistress, is subjected to the sexual advances of the latter's son and heir, Mr B——. Although she admires her master, the principled Pamela resists all his efforts to seduce her with such spirit and steadfastness that his lust is converted into love and he eventually makes her his wife. The story, which Richardson claimed was based on an actual case, is told entirely in the form of letters and journal entries, mostly written by the heroine; and it initiated a long line of sentimental epistolary novels, among them the first version of *Sense and Sensibility*, called *Elinor and Marianne*. Richardson's epistolary technique became obsolete with the development (in which Jane Austen played a crucial part) of more subtle and flexible methods of representing a character's thoughts and feelings in literary narrative. The basic structure of *Pamela* as a love story has, however, had a remarkably long life and proved adaptable to many literary purposes, high and low. Though invented by a male author, it is an essentially feminine kind of fiction, usually written by women, centred on a heroine rather than a hero, and directed particularly at a female audience. It arose at a time when women were beginning to assert their right to choose their partners in marriage but were restricted by social convention to a very passive role in the courtship process. The 'happy ending' of the didactic love story rewards the heroine, who copes with various emotional, social, economic and ethical obstacles to union with the man she loves without losing her integrity. If there were no obstacles, of course, there would be no story.

Structurally, then, the love story consists of the delayed fulfilment of a desire. The delay puts the heroine under stress and thus generates the 'sentiment' – that is, the representation of feelings, anxieties and moral choices that is the real source of interest and value in the sentimental novel. In *Pamela*, the cause of delay is very simple: Mr B—— wants extramarital sex, but Pamela wants love and marriage, and eventually she wins. This plot was too explicitly sexual, and perhaps too democratic in its implications (Pamela is promoted from the bottom to the top of the class system by sticking to her principles), for Richardson's more genteel, mainly female successors in the sentimental novel tradition, such as Fanny Burney, Maria Edgeworth and Jane Austen. The heroine, though often inferior to the hero in social status and fortune, is not as remote in class terms as Pamela was from Mr B—— before her marriage. The hero is not morally compromised by having designs on the heroine's purity, and illicit sexuality is displaced on to other characters – a seducer whose designs are frustrated by the hero, for instance, or a seductress or 'fallen woman' who throws into relief the heroine's moral integrity. The necessary delay in the union of hero and heroine then has to be contrived by other means. For example, the lovers get off on the wrong foot, and one or both take some time to recognize the true nature of their feelings; they are alienated by misunderstandings, by other characters' intrigues, by apparently insurmountable obstacles to do with fortune, family prejudice and the like. In many of these novels (e.g. Fanny Burney's *Evelina* [1778] and Maria Edgeworth's *Belinda* [1801]), some of the romance motifs that Richardson had rigorously excluded from his *Pamela* begin to seep back into the sentimental novel as a way of resolving the plot in a flurry of wills, confessions, discoveries of long-lost daughters/sons/parents and so on. Jane Austen did not use such devices; indeed, she pointedly abstained from them. But all her novels have the basic structure of the didactic love story that derived from Richardson, albeit with much variation, modification, displacement and even inversion of its basic components.

Of all Jane Austen's works, perhaps *Pride and Prejudice* cleaves most closely to the paradigm of the classic love story. Here the delay of the lovers' union is caused by their mutually unfavourable 'first impressions' (the original title of the novel). Darcy offends Elizabeth by his arrogance, by his interference in the promising relationship between Mr Bingley and her sister Jane, and by his alleged ill-treatment of Wickham. She refuses his first, totally unexpected proposal of marriage, thus demonstrating her integrity as well as her impulsiveness, because the match is a tempting one in material terms. When, for a number of reasons, her feelings toward Darcy change, she is rewarded with a second chance to accept him. Elizabeth rejects the cynical *realpolitik* of the marriage market as expounded and practised by Charlotte Lucas; she also survives unscathed the temptations of the erotically attractive but immoral male, represented by Wickham. Wickham demonstrates his dangerous power on Elizabeth's younger sister, Lydia, and Darcy's moral rescue operation in this crisis precipitates his union with the grateful and admiring Elizabeth – a good example of the displacement of the Richardsonian seduction plot on to secondary characters. Something similar happens at the end of *Mansfield Park*, where the adultery of Henry Crawford with Maria Bertram and Mary Crawford's failure to condemn it 'justify' Fanny's earlier refusal of Crawford and precipitate her union with Edmund. The peripeteia (the surprising but satisfying reversal of expectation) in Jane Austen's plots very frequently takes the form of sexual misbehaviour, or something like it (such as Lucy Steele's marriage to Robert Ferrars in *Sense and Sensibility*).

The classic love story consists of a delay not only of the heroine's desire but also of the reader's desire – to know the answer to the basic question raised by the narrative: will the heroine get the man she wants? There are three principal sources of interest in narrative: suspense, mystery and irony. Suspense raises the question: what will happen? Mystery raises the question: why did it happen? When the reader knows the answer to the questions but the characters do not, irony is generated. Thus, all rereadings of novels tend to create an effect of irony, but this is especially true of Jane Austen's novels, which are permeated with irony, rhetorical as well as dramatic, and which can sustain an infinite number of readings. On first reading they tend, like most love stories, to engage the reader's interest through suspense rather than mystery. *Emma* is an exception, since it is full of enigmas (Why is Mr Elton so keen to attend the Westons' dinner party when Harriet is ill? Who sent the piano to Jane Fairfax? What are Frank Churchill's real feelings about Emma?) This follows from the fact that Emma does not fall in love until the book is almost over; therefore, the question: will she get the man she wants? cannot provide the main source of narrative interest. In *Pride and Prejudice*, too, though to a lesser extent, the heroine's knowledge of her own heart is delayed, and enigmas, mainly to do with Wickham and Darcy, supply narrative interest, together with the suspense plot concerning Bingley's intention toward Elizabeth's sister Jane. In the other novels Jane Austen makes relatively little use of mystery as a means of engaging the reader's interest, and in *Northanger Abbey* she mocked Mrs Radcliffe's rather mechanical reliance on this device in *The Mysteries of Udolpho* (1794).

In *Northanger Abbey*, Jane Austen played a delightful (and risky) double game with both the conventions of the sentimental novel and the conventions of traditional romance that were beginning to reinvade it through the contemporary cult of the Gothic – a process in which Mrs Radcliffe played a crucial role. At first sight, Jane Austen seems to be simply justifying the former at the expense of the latter. The famous conclusion to chapter 5, in which the narrator defends the novel as a form 'in which the greatest powers of the mind are displayed, in which the most thorough knowledge of human nature, the happiest delineation of its varieties, the liveliest effusions of wit and humour are conveyed to the world in the best chosen language' (*NA*, p. 38),[1] explicitly cites titles by Fanny Burney and Maria Edgeworth. Catherine's naive addiction to the Gothic novel retards the happy consummation of her love for Henry Tilney – first, by leading her into uncritical friendship with Isabella Thorpe and her brother John, whose intrigues constantly threaten her happiness, and second, by tempting Catherine into a ludicrous suspicion, during her stay at Northanger Abbey, of General Tilney's having murdered his wife, thus herself temporarily forfeiting Henry's good opinion.

But as several commentators have observed, Catherine's opinion of the general is not totally unwarranted, since he shows himself to be a thoroughly nasty man. Furthermore, the conventions of the more realistic sentimental novel are themselves subjected to ironic undermining – none more devastating than the passage in which the narrator tells us that Henry Tilney's affection for Catherine 'originated in nothing better than gratitude, or, in other words, that a persuasion of her partiality for him had been the only cause of giving her a serious thought' (*NA*, p. 243); and none more witty than the narrator's admission that the anxiety of Henry and Catherine about the general's opposition to their marriage 'can hardly extend, I fear, to the bosom of my readers, who will see in the tell-tale compression of the pages before them, that we are all hastening together to perfect felicity' (*NA*, p. 250). It seems that there is no great 'virtue' in this heroine, and the narration of her 'reward' is almost contemptuously offhand, making the reader feel guilty at the pleasure he takes in it and sending him back, perhaps, to reread that highly equivocal defence of the novel as a genre in chapter 5.

Of all Jane Austen's novels *Northanger Abbey* is the only one that lends itself to a modern deconstructive reading, for it does seem to deny the reader any sure ground for interpretation and discrimination and to make explicit the impossibility of getting the world into a book. The other novels take the paradigm of the didactic love story more seriously, invest it with deeper significance, and centre it on heroines of more worth than Catherine Morland – but without sacrificing comedy and humour.

Comedy is not easily combined with the sentimental novel. *Pamela* is only unintentionally funny, a weakness Henry Fielding riotously exploited in *Shamela* (1741) and *Joseph Andrews* (1742). His own most sentimental novel, *Amelia* (1751), is his least amusing. In Richardson's *Clarissa* (1747–8) and in Rousseau's *La Nouvelle Héloïse* (1761), the sentimental pursuit of personal authenticity leads to tragedy, or at least pathos, to gestures of renunciation and loss, in which neither Jane Austen nor her heroines are interested. Emma's happiness – her eventual marriage to Knightley – entails disappointment for Harriet Smith, whose misplaced hopes of marrying him were unintentionally encouraged by Emma herself. Emma is sorry for Harriet, but not extravagantly so:

> For as to any of that heroism of sentiment which might have prompted her to entreat [Knightley] to transfer his affection from herself to Harriet, as infinitely the most worthy of the two – or even the more simple sublimity of resolving to refuse him at once and for ever, without vouch-safing any motive, because he could not marry them both, Emma had it not.
>
> (p. 431)

Both Fanny Burney and Maria Edgeworth leavened the sentimental novel with comedy, and Jane Austen undoubtedly learned from them; but their comedy is, compared with hers, more in the nature of 'comic relief' from the main story and often takes a rather robust, farcical form reminiscent of the comic fiction of Fielding, Sterne and Smollett, which itself derived ultimately from Rabelais, Cervantes and the picaresque tradition. Jane Austen's comedy seems more theatrical in its origins, reminding us faintly of Congreve, Molière and even Shakespeare.

One of the most venerable distinctions in general poetics is that drawn by Plato in Book III of *The Republic*, between diegesis (description of actions by an authorial narrator) and mimesis (representation of action through the imitated speech of characters). Drama is pure mimesis, in this sense, but the epic, and the novel which formally derives from it, combine diegesis and mimesis. Among the classic novelists, Jane Austen tends toward a dominantly mimetic method. Her stories are unfolded in a series of scenes, with a minimum of authorial description, and her skill in revealing character through speech is justly celebrated. Many passages from the earlier novels (e.g. the discussion between Mr and Mrs John Dashwood in chapter 3 of *Sense and Sensibility*, and the dialogues between Mr and Mrs Bennet in *Pride and Prejudice*) could be performed as written (and have been, on radio, television and film). Action, in Jane Austen's novels, is social interaction of people in pairs, in groups, in social situations such as parties, dinners, balls, courtesy calls, walks and excursions – situations that lend themselves naturally to 'scenic' presentation and emphasize 'manners'. This is one reason why the comedy in Jane Austen does not seem tacked on to the love story but permeates it. This is true even of *Mansfield Park*, the most earnest of the novels and often disliked on that account. The comings and goings in the 'wilderness' at Sotherton (rather reminiscent of Shakespeare's Forest of Arden), for instance, and the whole saga of the theatricals, are exquisitely comic in a highly dramatic way, culminating in the wonderfully funny moment when the astonished Sir Thomas Bertram, unexpectedly returned home from the West Indies, interrupts Mr Yates rehearsing his part in *Lovers' Vows:*

> He stept to the door . . . and opening it, found himself on the stage of a theatre, and opposed to a ranting young man, who appeared likely to knock him down backwards. At the very moment of Yates perceiving Sir Thomas, and giving perhaps the very best start he had ever given in the whole course of his rehearsals, Tom Bertram entered at the other end of the room; and never had he found greater difficulty in keeping his countenance. His father's looks of solemnity and amazement on this his first appearance on any stage, and the gradual metamorphosis of the impassioned Baron Wildenhaim into the well-bred and easy Mr. Yates, making his bow and apology to Sir Thomas Bertram, was such an exhibition, such a piece of true acting as he would not have lost on any account. It would be the last – in all probability the last scene on that stage; but he was sure there could not be a finer.
>
> (pp. 182–3)

Here Jane Austen very characteristically turns the conventions of a falsifying kind of art inside out in order to reinforce the truthfulness of her own representation of experience. The encounter between Mr Yates and Sir Thomas takes place on the interface between life and art and is equally disconcerting to both parties on that account. Sir Thomas walks unintentionally on to a stage for the first time in his life and becomes willy-nilly an actor in a scene, just as Yates is startled by the reality of the encounter out of the artificial rant and exaggerated gesture of melodrama into a genuine 'start' from which he recovers by a piece of 'true' social acting. The touch of genius in the passage is, however, the introduction of Tom Bertram as a kind of audience for this piece of real-life theatre. It is through his eyes that we see and relish the ironies of the spectacle – and to recognize that fact is to recognize that, scenic as it is, Jane Austen's fiction is an achievement of narrative, not dramatic art. This kind of focalizing of the action through an individual viewpoint is peculiar to written narrative and is one of the constituents of fictional 'realism'.

The realism of Jane Austen's novels, the illusion of life that they create, has always been one of the chief attractions of her work to many generations of readers, from Sir Walter Scott's tribute, in his journal of 1826, to 'the exquisite touch, which renders ordinary commonplace things and characters interesting, from the truth of the description and the sentiment', to Arnold Kettle's declaration, in 1951, that '*Emma* is as convincing as our own lives, and has the same sort of concreteness'.[2] More recently, realism as a literary effect has fallen into disfavour. Post-structuralist criticism, especially that which derives from the work of Roland Barthes, has identified the 'classic realist text' as an instrument of ideology, a genre founded on bad faith, on the pretence that bourgeois culture is 'natural', using the dominance of the authorial voice over all the other discourses in the text to limit meaning in the interests of control, repression and privilege. It cannot be denied that Jane Austen took for granted the existence of class-society (though she did not see it as fixed or static), that she subscribed to the Christian-humanist notion of the autonomy and responsibility of the individual self, and that her novels unequivocally endorse certain values and reject others. If these are grounds for condemnation, then she stands condemned – though it seems a perverse and anachronistic judgement. Jane Austen's admirers have, however, often seemed handicapped in defending and celebrating her art by the poverty of their critical tools for analysing it. Without a metalanguage (a language for talking about an object language – in this case the language of literary realism), criticism is apt to find itself reduced to mere paraphrase, retelling Jane Austen's stories in language that is of the same kind as hers but inferior in eloquence, precision, and wit. Part of the problem is that realism is a literary effect that works by disguising its own conventionality. Some of the concepts and methods of structuralist and formalist criticism may help us to see through that disguise and understand how Jane Austen constructs a fictional world 'as convincing as our own lives'.

For example, Roland Barthes's analysis of the classic realist text in *S/Z* as a 'braiding' of multiple codes of signification – some having to do with the raising and resolution of narrative questions, some contributing to the creation of character, others imparting through devices of connotation the underlying themes and values of the story – all bound together in a kind of aesthetic 'solidarity', so that any segment of the text can be shown to be communicating several messages simultaneously: this would seem to be highly relevant to Jane Austen's fiction, in which every detail, every nuance of gesture and conversation, is charged with significance. One must make the reservation, however, that the codes of connotation in Jane Austen operate under much stricter constraints and offer the critic much less opportunity for exegetical display than Balzac (the subject of *S/Z*). Another way of putting this is to say that Jane Austen's novels exhibit in a very pure form the dominance of metonymy over metaphor that Roman Jakobson argued is characteristic of realism as a literary mode.[3] Metonymy is a trope that works by manipulating relationships of contiguity (as opposed to metaphor, which manipulates relationships of similarity). 'Metonymic' discourse thus emphasizes sequence and causality, and Jane Austen's novels illustrate this bias very well. Her novels have a seamless quality, one episode leading logically and naturally to the next. She is particularly artful in the way she introduces, or reintroduces, one character to fill the space left in the story by another. Thus, in *Emma*, when the enigma of Mr Elton's equivocal behaviour toward Emma and Harriet is solved to their mutual embarrassment and mortification and he departs from Highbury in a huff, the advent of Jane Fairfax and Frank Churchill, heralded many pages previously, provides a new focus of attention; and when Churchill, in turn, leaves the scene of Highbury, back comes Mr Elton with Mrs Elton (whom he has very plausibly married on the rebound from Emma). The reader of Jane Austen never feels, as he so often does with classic fiction, that the action has been patently contrived, new characters invented, new settings provided, to satisfy the exigencies of the plot and theme or simply to preserve the momentum of the text. Motivation of character conforms scrupulously to a code of psychological causality. In reading sentimental fiction by Jane Austen's contemporaries, one's credulity is frequently strained by the ability of hero and heroine to misunderstand each other (Fanny Burney's *Camilla* is a particularly flagrant example of a novel kept going, for some nine hundred pages, virtually by this means alone); but the mistakes and misjudgements of Jane Austen's characters satisfy the modern reader's most stringent standards of plausibility.

Metaphor and metaphorical symbolism are used very sparingly by Jane Austen, and under strict constraints. Mark Schorer showed how, in *Emma*, buried or 'dead' metaphors drawn from the language of commerce and property imply a scale of values that contrasts ironically, and almost subliminally, with the emotional and moral issues to which they are applied,[4] and I have written elsewhere about the extraordinarily subtle and delicate way in which the pathetic fallacy is used in the same novel to mark the transition of the heroine from despair to joy.[5] Even in *Persuasion*, by general consent the most 'poetic' or 'romantic' of the novels, the seasonal symbolism that attaches to the heroine's progress from an autumnal mood of resignation to a joyful 'second spring of youth and beauty' (*P*, p. 124) arises metonymically out of the actual seasonal span of the main action; and the metaphor of 'bloom' that articulates this theme most insistently (Anne is said to have lost her bloom at the beginning of the novel but to have recovered it by the end) is so conventional as scarcely to be perceived as a figurative expression.

One of the most fruitful concepts in modern narrative theory has been the Russian formalist distinction between *fabula* (the story as it would have been enacted in real time and space) and *sjuzet* (the story as it is represented in the text). In the case of fiction (as distinct from historiography), the *fabula* is not a prior reality but an extrapolation from the *sjuzet*, to be used as a tool of comparison. By observing how the narrative text selects, manipulates and 'deforms' the raw material of the *fabula*, we can uncover the formal choices that realistic illusion tends to disguise and relate those choices to the thematic and affective properties of the text. These choices crucially concern the handling of time, and what in Anglo-American criticism is loosely called 'point of view' (loosely, because it concerns not merely the perspective from which the action is seen but also the voice in which it is narrated).

Gérard Genette has identified three categories of time in which there may be more or less disparity between *fabula* and *sjuzet:* order, duration and frequency.[6] Jane Austen's narratives rarely deviate from chronological order. If there is a retrospective account of some event antecedent to the main action or a delayed explanation of some event in the main action, either it is incorporated into the time span of the main action in the form of a letter (e.g. Darcy's letter to Elizabeth explaining his involvement with Wickham; *PP*, pp. 196–203) or in dialogue (e.g. Willoughby's apologetic confession to Elinor; *SS*, pp. 319–29), or it is briefly summarized in a non-scenic way by the authorial narrator (e.g. the account of Anne Elliot's former relationship with Wentworth at the beginning of chapter 4 of *Persuasion*). In other words, there is a minimal disturbance of chronological order in Jane Austen's novels. We don't encounter in them the effect of flashback, in which the temporal progress of the main action is suspended and for a while effaced by the scenic presentation of an earlier event; nor do we encounter anything like a 'flashforward' – a proleptic glimpse of what is to come. The former effect is characteristic of fiction in which reality is seen as highly subjective – *Tristram Shandy*, for example, or the modern stream-of-consciousness novel; the latter effect is one in which the author as omniscient maker and manipulator of the fiction is apt to show his hand. By eschewing both these effects, Jane Austen strengthens the correspondence between her fictional world and the public, 'common-sense' notion of time as a plane on which we all move, from a known past toward an unknown future, according to a logic of causality that becomes intelligible only in retrospect.

By 'duration' Genette means the relationship between the time putatively occupied by the action of the *fabula* and the 'reading time' it is accorded in the text. The main action of Jane Austen's novels never occupies more than a year, and usually rather less. *Emma*, for instance, begins with Mrs Weston's marriage in the autumn and ends with the heroine's marriage the following autumn. *Persuasion* begins in autumn and ends the following spring. *Mansfield Park* stands out from the other novels in having a longish prelude describing Fanny's background and how she was adopted as a young child by the Bertram family, but the main action properly begins with the arrival of the Crawfords at *Mansfield Park* 'in the month of July, and Fanny had just reached her eighteenth year' (*MP*, p. 40). It ends the following summer. Why is there this consistency in the time span of Jane Austen's novels? Perhaps six months is about the shortest time in which to portray plausibly the development of a meaningful relationship between hero and heroine, particularly if it entails a revolution in feeling, as in Elizabeth Bennet's attitude to Darcy, Edmund Bertram's to Mary Crawford and Fanny, Wentworth's to Anne Elliot; and anything longer than twelve months would draw attention to ellipses in the temporal continuity of the narrative and slacken its grip on the reader.

The tempo of a fictional narrative can seem faster than reality (e.g. the thriller) or slower (the stream-of-consciousness novel) or to move at about the same pace. Jane Austen's novels seem to have the tempo of life itself, yet their stories occupy several months, and the reading of them takes only a few hours. The illusion is achieved by the highly selective and dominantly scenic presentation of experience. Jane Austen notoriously – it is one of the chief causes of critical controversy about her – left out a great deal from her novels: physical love, the work men do, historical events, 'local colour'. Her novels are concerned with the personal and social relations of young middle-class women confined to a very limited field of activity. The plot, which is concerned ultimately with the choice of husband, is furthered in a series of social encounters or 'scenes' that, because of the amount of direct speech in them, create the effect of more or less neutral duration, neither noticeably slower or faster than the tempo of 'reality'; and because of the habitual, repetitive quality of these scenes, we are scarcely aware of the intervals between them.

Consider, for example, the events in the second volume of *Emma* (chapters 19–36 in most modern editions): Emma and Harriet visit the Bateses and hear of Jane Fairfax's impending arrival; they visit again and meet Jane; Knightley calls at Hartfield, and so does Miss Bates, with news of Mr Elton's marriage; Harriet visits the Martins; Frank Churchill arrives and visits Hartfield and walks in the village with Emma; all the principal characters meet at the Coles's dinner party; Emma, Harriet, Mrs Weston and Frank Churchill call on the Bateses; discussions take place at Randalls and the Crown Inn about the proposed ball; Frank Churchill, summoned by his aunt, calls at Hartfield to say goodbye; Emma meets Mrs Elton and gives a dinner party in her honour. Two or three months have passed, yet we have no sense of the acceleration of the normal tempo of life.

By 'frequency', Genette refers to the ratio between the number of times an event occurs in the *fabula* and the number of times it is narrated in the *sjuzet*. As we might expect, Jane Austen generally follows the historical, 'common-sense' norm of one-to-one. She does, however, use summary (narrating once what happened several times) in linking passages and to express with sometimes disconcerting candour the tedium and repetitiveness of the social round to which her heroines are confined – for example, 'that kind of intimacy must be submitted to, which consists of sitting an hour or two together in the same room almost every day' (*SS*, p. 124). Jane Austen seldom repeats the narrative presentation of a single event, unless we count Emma's reflections on the Elton–Harriet débâcle (*E*, pp. 134–9) or Edmund's and Fanny's inquests on the behaviour of Mary Crawford (*MP*, pp. 63–4). She never presents successive accounts of the same event as experienced by two or more characters, in the manner of Richardson. This brings us to the topic of 'point of view'.

The great advantage of Richardson's epistolary technique – and the reason it enjoyed such a vogue – was that it short-circuited the simple alternation of diegesis and mimesis, author's voice and characters' voices, in traditional narrative by making the characters tell their own story virtually as it happened. The gain in immediacy and realistic illusion was enormous, but the technique had certain disadvantages, which, we may speculate, caused Jane Austen to abandon it after some early experiments. The machinery of correspondence was clumsy, uneconomical, and likely to strain credulity, while the elimination of the authorial voice from the text deprived it of an important channel of meaning. The nineteenth-century novel developed a new and more flexible combination of author's voice and characters' voices than the simple alternation of the two one finds in traditional epic narration, from Homer to Fielding and Scott – a discourse that fused, or interwove, them, especially through the stylistic device known as 'free indirect speech'. This technique, which Jane Austen was the first English novelist to use extensively, consists of reporting the thoughts of a character in language that approximates more or less closely to their own idiolect and deleting the introductory tags, such as 'he thought', 'she wondered', 'he said to himself' and the like, that grammar would normally require in the well-formed sentence. For instance, after Mr Elton's unwelcome declaration to Emma, the next chapter begins: 'The hair was curled, and the maid sent away, and Emma sat down to think and be miserable. – It was a wretched business, indeed! – Such an overthrow of every thing she had been wishing for! – Such a development of every thing most unwelcome! – Such a blow for Harriet! That was the worst of all' (E, p. 134). Free indirect speech, which enters this passage at the second sentence, allows the novelist to give the reader intimate access to a character's thoughts without totally surrendering control of the discourse to that character (as in the epistolary novel). The passage continues in a more summary and syntactically complex style, in which the narrator's judicial authority is perceptible, though Emma's consciousness remains focal:

> Every part of it brought pain and humiliation, of some sort or other; but, compared with the evil to Harriet, all was light; and she would gladly have submitted to feel yet more mistaken – more in error – more disgraced by mis-judgement, than she actually was, could the effects of her blunders have been confined to herself.

> (E, p. 134)

Free indirect speech, combined with presentation of the action from the spatio-temporal perspective of an individual character (the usual meaning of 'point of view' in literary criticism) allows the novelist to vary, from sentence to sentence, the distance between the narrator's discourse and the character's discourse, between the character's values and the 'implied author's' values, and so to control and direct the reader's affective and interpretive responses to the unfolding story. Thus, for instance, we identify, and identify with, Elinor rather than Marianne as the heroine of *Sense and Sensibility* because we see much more of the action from Elinor's perspective, because we have much more access to her private thoughts, and because there is much greater consonance between the narrator's language and the language of Elinor's consciousness. Marianne's unhappiness at Willoughby's desertion is consistently ironized, implicitly judged as self-indulgent, by an authorial rhetoric of oxymoron: 'this nourishment of grief was every day applied. She spent whole hours at the pianoforté alternately singing and crying' (p. 83); 'in such moments of precious, of invaluable misery, she rejoiced in tears of agony to be at Cleveland' (p. 303). Compare Elinor, confronted with apparent proof of Lucy Steele's engagement to Edward Ferrars: 'for a few moments, she was almost overcome – her heart sunk within her, and she could hardly stand; but exertion was indispensably necessary, and she struggled so resolutely against the oppression of her feelings, that her success was speedy, and for the time complete' (p. 134).

There is considerable variation between the novels in the amount of switching from one character's perspective to another's and in the degree to which the narrator explicitly invokes her authority and omniscience. In *Pride and Prejudice*, for instance, such effects are frequent. Although Elizabeth is the dominant centre of interest, and consciousness, the narrative frequently moves away from her perspective. Here is a characteristic shift:

> Occupied in observing Mr. Bingley's attentions to her sister, Elizabeth was far from suspecting that she was herself becoming an object of some interest in the eyes of his friend. Mr. Darcy had at first scarcely allowed her to be pretty . . . But no sooner had he made it clear to himself and his friends that she had hardly a good feature in her face, than he began to find it was rendered uncommonly intelligent by the beautiful expression of her dark eyes
>
> (*PP*, p. 23)

It is important to the effect of the novel that the reader should know this and Elizabeth should not. A little later in the same scene, Elizabeth is 'eagerly succeeded' at the piano by her sister Mary.

> Mary had neither genius nor taste; and though vanity had given her application, it had given her likewise a pedantic air and conceited manner, which would have injured a higher degree of excellence than she had reached. Elizabeth, easy and unaffected, had been listened to with much more pleasure, though not playing half so well.
>
> (*PP*, p. 25)

This brutally frank comparison of the sisters comes to us straight from the authorial narrator, and Elizabeth is not compromised, here or elsewhere, by any suspicion of vanity or disloyalty to her mostly tiresome family. Throughout the novel the reader is put in a privileged position of knowing more than any of the characters know individually.

Emma follows an antithetical method. It is not quite true to say, as F. R. Leavis did, that 'everything is presented through Emma's dramatised consciousness'.[7] There are two important scenes in which Emma is not present and therefore, axiomatically, cannot provide the point of view. The first of these is chapter 5 of volume 1, a dialogue between Mr Knightley and Mrs Weston about Emma that remains wholly 'objective' until the last paragraph, which gives us a hint of Mrs Weston's private hopes of a match between Emma and Frank Churchill. In the fifth chapter of volume 3, there is a shift of point of view to Knightley, when he begins to suspect Frank Churchill of 'some double dealing in his pursuit of Emma' (p. 343) and 'of some inclination to trifle with Jane Fairfax'. (In the following chapter Mrs Elton plans her strawberry-picking expedition when Emma is absent, but this scene is less important hermeneutically.) There are also some very clear authorial comments about Emma's character at the outset of the novel that should put the reader on his guard against identifying too readily with her attitudes and opinions: for example, 'The real evils indeed of Emma's situation were the power of having rather too much her own way, and a disposition to think a little too well of herself' (p. 5). But with these reservations it is true that the action of the novel is narrated wholly from Emma's perspective, so that the reader is obliged, on first reading at least, to share her limited knowledge and perhaps her mistakes and surprises. There is, to my knowledge, no precedent for such a novel before *Emma* – that is, a novel in which the authorial narrator mediates virtually all the action through the consciousness of an unreliable focalizing character. The effect is not only a wonderful multiplication of ironies and reversals but also an intensification of what Henry James called the sense of felt life – a more intimate relationship between fictional discourse and the processes of human consciousness. And not until Henry James himself, perhaps, was there a novelist in the English language who equalled the skill and subtlety with which Jane Austen carried out this difficult technical feat. To make that comparison inevitably recalls the astonishing perversity of James's own observation that 'Jane Austen was instinctive and charming . . . For signal examples of what composition, distribution, arrangement can do, of how they intensify the life of a work of art, we have to go elsewhere.'[8] He never said an untruer word.

Chapter 9

The art of ambiguity

The Spoils of Poynton

The Spoils of Poynton, first published in 1897, occupies a uniquely interesting place in the long history of Henry James's literary career. It was the first substantial piece of fiction that he wrote after the collapse of his ambitions to find fame and fortune as a playwright, and the first to be written in what has come to be known as his 'later' manner. These two facts are connected.

In 1890 James was commissioned to adapt his early novel *The American* (1877) for the stage. It had a qualified success, and the experience encouraged him to try writing original plays. His career as a novelist was in the doldrums. The reception of his last two major works, *The Princess Casamassima* (1886) and *The Tragic Muse* (1890), had been disappointing, both critically and commercially. He was worried and piqued by the small financial reward he derived from his books. He saw in the theatre the chance to make a lot of money in a short space of time, enough to ensure 'real freedom for one's general artistic life'.[1] He accordingly wrote three comedies in the next few years, none of which managed to find a producer. All his hopes now hung upon the success of *Guy Domville*, a costume drama set in eighteenth-century England about a young Catholic gentleman who is torn between his vocation to become a priest and a felt obligation, on the sudden death of his elder brother, to marry and ensure the continuation of the family. A popular actor-manager, George Alexander, accepted the play for production at the St James's theatre in London early in 1895.

The story of the first night of *Guy Domville*, superbly narrated by Leon Edel in his *Life of Henry James*,[2] is itself as full of suspense, pathos, comedy and irony as any novel. Among the newspaper critics present, at that time unknown to each other and to James, were three men shortly destined to become the most celebrated writers of the age – George Bernard Shaw, Arnold Bennett and H. G. Wells. They appreciated James's intelligent dialogue, as did most of the stalls, well packed with James's friends and admirers of his fiction. The gallery, however, was impatient with the play's clumsy stagecraft and began to barrack the production in its later stages. James himself, unable to bear the strain of sitting through the performance, had spent the evening watching Oscar Wilde's highly successful *An Ideal Husband*. With the applause for this play still ringing in his ears, James walked the short distance to the St James's theatre, arriving in the wings just as Alexander was taking his bow. The actor-manager, either foolishly or mischievously, led James on to the stage, where this most sensitive and dignified of writers was roundly booed by the gallery.

Guy Domville was a flop and had to be hurriedly replaced (ironically enough by Wilde's *The Importance of Being Earnest*), but it was the personal humiliation of the first night that determined James to abandon his theatrical ambitions. It was one of the darkest episodes of his literary life. Yet he was able to turn this apparent failure to positive account. He returned to writing fiction with a confirmed sense that this was his true *métier*, but he began to develop a new kind of narrative method that owed much to his experiments with drama – first in short novels such as *The Spoils of Poynton* and *What Maisie Knew* (1897), and eventually in the three great masterpieces of his mature years, *The Wings of the Dove* (1902), *The Ambassadors* (1903) and *The Golden Bowl* (1904).

On superficial inspection the later novels of Henry James seem anything but theatrical. They are much concerned with consciousness, with representing mental acts of perception, speculation and inference; and usually the story is conveyed to us through the consciousness of a single character whose understanding of the actions and motives of the others is necessarily limited and often unreliable. These are effects that are very difficult to achieve in the theatre, except by the comparatively clumsy conventions of the soliloquy and the aside.

What Henry James's later work owes to drama is essentially structural, what he himself referred to as 'the scenic method'. The story is unfolded in a series of scenes or dramatic encounters between the main characters, in which the issues of the plot are discussed or alluded to in dialogue. The import of what is said is often obscure or problematical, and the effort of interpreting it is depicted in the consciousness of the central or focalizing character, rendered in prose of great complexity and delicacy of nuance.

This method constitutes a considerable modification of the form of the classic nineteenth-century novel on which James's earlier fiction was modelled. Instead of an even balance between 'telling' and 'showing', between expansive authorial description and commentary on the one hand, and the dramatic interaction of characters on the other, the balance had shifted radically in favour of 'showing'. The authorial voice rarely intrudes, and when it does its comments are ambiguous. Instead of being given a detailed visual description of the physical setting of the action and appearance of the characters, we get only the *impressions* of the focalizing character. (Fleda's enraptured introduction to Poynton at the beginning of chapter III is a good example – there is not a single reference to a specific object.) One consequence of this narrative method is that the interpretative effort required of the reader becomes equivalent to that required of the central character. To James it represented an enormous gain in intensity and economy of effect, very different from the 'loose baggy monsters' of classic nineteenth-century fiction, from Balzac to George Eliot; and it was a gain he attributed to his experience of writing plays. 'When I ask myself what there may have been to show for my long tribulation, my wasted years and patiences and pangs, of theatrical experiment,' James wrote in his notebook at the time of writing *The Spoils of Poynton*, 'the answer comes up as just possibly *this:* what I have gathered from it will perhaps have been exactly some such mastery of fundamental statement – of the art and secret of it, of expression, of the sacred mystery of structure.'[3]

Another distinction of *The Spoils of Poynton* is that James left a more detailed account of its genesis and composition in his Notebooks than of any other of his novels. This, as I shall suggest later, is a double-edged tool for interpreting the story, but, supplemented by the Preface James wrote for the New York edition of 1908, the Notebook entries afford an unequalled insight into the laboratory of the writer's mind.

The original 'germ' of the story came to James, as so often, in the form of an anecdote related at a dinner party, in 1893. It concerned a legal dispute between a Scottish widow and her son about the possession of the family house, which was full of 'valuable things' collected by the former. According to James's informant, the mother was prepared to deny her son's legitimacy to win her case, a melodramatic twist which James characteristically eschewed, along with other particulars, in his own working out of the situation. ('Clumsy Life at her stupid work,' as he disdainfully observes in the Preface.)

The potential story James saw in the anecdote was about the effect of aesthetic taste on personal relationships, arising from the injury to the mother's pride and possessiveness at being forced to relinquish the house she has made into a thing of beauty to a son who is not only indifferent to her connoisseurship, but who chooses an equally philistine wife, instead of the discriminating protégée the mother had intended for him. According to the Preface, James at first thought of the contents of the house themselves, the 'things', as being the centre of the story, but quickly realized that this would not do. The things were in themselves inarticulate, and to render them with the lavish descriptive detail of a Balzac would take up far too much space for what he then conceived of as a short story, and (more significantly) would work against the interests of 'the muse of dialogue'. Hence the 'growth and predominance of Fleda Vetch' as 'a centre' for the tale, a process which we can trace through its various stages in the Notebook entries from May 1895 when, a few months after the débâcle of *Guy Domville*, he commenced work on the story.

From the beginning James saw the mainspring of the narrative as the mother's removal of the 'things' from the house. Originally this was to have happened after the son's marriage, and Fleda was to have assisted in their restoration out of wholly altruistic motives. When the plot was revised so that Mrs Gereth made a pre-emptive strike, removing the things *before* the marriage, the question of their restoration became entangled with the question of Fleda's personal destiny, especially when James, rather to his own surprise, made Owen fall in love with her while engaged to Mona Brigstock. For Fleda the dispute between mother and son becomes morally complex because she stands to gain or lose by what she does or does not do in relation to it. The overarching narrative question of the text becomes, not what will happen to the things, but will Fleda come to possess them, along with her Prince Charming? For, like many other great English novels, from *Pamela* to *Mansfield Park* and *Jane Eyre*, *The Spoils of Poynton* is a variation of the Cinderella myth, albeit an ironic one. The crucial interpretative question is: at whom, or at what, is the irony directed?

Most of the critics who have commented on *The Spoils of Poynton* fall into two groups. Either they take Fleda to be the heroine of the story in the traditional sense – heroic in her readiness to sacrifice her own happiness rather than compromise her principles, sensitive and perceptive in her dealings with the other characters, to whom she is morally superior; or they have taken her to be neurotic and self-deceiving, pathologically fearful of sex, and contributing more harm than balm to the domestic row between the Gereths. According to the editors of the Notebooks, F. O. Matthiessen and Kenneth B. Murdock, Fleda is 'one of James's most extreme embodiments of imagination, taste and renouncing sensibility'.[4] Wayne Booth says she comes 'close to representing the author's ideal of taste, judgement and moral sense'.[5] Philip L. Greene asserts: 'James produces in Fleda Vetch a reliable reflector of his values. She is the renouncing sensibility who is capable of love.'[6] According to Nina Baym, on the other hand, Fleda is 'a stumbling bungler'.[7] According to William Bysshe Stein, 'She sacrifices her love for moral mummery' and 'her hypocritical respectability converts social behaviour into a game that is a comic perversion of life'.[8] John Lucas claims that 'Fleda invents most of her experience and in particular she invents Owen's love for her'.[9] This is only a sample of the contradictory opinions to be found in the criticism of *The Spoils of Poynton* (which has followed a very similar course to that of *The Turn of the Screw*, for similar reasons).

Both schools of thought can muster plausible arguments for their respective readings of the tale, and the impossibility of choosing between them has led some critics to conclude that there is something deeply unsatisfactory about the work. 'If there is a line in good literature between complexity and self-contradiction,' says A. W. Bellringer, 'the possibility is that James's treatment of his material has overstepped that line', and he cites the similar opinions of F. R. Leavis and Ivor Winters.[10] A number of recent critics, however, without discussing *The Spoils of Poynton* in detail, have in various ways suggested that James's later fiction constantly aspired to the condition of ambiguity – that the impossibility of arriving at a single, simple version of the 'truth' about any human action or experience is, in the broadest sense, what that fiction is about.[11] I shall argue that this is the appropriate perspective in which to read *The Spoils of Poynton*. What Fleda says to Mrs Gereth – 'You simplify far too much . . . The tangle of life is much more intricate than you've ever, I think, felt it to be' (p. 186)[12] – could be turned against many critics of the novel. It is, however, instructive to consider the arguments that have divided them.

What one might call the pro-Fleda party relies heavily on James's own remarks in the Preface and Notebooks. (The controversy is therefore a classic instance of a general theoretical question about the bearing of author-ial intention on interpretation.) It seems clear that James intended his readers to admire and identify with Fleda. 'Fleda becomes rather fine, DOES some-thing, distinguishes herself (to the reader),' he writes in the Notebook (p. 233). In the Preface, justifying his choice of Fleda as the story's centre of consciousness, he describes her as a 'free spirit' surrounded by 'fools' (p. 31).

The anti-Fleda party are likely to be anti-intentionalists, arguing that whatever James thought he was going to write beforehand, or thought he had written afterwards (many years afterwards in the case of the Preface), is irrelevant to the interpretation of what he did write. In the Notebook scenario for instance, Fleda was to have demonstrated her heroism by sending Owen away from Ricks with a firm recommendation that he should marry Mona immediately. She makes no such declaration in the text. Indeed, the Fleda of the text is generally notable for what she does not do, rather than for what she does. (Matthiessen and Murdock note how many positive actions in the scenario were finally treated negatively.[13]) Fleda vacillates, hesitates and delays rather than acts. Chapter IV concludes:

> She dodged and dreamed and fabled and trifled away the time. Instead of inventing a remedy or a compromise, instead of preparing a plan by which a scandal might be averted, she gave herself, in her sacred solitude, up to a mere fairy-tale, up to the very taste of the beautiful peace she would have scattered on the air if only something might have been that could never have been.
>
> (p. 62)

This is less damaging to Fleda if we read it as rendering a self-accusation rather than as an authorial judgement, but it does seem to hold her partly responsible for the family 'war' that follows.

As to the Preface, James's tributes to Fleda are in fact always equivocal, giving with one hand and taking away with the other. 'Fleda almost demon-iacally both sees and feels, while the others but feel without seeing' (p. 31). This assertion of Fleda's superior sensibility is qualified by an adverb that suggests all the hysteria and capacity for mischief unsympathetic readers have attributed to her. Such readers are however unable, or unwilling, to entertain both terms of the paradox; and in seeking to establish that Fleda is a deeply flawed character whose exposure is the whole point of the novel they usually overstate the case and make assumptions and inferences quite unwarranted by the text.

Central to this reading is the claim that Fleda is neurotic about sex, though the precise diagnosis of her condition varies. Either she wants Owen as a husband only as a means of bettering herself, or she desires him sexually but is guilty about her desire and represses it, or she doesn't really want a heterosexual relationship but a lesbian or mother–daughter one with Mrs Gereth. There is some evidence for all of these interpretations (and some counter-evidence, as we shall see). In the first chapter Fleda is shown as rather priggishly disapproving of Owen's 'romping' with Mona, and Mona's physical charms and putative 'permissions' figure prominently in Fleda's thoughts. She herself allows Owen only one embrace, and is most character-istically seen as running away from him or shutting doors in his face whenever he shows signs of becoming amorous. She is however constantly kissing or being kissed by Mrs Gereth.

Because of its subjective method of representing experience, the later fiction of Henry James lends itself to psychoanalytical interpretation. Whether Owen's umbrella and the Maltese cross are phallic symbols; whether, as Arnold Edelstein has ingeniously argued,[14] Fleda is arrested at the anal stage of personal development, seeking a mother-substitute in Mrs Gereth, but forfeiting her regard because she 'holds on' (to her modesty) when Mrs Gereth urges her to 'let herself go', and lets go of Owen when Mrs Gereth wishes her to hold on – these are interpretations which it is impossible absolutely to prove or falsify, and their persuasiveness will depend ultimately on the credence the reader gives to the Freudian discourse itself. But there are limits to interpretative licence. When William Bysshe Stein,[15] for instance, bids us note Fleda's 'insidious conversion of [Owen's] quick speech into an erotic association' in her reflection that 'It was usually as desperate as a "rush" at some violent game', we must protest that there is nothing erotic about a game like football or rugby which is obviously being alluded to here, one of a string of sporting motifs associated with Owen.

Fleda is certainly sexually inexperienced, and this contributes to the difficulties in which she finds herself. She lacks confidence in her physical attractiveness, and is disturbed by Mrs Gereth's hints that she should use it to captivate Owen. Her one embrace with Owen is, however, passionate, and rendered with an orgasmic lyricism rare in James's writing:

He clasped her, and she gave herself – she poured out her tears on his breast. Something prisoned and pent throbbed and gushed; something deep and sweet surged up – something that came from far within and far off, that had begun with the sight of him in his indifference and had never had rest since then. The surrender was short, but the relief was long: she felt his warm lips on her face and his arms tighten with his full divination.

(p. 161)

Defending herself later against Mrs Gereth's accusation that she has lost Owen by her scruples and her reserve, she says: 'I don't know what girls may do; but if he doesn't know that there isn't an inch of me that isn't his – !' (p.181). The conjunction of Fleda's confession of sexual inexperience with the assertion of her passion is significant. James was intensely and sympathetically interested in the plight of the genteel young woman or adolescent girl in late Victorian society who, brought up largely in ignorance of the sexual life, has to make her way in a knowing and corrupt adult world. He returned to this theme again and again – sometimes combined with the 'international theme', as in *Daisy Miller* and *The Portrait of a Lady*, sometimes more directly as in *What Maisie Knew* and *The Awkward Age* – often increasing the vulnerability of the heroine by making her motherless, like Fleda Vetch. Critics who regard Fleda as neurotic are apt to be judging her in the light of modern sexual mores.

Her defenders often cite the speech just quoted as evidence that, within the limits of her experience, she is capable of genuine passion. But when we look at those words in context we find that their import, typically, is qualified by a suggestion of calculation on Fleda's part:

'I don't know what girls may do; but if he doesn't know that there isn't an inch of me that isn't his – !' Fleda sighed as if she couldn't express it; she piled it up, as she would have said; holding Mrs Gereth with dilated eyes she seemed to sound her for the effect of these professions.

There is a small but significant deviation in the narrative discourse, here, from Fleda's 'point of view', which frames the story after the first chapter. We glimpse Fleda momentarily from some impersonal vantage-point, with her dilated eyes anxiously calculating whether Mrs Gereth is convinced. She is not. Fleda feels 'more and more in her companion's attitude a quality that treated her speech as a desperate rigmarole and even perhaps a piece of cold immodesty' (p. 181). There is a poignant irony in that final phrase, since Mrs Gereth has frequently appeared in relation to Fleda as a kind of bawd or female pander. Fleda's aposiopesis (i.e. a sentence left incomplete for rhetorical effect) echoes another in Mrs Gereth's speech a few pages before:

'When once I get you [and Owen] abroad together – !' Mrs Gereth checked herself as if from excess of meaning; what might happen when she should get them abroad together was to be gathered only from the way she slowly rubbed her hands.

(p. 173)

The 'sounding' of other people's unspoken thoughts by observation of their body language, facial expressions or oblique hints and allusions in speech, is a characteristic activity in Fleda Vetch, as of most Jamesian protagonists. It is how she first becomes aware that Owen is attracted to her – in chapter VI when, on meeting her in Oxford Street, he insists on escorting her on her shopping expedition and back across the Park to Kensington. 'He wanted to stay with her – he wanted not to leave her: he had dropped into complete silence but that was what his silence said' (p. 76). Is it? At this point the reader has no way of knowing. It could be wishful thinking, since we already know that Fleda has indulged in a fantasy of winning Owen's love. The same question is raised, even more acutely, in chapter VIII when, towards the end of Owen's interview with Fleda at Ricks, he shuts the door which she has opened to let him out of the drawing room.

He had done this before she could stop him, and he stood there with his hand on the knob and smiled at her strangely. Clearer than he could have spoken it was the sense of those seconds of silence.

'When I got into this I didn't know you, and now that I know you how can I tell you the difference? And *she's* so different, so ugly and vulgar, in the light of this squabble. No, like *you* I've never known one. It's another thing, it's a new thing altogether. Listen to me a little: can't something be done?'

(p. 99)

It is easy to assume that because they appear in quotation marks these words were actually spoken by Owen. Even as careful a reader as Bernard Richards seems to make this mistake, describing the italicized '*she*' as: 'a typical Jamesian device: the unspecified pronoun. It is quite probable that Owen is referring to his mother, but readers who want a romance between Owen and Fleda will assume that he has Mona in mind.'[16] In fact these words are Fleda's verbalization of what she thinks, or would like to think, Owen's silence means, and it is the truth of her interpretation, not the reference of the pronoun, that is doubtful (Fleda is obviously interested in how Owen compares herself to Mona.) That Owen himself has not spoken is confirmed as the passage continues: 'It was what had been in the air in those moments at Kensington, and it only wanted words to be a committed act. The more reason, to the girl's excited mind, why it shouldn't have words' (p. 99).

Critics who would have us believe that Owen's attraction to Fleda is a complete fabrication of her 'excited mind' have, however, some difficulty in explaining away his declaration and proposal of marriage in chapter XVI.

According to Robert C. McLean, Owen is deceiving Fleda in order to get the spoils back.[17] This interpretation requires us to believe that, had Fleda accepted his suit, Owen, with the collusion of the Brigstocks, would have broken off his engagement to Mona, and engaged himself to Fleda, for just so long as it took his mother to return the spoils to Poynton, and then reversed the process, with all the scandal and dishonour to himself that would entail. This seems improbable, to say the least, and inconsistent with McLean's own judgement that Owen is 'the most humane figure in the book'.[18]

But if Owen's declaration of love for Fleda is not a callous trick, why does he marry Mona after all? Fleda suggests that he recognized where his duty lay, but her words sound more like a self-justification: 'That he has done it, that he couldn't *not* do it, shows how right I was' (p. 196). Mrs Gereth has a coarser explanation: taking advantage of Fleda's foolish scruples, Mona compromised Owen into marrying her by seducing him. This theory is somewhat undermined, however, when her confident assertion that Owen 'hates' Mona for this ploy and will not cohabit with her, is falsified, as she herself later admits.

Owen's motivation remains an enigma till the end, but the most likely explanation is that he is a weak and, in personal relations, cowardly man. Mrs Gereth calls him 'disgustingly weak' (p. 186) and Fleda accepts the verdict, adding only that 'it's because he's weak that he needs me' (p. 186). This has been Fleda's attitude to Owen from her very first encounter with him, when he strikes her as being 'absolutely beautiful and delightfully dense . . . She herself was prepared, if she should ever marry, to contribute all the cleverness, and she liked to figure it out that her husband would be a force grateful for direction' (p. 40). Such, apparently, has also been the nature of the marriage between Mrs Gereth and her late husband, and such, we may guess, will be the marriage of Mona and Owen. One of the many ironies of *The Spoils of Poynton* is the spectacle of three, in their different ways, strong-willed women fighting for the allegiance of a decidedly weak man.

The mystery of Owen's motivation is sealed by the wonderfully ambiguous conclusion of his letter asking Fleda to choose some treasure from Poynton as a gift: 'You won't refuse if you'll simply think a little what it must be that makes me ask' (p. 209). It is an epitome of the whole book, and Fleda enacts in relation to it our own experience of reading the book: 'Fleda read that last sentence over more times even than the rest: she was baffled – she couldn't think at all of what in particular made him ask. This was indeed because it might be one of so many things.'

Reviewing the critical discussion of *The Spoils of Poynton* reveals the difficulties and dangers of reading this text with the aim of wresting from it a single answer to the questions it raises. It is possible to make a plausible

case for almost any answer by selective quotation, but as soon as we return
to the text itself we find that nearly every speech or action is capable
of a double interpretation, and that every hint is balanced by a counter-
suggestion. At the heart of the story is the ambiguity of Fleda's character
and conduct. Does it arise from authentic conflict or neurotic contradiction?
Is her anxiety to protect her 'secret' (i.e. that she loves Owen) reasonable and
honourable (given that he is engaged to another woman) or obsessive and
perverse (given that she has reason to think he loves herself and is disillusioned in the other woman)? Is her refusal to take any of the several
opportunities she has to attach Owen to herself and detach him from Mona
indicative of high moral principle and selflessness, or of moral egotism and
sexual neurosis? Is her sudden change of mind in chapter XVIII, when she
declares herself ready to 'go to the Registry Office' and takes steps to
recall Owen, an example of moral pragmatism, responding to Mrs Gereth's
changed status as the 'victim' of the situation,[19] or is it typical of her
confused and illogical mind that she acts when it is too late to have any
effect? To read the text carefully is to be swayed back and forth between
these alternatives, without ever finding a conclusive answer.

Some deep imaginative fascination with symmetrically opposed ideas has
left its mark on every level of the text. Rhetorical figures of parallelism and
antithesis abound, for example:

If he didn't dislike Mona what was the matter with him? And if he did,
Fleda asked, what was the matter with her own silly self?

(p. 105)

If her friend should really keep the spoils she would never return to her.
If that friend should on the other hand part with them what on earth
would there be to return to?

(p. 132)

'Where is . . . your freedom? . . . If it's real there's plenty of time, and if
it isn't there's more than enough.'

(p. 162)

'If he's at Waterbath he doesn't care for you. If he cares for you he's not
at Waterbath.'

(p. 186)

This last is a good example of the figure of chiasmus (repetition of words
or phrases in reverse order) which Ralf Norrman has plausibly argued is
the key to James's imagination.[20] The plot of *The Spoils of Poynton* exhibits
the same pattern in the movement of the spoils themselves: present at
Poynton – absent from Poynton – present at Ricks: absent from Ricks –
present at Poynton – absent from Poynton. This brings us to the ending
of the story, which is as ambiguous as everything else about it.

Fleda eagerly accepts Owen's offer of a souvenir from Poynton: 'The passion for which what had happened had made no difference, the passion that had taken this into account before as well as after, found here an issue that there was nothing whatever to choke' (p. 209). The passage is typically complex and allusive, but evidently means that Fleda, who still loves Owen, in spite of his marriage, a contingency she had always taken into account, sees no reason why she should not find some relief or satisfaction of her feelings by accepting a precious gift from Poynton. When she goes to the house, in a state of high excitement, to make her choice (she inclines to the Maltese cross), she finds that Poynton and all its contents have been destroyed by fire, a disaster that is attributed by the station-master partly to the carelessness of the servants left in charge by the absent Owen and Mona. 'Mixed with the horror, with the kindness of the station-master, with the smell of cinders and the riot of sound was the raw bitterness of a hope that she might never again in life have to give up so much at such short notice' (p. 213).

This conclusion can be and has been interpreted in a number of different ways: as vindicating Mrs Gereth by showing that Owen and Mona are unworthy custodians of Poynton; as implying that Fleda is responsible for the disaster because she could have been mistress of Poynton; as punishing Fleda for her pride and folly by denying her the much-desired present; as vindicating Fleda's refusal to compromise her moral principles for the sake of worldly goods; as impressing Fleda with a final, painful awareness of the meaning of renunciation; as a judgement on all the chief characters for their egotistical obsession with the 'things'.

It is important to realize that the latter are not major works of art, but what are usually called 'antiques'. Discussing the original germ of the story in the Preface, James observes:

> One thing was 'in it' . . . on the first blush . . . the sharp light it might project on that most modern of our current passions, the fierce appetite for the upholsterer's and joiner's and brazier's work, the chairs and tables, the cabinets and presses, the material odds and ends, of the more labouring ages.

> (p. 26)

Although this theme was overlaid, in the development of the story, by a concern with character, it never disappeared entirely, and the terms in which James describes it here are extremely interesting. His use of the epithet 'labouring' suggests a quasi-Marxist explanation of the modern cult of antiques, while his references to 'passion' and 'fierce appetite' hint at a Freudian diagnosis.

The cult probably had its origins in the aesthetic nostalgia of the Romantic Revival. Later in the nineteenth century, the Pre-Raphaelite Movement, art historians like Ruskin, aesthetes like Pater and Wilde, and the Arts and

Crafts Movement led by William Morris, all contributed to a growing
enthusiasm among people with claims to good taste for domestic artefacts
of pre-industrial design or manufacture. By the time James was writing *The
Spoils of Poynton*, as Bernard Richards observes,[21] magazines were springing
up to cater for the new passion for collecting (*The Studio* in 1893, *The
Connoisseur* in 1901, for instance).

The overt justification for collecting antiques is that the artefacts of the
past are aesthetically superior to those of the present. But James's description of the past as 'the more labouring ages' implies another explanation:
the value of the antique is a function of the difference between pre- and
post-industrial methods of production. As industrial techniques of mass-
production made domestic furnishings and ornaments cheaply and plenti-
fully available, the upper classes could only demonstrate their superior
status in this sphere in one of two ways – either by conspicuous consump-
tion of the products of the new technology, or by collecting the artefacts
of pre-industrial times and, preferably, foreign countries. Waterbath epitomizes the first way, and Poynton the second. That the former is the object
of irony in *The Spoils of Poynton* hardly needs to be stated: some of its
funniest pages concern the vulgarity of Waterbath and its inhabitants. But
it is a vulgarity perceived by Mrs Gereth and Fleda Vetch, and if we identify
too uncritically with their attitude we miss the more subtle irony directed
at Poynton and the cult of its 'things'.

The cult of antiques might be described as a special case of what Marxist
theory calls 'commodity fetishism' and 'reification'. Commodity fetishism is
the tendency of commodities to conceal the social nature of their production
behind their exchange value, and reification (literally, 'making into a thing')
is the false consciousness that allows this to happen by treating economic
laws and institutions as if they were absolute and unchangeable.[22] By surrounding themselves with commodities produced in the pre-industrial past,
that have acquired the status of art, the Mrs Gereths of this world can
suppress the knowledge that they inhabit a capitalist society based on the
exploitation of labour; and their obsessive collecting is a kind of inverted
reification, treating 'things' as absolute and irreplaceable.

'Fetishism' also has a meaning in Freudian discourse which seems relevant, namely, the displacement of erotic desire on to some non-sexual part
of the human body (for example, the foot) or inanimate object (for example,
clothing). *The Spoils of Poynton* is a story of erotic desire displaced on to
'things'. All the energy of Mrs Gereth's marriage went into collecting
'things'. Mona is ineligible as a mate for Owen, in his mother's view,
because she does not appreciate the 'things', yet she covets them enough
to make their possession a condition of her marriage. Fleda is made available
to Owen as an alternative partner only by virtue of sharing Mrs Gereth's
taste, and reflects that, if she had been in a position to actually marry
Owen, 'she might, should she have wished to keep her secret, have found

it possible to pass off the motive of her conduct as a mere passion for his property' (p. 58). 'Passion' is a floating signifier in *The Spoils of Poynton*, attaching itself now to sexuality, now to decor, and trailing with it connotations of religious ecstasy and suffering. As noted above, Fleda's 'passion' seeks its final outlet in the acquisition of one of the 'things' at Poynton, and if we see the Maltese cross as symbolically phallic rather than sacrificial, we may accuse Fleda of sexual fetishism too.

The word 'fetish' literally denotes an object invested with magic or supernatural properties in primitive religion, and when we say colloquially that somebody 'makes a fetish' of something, we mean they attribute an exaggerated or irrational importance to it. The religious imagery associated with the beauty of Poynton is characteristically ambiguous in import, but there are frequent suggestions that Mrs Gereth's obsession has warped her human nature. Fleda, for instance, early on recognizes

> the poor lady's strange, almost maniacal disposition to thrust in everywhere the question of 'things', to read all behaviour in the light of some fancied relation to them. 'Things' were of course the sum of the world; only, for Mrs. Gereth, the sum of the world was rare French furniture and oriental china.
>
> (p. 49)

It is a measure of Fleda's moral superiority that she can take no pleasure in the things when they are illicitly removed to Ricks: 'there was a wrong about them all that turned them to ugliness' (p. 85). They become 'a torment of taste' (p. 86).

James originally thought of calling his tale 'The house beautiful', the Paterian title of a lecture Oscar Wilde was trailing around the country in 1893.[23] When it was serialized in the *Atlantic Monthly* he called it *The Old Things*, and finally settled on *The Spoils of Poynton* for the first book publication. The shift from a metonymic to a metaphoric title suggests a wish to moralize the theme. The 'things' are 'spoils' in a multiple sense: they are booty brought back by Mrs Gereth from her Continental travels, they are the cause of a war between the principal characters to possess them (imagery of battle is persistent) and they are finally 'spoiled' by the fire.

This conclusion to the tale must carry some implication of *vanitas vanitatum*. 'Vanity of vanities, all is vanity. What profit hath a man of all his labours which he taketh under the sun?' asks the preacher in *Ecclesiastes*. Mrs Gereth, whose marriage had seemed to her 'a long sunny harvest of taste and curiosity' (p. 41), comes to acknowledge the force of this question. In that remarkable scene in chapter XVIII, when she faces the prospect of losing the 'war', she reproaches herself for having adopted Fleda as her protégée in these terms: 'It was your clever sympathy that did it – your beautiful feeling for those accursed vanities' (p. 185). To Fleda, Mrs Gereth in final defeat seems to 'represent the final vanity of everything' (p. 196).

Yet Fleda herself, a page or two earlier, consoles herself, in the ominous silence and absence of Owen, by imagining the restoration of the spoils to Poynton in rapturous religious language:

> It was really her obliterated passion that had revived, and with it an immense assent to Mrs. Gereth's early judgment of her. She equally, she felt, was of the religion, and like any other of the passionately pious she could worship now even in the desert. Yes, it was all for *her*; far round as she had gone she had been strong enough: her love had gathered them in . . . They were nobody's at all – too proud, unlike base animals and humans, to be reducible to anything so narrow. It was Poynton that was theirs; they had simply recovered their own. The joy of that for them was the source of the strange peace that had descended like a charm.
>
> (p. 194)

It is difficult to decide whether this flight of fancy is sublime or ridiculous – and whether its reversal in the last chapter is a spectacle of tragic suffering or poetic justice.

In the first edition of *The Spoils of Poynton* James frequently describes his characters as 'hesitating'. The text itself is continually hesitating between alternative meanings, and the attentive reader perforce must do the same. In the New York edition of 1908, S. P. Rosenbaum has noted, James substituted several variations for the verb 'hesitated': 'gasped', 'wondered', 'debated', 'dropped', 'faltered', 'cast about', 'hung fire', 'hung back', 'took it so', 'rather floundered', 'thought again', 'waited for thought', 'had a pause', 'failed of presence of mind for a moment' and 'seemed for an instant to have to walk round it'. These verbs also apply well enough to the experience of reading *The Spoils of Poynton*.

Chapter 10

Indeterminacy in modern narrative
Reading off 'Mrs Bathurst'

If Rudyard Kipling is not usually thought of as a modern writer in the sense of modern*ist*, it is because his work seems, superficially, to belong to a traditional kind of storytelling discourse familiar from the nineteenth-century novel, in which a lucid, literary and reassuringly normative author-ial narration frames and judges the speech and actions of characters who belong to distinct and recognizable social and ethnic types. This impression is, however, misleading. It is true that Kipling does not indulge in the kind of stylistic experiment by means of which writers such as Joyce, Woolf and Lawrence represented the subjectivity of experience and the relativity of 'truth'. But the relationship between the story and the telling of it in Kipling's work is often highly problematical, making the latter as teasingly ambiguous, as difficult and 'polysemous' as that of the acknowledged modern masters.

The short story 'Mrs Bathurst' (1904) is a particularly striking instance of this aspect of Kipling's art, one which has fascinated and, on occasion, exasperated several generations of readers. In what follows, I aim, not to provide a new or definitive solution to its enigmas, but rather, by bringing to bear upon it the apparatus of modern narratological theory, to uncover the means by which these enigmas are generated, and thus to throw light on the production of meaning in modern narrative in general. What such a study of the story shows is that, paradoxically, indeterminacy of meaning leads to an *increase* of meaning, because it demands more interpretative effort by the reader than does traditional narrative.

Seymour Chatman has represented the chain of communication that oper-ates in narrative by the following diagram:

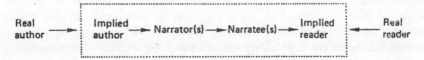

The box represents the boundaries of the text. The categories within the box are aspects of the text. The real author and the real reader are outside the text.[1]

The real author is the actual historic individual who produced the text, in this case Rudyard Kipling (b.1865, d.1936), about whom we know or can discover quite a lot of information. The real reader is any individual who reads the text, each, like the real author, having his or her own unique history and a finite biological life. The implied author and the implied reader, however, live as long as the text lives. The implied author is the creative mind implied by the existence of the text, to whose original activity we attribute the effects and values we, as readers, discover in it. A reader of 'Mrs Bathurst' who knew nothing about the real Rudyard Kipling, and had indeed never heard of him before, could nevertheless make meaningful assertions about Kipling as the implied author of the tale – statements such as, for instance, 'In "Mrs Bathurst" Kipling fails to tell us enough about the main protagonists of the story to engage our interest', or 'In "Mrs Bathurst" Kipling exploits the recent invention of the cinema to subtle effect.' Such statements about the implied author invariably use the present tense, to indicate that they refer to the author inscribed in the text, not the real author.

Much controversy about the concept of authorial intention arises from a confusion between the real author and the implied author. A literary text is an intentional act – it does not come into existence by accident. It is therefore entirely logical and natural to presume that every component of a literary text has or ought to have some kind of point or function or purpose. Of course, we must beware of presuming that there is only *one kind* of point, purpose, function. Critics who complain about 'Mrs Bathurst' that, for example, the Boy Niven episode is irrelevant to the main story are perhaps guilty of such a mistake. But it is entirely reasonable to ask the question, why did Kipling, Kipling the implied author, introduce this episode into his text? This is, in a sense, a question about intention. It is also a question about cause and effect. The critic who wishes to defend the inclusion of the episode will do so by identifying some effect of which it is the cause. He may say, for instance, that it is thematically proleptic – that it foregrounds, in anticipation, the themes of desertion, of quest, of trust and credulity, which are central to the story of Vickery and Mrs Bathurst.

Another kind of criticism will take this question to the real author, either by questioning him directly, if he is alive and willing to answer, or by investigating his diaries, letters, reported conversation and so on, for evidence of what he intended. In doing this, in moving from the author inscribed in the text to the real author, criticism risks committing what has been called the intentional fallacy.[2] If you ask a real author what he intended by a particular scene or episode or sentence and he says, 'I intended to produce an effect *x*', his stated intention is of no consequence to criticism if the episode does not in fact produce that effect; and if it does, there is no point in asking him – unless it happens that you failed to observe this effect by independent reading. The point is not that the real author's comments are without interest but that they do not have absolute authority.

As far as I am aware, Kipling gave away little extra-textual information about 'Mrs Bathurst' other than to say that its genesis was the combination of the memory of a woman serving in a bar in Auckland, New Zealand, and a serviceman's remark, overheard in South Africa, about some other woman, that 'she never scrupled to feed a lame duck or set 'er foot on a scorpion at any time of 'er life' – words, of course, spoken by Pritchard in the text.[3]

Most writers are in fact chary of giving unequivocal answers to direct questions about what they meant or intended by a particular work or part of a work, because of an intuitive sense that by doing so they might be impoverishing, limiting, closing down the possible meanings that their writing might produce. Henry James's prefaces tell us much about the technical problems and choices faced by the practising novelist, but do not resolve the ambiguities of tales like *The Turn of the Screw* or *The Spoils of Poynton*. Joyce 'leaked' the design of *Ulysses* to the world via his friend Stuart Gilbert, thus leaving readers free to ignore this information if they wish. Samuel Beckett has hung over his work the mocking sign, 'No symbolism where none intended'. Modern writers have, in short, tended to endorse, however obliquely, the anti-intentionalist approach to the problem of meaning in literary texts. They know from experience that we discover what we want to say in the process of saying it. Most statements of authorial intention are in fact *post facto* acts of self-commentary and self-criticism.

The intentional fallacy implies a model of communication according to which the writer conceives of a pre-verbal meaning, wraps it up in a package of story, character and trope, and leaves it about for a reader to find, who unwraps the package, throws away the wrapping, and extracts the original pre-verbal meaning. This is as false to the reading experience as it is to the writing process. The reader produces the meaning of a text by responding to its linguistic and discursive cues, by translating its words into his own words, which in their most formalized state constitute the *critical* text. The critical text does not, of course, have the same meaning as the original: it could only do so by being indistinguishable from it, and therefore useless.

The 'real reader' in Chatman's scheme is, as explained above, any real historic individual who reads the text at a particular time. The 'implied reader' is the ideal reader of the text, the reader whom the implied author seems to invite to collaborate in the production of the text's meaning, the reader whom criticism usually refers to as 'we' or 'one' rather than 'I', using the present tense rather than the preterite. Each real reader tries to become the implied reader that is inscribed in the text. On one very simple level, recognized in traditional literary education, this will entail informing ourselves of historical data – about manners, morals, social and political context, meaning of words – which the original audience would have been familiar with, but which have been lost or obscured with the passing of time. To give a banal example, 'Mrs Bathurst' assumes the reader's familiarity with the Boer War, about which a reader today may know little or nothing.

But the effort of the real reader to become the implied reader is not merely a matter of acquiring relevant historical information: it is also a synthesizing and interpretative effort. The reader is involved in a her-meneutic activity, exercising what Jonathan Culler has called a literary competence, that is analogous to linguistic competence – making connec-tions, drawing inferences, forming and constantly modifying hypotheses, in order to produce the meaning of the text. As Wolfgang Iser (who was, I think, the first to put forward the concept of the 'implied reader') has pointed out, there is an inevitable degree of indeterminacy in all literary texts, due to the fact that the statements they make are not subject to ordinary criteria of verification and falsification, but there are also certain limits on the freedom of interpretation imposed by the formal properties of the text.[4] Modern texts, of which 'Mrs Bathurst' is an example, seem to cultivate rather than control indeterminacy, and therefore generate plurality of meaning. We might say, then, that the implied reader of 'Mrs Bathurst' is one who, denied the satisfaction of a 'closed' narrative meaning, will not reject the text in disgust, but accept the denial of such satisfaction as itself meaningful – and, paradoxically, satisfying.

Narrative consists essentially in the representation of process. It obtains and holds the interest of its audience by raising questions in their minds about the process it describes, and delaying the answers to those questions, or raising new questions as others are answered. The questions are basically of two kinds: what happens next? which generates suspense; and what happened in the past, and why? which generates mystery. (Roland Barthes calls them the proaeretic and hermeneutic codes, respectively.[5]) When all the questions are answered, the narrative must end. It is characteristic of the modern text, however, that it ends *before* all the questions are answered.

'Mrs Bathurst' is essentially a mystery story. The basic narrative questions it raises belong to the order of enigma; why did Vickery desert within eighteen months of qualifying for pensioned retirement? What passed between him and Mrs Bathurst? What became of them subsequently? We get only partial answers to these questions. We discover that he was on the verge of losing his sanity at the time of his desertion, evidently because of despair or guilt about his relationship with Mrs Bathurst, which, since he was married until very recently, was in some degree illicit; and we are given convincing evidence that he died, struck by lightning in a teak forest in the South African interior, in the company of an unidentified second person. Even these partial answers are elaborately delayed. Not only that, but it is a long time before we discover what the questions – the basic narrative questions – *are*, and therefore what the story is supposed to be *about*. There are a number of false starts to this story which has False Bay as its immediate setting: the story of the narrator's missed appointment with HMS *Peridot;* the story of Sergeant Pritchard and the maidservant who gave him a bottle of beer, mistaking him for someone called MacClean; the story of Boy Niven who led a party of British servicemen on a wild-goose chase in search of a non-existent farm on an island off Vancouver in 1887. All of these stories, which are introduced with elaborate specificity as to time and place and proper names, all of which information the conscientious reader files away in the expectation that it is going to be significant, turn out not to be *the* story at all, but part of the frame of the story.

The Russian formalists distinguished between what they called the *fabula* and *sjuzet* of narrative. The *fabula* is the raw material, the basic story stuff, the story as it would have been enacted in real time and space. The *sjuzet* is the actual narrative text in which the story is represented, with all the gaps, elisions, rearrangements, selections and distortions involved in that process. Seymour Chatman translates these terms as 'story' and 'discourse'. In 'Mrs Bathurst' we have a text in which there is an enormous disparity between the story and the discourse. The most crucial parts of the story, those concerning the relationship between Vickery and Mrs Bathurst, are never actually represented or reported in the discourse, and are therefore irrecoverable. The discourse itself consists of the testimonies of Pyecroft, Pritchard and Hooper about such limited access as they had to the lives of Vickery and Mrs Bathurst: these testimonies are like pieces of a jigsaw puzzle, most of which is missing. The consequence of all this is to displace the attention of the reader from the story to the discourse – not merely to the rhetoric of the discourse (though this is certainly the case, and a characteristic effect of modern narrative) but also to what might be called the story of the discourse: that is, the story of the interaction of the men who are pooling their knowledge about Vickery and Mrs Bathurst. If the core story is one of mystery, we might say that the frame story is one of suspense: will they solve the mystery? what object will Hooper produce from his pocket? are the questions it raises. The answers are as inconclusive as the answers to the questions in the core story.

At this point we must introduce the two middle terms in Chatman's schema: narrator and narratee. He says they are optional. I would agree as regards the narratee, who is any recipient of the narrative explicitly evoked in the text – for example, the 'dear reader' of much classic fiction, or the listeners to Marlow's yarn on the deck of the *Nellie* in *Heart of Darkness*. But to me the existence of a narrative implies the existence of a narrator, however objective and impersonal. This quibble is, however, immaterial in relation to 'Mrs Bathurst'. A striking feature of this text is that all the characters who belong spatio-temporally to the discourse – the anonymous 'I', Hooper, Pritchard and Pyecroft – double the roles of narrator and narratee at different stages of the text. The narrative therefore has a 'Chinese box' structure, consisting of several stories inside one another, which reveal themselves as frames for the real story, the story of Vickery's entanglement with Mrs Bathurst, which is at the centre of the last box, which is a hole, an absence, an insoluble enigma.

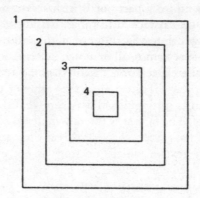

1. The narrative of 'I', addressed to the reader. (This is 'the story of the discourse'.)
2. Pritchard's narrative, about his acquaintance with Mrs Bathurst in Auckland, addressed to 'I', Pyecroft and Hooper.
3. Pyecroft's narrative about Vickery in Cape Town, addressed to 'I', Pritchard and Hooper.
4. Hooper's narrative, about the discovery of the corpses in the teak forest, addressed to 'I', Pritchard and Pyecroft.

The 'I' figure actually narrates the whole text, but since so much of his narration consists of the quoted direct speech of the other narrators, and he does not offer any judgement or interpretation of the core story, he does not have a dominant role in the production of meaning. Who is he? In the absence of any strong indications to the contrary it is perhaps natural to identify him with the real author whose name appears on the title page of the book in which the story appears: Rudyard Kipling. But he is never named either here or in the several other stories in the same collection, *Traffics and Discoveries* (1904), in which he is recognizably the same narrator (some of these stories also concern Pyecroft). He is not named, or referred to as 'Mr Kipling' by the other speakers, because to have done so would have produced a disturbing anomaly, putting on the same ontological plane a person with historical provenance (Rudyard Kipling) and characters who have only a fictitious existence. We identify the 'I' narrator, I think, as a fictional persona of the real Kipling; he corresponds to Kipling the traveller, Kipling the military journalist, Kipling the collector of interesting stories, and to that extent he lends credibility, reliability, authority to the tale that is unfolded about Vickery and Mrs Bathurst. But the fact that he is not named tacitly signifies that he is essentially a function of the story, as fictitious in his way as the other characters and, like them, a creation of the implied author. The 'I', as was observed earlier, keeps a very low profile as narrator of the whole text: we are more aware of his function as narratee to the other narrators. He is thus a kind of surrogate for the real reader, and perhaps a model for the implied reader: curious, patient, attentive to nuances of voice and expression in the other narrators. Only in the opening couple of pages can we say that the implied author has smuggled some of his own artistic designs into the text under the guise of the 'I' narrator's apparently innocent description of scene and setting, and probably we only become aware of that on a second or subsequent reading:

> The day that I chose to visit H.M.S. *Peridot* in Simon's Bay was the day that the Admiral had chosen to send her up the coast. She was just steaming out to sea as my train came in, and since the rest of the Fleet were either coaling or busy at the rifle-ranges a thousand feet up the hill, I found myself stranded, lunchless, on the sea-front with no hope of return to Cape Town before 5 p.m. At this crisis I had the luck to come across my friend Inspector Hooper, Cape Government Railways, in command of an engine and a brake-van chalked for repair.
>
> 'If you get something to eat,' he said, 'I'll run you down to Glengariff siding till the goods comes along. It's cooler there than here, you see.'
>
> I got food and drink from the Greeks who sell all things at a price, and the engine trotted us a couple of miles up the line to a bay of drifted sand and a plank-platform half buried in sand not a hundred yards from the edge of the surf. Moulded dunes, whiter than snow, rolled far inland up a brown and purple valley of splintered rocks and dry scrub. A crowd of Malays hauled at a net beside two blue and green boats on the beach; a picnic party danced and shouted barefoot where a tiny river trickled across the flat, and a circle of dry hills, whose feet were set in sands of silver, locked us in against a seven-coloured sea. At either horn of the bay the railway line, cut just above high-water mark, ran round a shoulder of piled rocks, and disappeared.
>
> (p. 345)[6]

On the level of narrative these paragraphs serve simply to raise and answer the question: how will the narrator be diverted? which is a reflection or repetition of the question that brings the reader to the text: how shall I be diverted? The story begins with the frustration of the narrator's attempt to visit a ship of the Fleet. He is left alone, 'stranded, lunchless, on the sea-front, with no hope of return to Cape Town before 5 p.m.', threatened by loneliness and *ennui*. The tiny crisis in the narrator's life is resolved by the happy appearance of a friend, Inspector Hooper, who offers company and a shared meal in a congenial setting. This creates a mood conducive to the telling, and reception, of a story. Many tales are framed in a similar way in the history of literature, by the occurrence of some space or gap in the

narrator's and narratee's lives – at an inn on a pilgrimage, in a palace closed
against the plague, on the deck of a becalmed ship.

But the particular terms in which this little crisis and its resolution are
realized also subtly establish a structural opposition between land and sea
which proves to be of considerable importance to the core story of Vickery
and Mrs Bathurst. On the level of narrative, the beginning of the second
sentence, 'She was just steaming out to sea as my train came in', merely
repeats the information contained in the first sentence. But the parallelism
of the syntax, as well as enforcing the irony of the narrator's frustration,
also strengthens the opposition between train and ship, an opposition which
is a matter of resemblance as well as difference, since both are methods of
transport that 'steam'. Having been disappointed by the disappearance of
the ship he had planned to visit, the narrator is rescued by the appearance
of his friend Mr Hooper, 'in command of an engine and a brake-van chalked
for repair'. Not 'in charge of' but 'in command of' – a phrase more usually
applied to a ship than to a train. And this train takes the narrator, rather
unexpectedly, to a beach, to a 'plank-platform half buried in sand not a
hundred yards from the edge of the surf'. The setting in which the story
of Vickery and Mrs Bathurst is narrated is, therefore, the interface between
land and sea, between trains and ships. 'At either horn of the bay', we are
told, 'the railway line, cut just above high-water mark, ran round a shoulder
of piled rocks, and disappeared', – just as Vickery disappeared, on the
railway. Pyecroft's last memory of him is as "e went clickin' into Simonstown station' (p. 366). Vickery is, of course, like Pyecroft, a sailor, and his
tragedy or folly or crime or whatever it is – let us call it his 'fall' – is
depicted as the exchange of the sea and his ship for the land and the railway
line, beside which he meets his death. The exchange symbolizes the disorder
in his life; it carries no evaluative overtones, no suggestion that the railway
is a morally inferior institution. The story accords as much respect to Mr
Hooper, representing the professional code of the railway, as to Pyecroft,
representing the Navy. Nor does the symbolism help in any way to resolve
the basic enigmas of the narrative. It functions as a formal device, essentially
a metaphorical device of equivalence, which imparts order and unity to data
that remain puzzlingly disparate and inconclusive on the metonymic level
of cause and effect.

This structural opposition between land and sea reappears in the crucial,
tantalizing and mysterious heart of the tale, the newsreel in which Mrs
Bathurst makes her fleeting appearance. It includes pictures of the two
modes of transportation that are juxtaposed in the second sentence of the
story: 'a troopship goin' to the war – marines on parade at Portsmouth,
an' the Plymouth Express arrivin' at Paddington' (p. 358). As several critics
have observed, this must be one of the earliest literary texts to exploit the
new invention of the motion picture, and it does so to very interesting and
subtle effect. I have described 'Mrs Bathurst' as a frame-tale which calls

attention to its frame; and Kipling also emphasizes this aspect of the cinematic image – that it can only show us what happens within the frame of
its picture:

> 'Then the doors opened and the passengers came out and the porters got
> the luggage – just like life. Only – only when anyone came down too far
> towards us that was watchin', they walked right out o' the picture, so to
> speak.'

(p. 360)

That is what Mrs Bathurst does when she appears on the screen: 'She
walked on and on till she melted out of the picture' (p. 361). And it is,
metaphorically speaking, what Vickery does: he steps out of the frame of
Pyecroft's perception at Simonstown station.

In this remarkable passage Kipling manages vividly to convey the disconcerting effect of the cinematic image – at once lifelike and insubstantial –
when it was still a novelty, and to turn this experience into a poignant
symbol of both the pain of disappointed desire and the mystery of human
motivation. To Vickery, watching the newsreel, Mrs Bathurst is both present and absent, near and far. He can see her, but she, peering out of the
screen with her 'blindish look', cannot see him. From her expression,
Pyecroft infers that she is looking for someone, and Vickery affirms that
she is looking for him. This motif of interpreting someone's intentions from
their countenance is repeated when Pyecroft and the cox, Lamson, scrutin-
ize the captain's expression after the latter's interview with Vickery. 'Mrs
Bathurst' is, indeed, in one sense a story about the difficulty of interpretation, and Pyecroft challenges us as well as the other characters in the
brake-van when he concludes his account of Vickery's strange behaviour
with the question, 'How do you read it off?' (p. 366).

How *do* we read it off? There is no difficulty in saying what 'Mrs
Bathurst', in a general sense, is about: it is about the tragic and destructive
consequences that may ensue when a man becomes infatuated with a woman
who, though morally blameless, is so powerfully attractive to the man that
he will abandon all scruples, honour and material security on her account.
Like other tales of Kipling, this one suggests that very ordinary humble
people may enact tragedy. That Vickery's last recorded words are Hamlet's,
'The rest is silence', makes this point. So does Vickery's remark to Pyecroft,
'What 'ave *you* to complain of? – you've only 'ad to watch. I'm *it*' (p. 366),
irresistibly recalling Faustus's words, 'Why this is hell, nor am I out of it.'
So does the densely obscure epigraph to the story – a fragment of an old
play, in actuality written by Kipling himself, describing the death of a
groom or clown which, it is said, would have excited more attention if it
had been suffered by a prince.

'Mrs Bathurst' is a tragedy of love and death, but its details are obscure
and ambiguous. It seems safe to infer that Mrs Bathurst and Vickery were

lovers, that he deceived her about the fact that he was married, that she came to England with the intention of meeting him. What we cannot ascertain is whether Vickery discovered that she came to England only when he saw the newsreel, or whether, after the moment recorded on the newsreel, they actually did meet in England. If the latter is the case, she would, presumably, have discovered that he was married, and, given her character, have broken off their relationship – perhaps, it has even been suggested, she died as a result of the shock, so that her apparition on the screen affects Vickery as a kind of ghost, 'looking for him' in an accusing, haunting fashion. If the former is the case, then Vickery is presuming that she will have found out that he was married, either before or after his wife died in childbirth. (Could the shock of the revelation have brought on the wife's death?)

The indeterminacy of the story is partly due to the indeterminacy of its chronology. It would seem that Vickery and Pyecroft saw the newsreel in December 1902, since we are told that it was just before Christmas, and shortly afterwards Vickery is sent to recover some ammunition 'left after the war in Bloemfontein Fort' (p. 365). The Boer War ended in May 1902. The newsreel, however, seems to have been filmed while the war was still going on, since it includes a shot of a troopship 'goin' to the war'. We don't know when Vickery left England – whether it was before or after Mrs Bathurst discovered he was married. Perhaps his ship was steaming out to sea from Portsmouth as her train was coming into Paddington station. But when he sees her on the screen, he must know, or have inferred, that there is no possibility of their union, either because she is dead or because of an irreparable breach between them. Otherwise, why should he desert, within a few months of his pensioned retirement, when he is free to marry her because of the death of his wife? Evidently Vickery is harrowed by guilt in relation to Mrs Bathurst, and feels he is on the verge of going mad and murdering someone, and persuades his captain to connive at his desertion by sending him up country, alone. He may, of course, be quite mistaken about Mrs Bathurst's reaction. The epigraph hints at this: 'She that damned him to death knew not that she did it, or would have died ere she had done it. For she loved him' (p. 343).

It has been suggested by some readers that Vickery and Mrs Bathurst were united – that the mysterious figure found dead beside Vickery by Hooper is Mrs Bathurst. It is true that Pritchard seems to leap to this conclusion, covering 'his face with his hands for a moment, like a child shutting out an ugliness. "And to think of her at Hauraki!" he murmured' (p. 369), and Hooper's description of the second figure as Vickery's 'mate' is nicely ambiguous as to sex. But this must be one last false clue put in by the implied author to tease the reader. There is no logical reason why Vickery and Mrs Bathurst should have met in this way and lived like tramps. It is in character for Vickery to have picked up some companion in his wanderings, as he picked up Pyecroft in Cape Town; and I am inclined to agree with Elliott L. Gilbert that this second corpse is introduced to indicate by its crouching posture that Vickery invited the fatal lightning stroke by standing upright beside the rail in the storm.[7] Thus his death is a kind of *liebestod*, comparable to Hamlet's leap into Ophelia's grave and subsequent expiatory death. The rest is silence.

I suggested earlier that there is in 'Mrs Bathurst', as well as a discourse about the story, a story of the discourse – a suspense story in which the most obvious narrative question raised is: what will Hooper produce from his waistcoat pocket? In the classic detective story we should expect the answer to this question to coincide with the solution of the mystery in the core story. In 'Mrs Bathurst' this coincidence both does and does not occur. We have every reason to believe that Hooper has in his pocket the false teeth which constitute incontrovertible evidence that the corpse in the teak forest was in fact Vickery's, and it is entirely natural that he should refrain from producing the gruesome relic out of respect for the feelings of Vickery's friends. There is no logical ground to doubt this testimony – Pyecroft has already confirmed the complementary evidence of the tattoo. Yet on the symbolic level the long-delayed gesture of Hooper's bringing his hand away from his waistcoat pocket – *empty*, can only have the effect of generating doubt and uncertainty in the reader's mind, and emphasizing the indeterminacy of the text.

Chapter 11

Milan Kundera, and the idea of the author in modern criticism

Milan Kundera was born in Brno, Czechoslovakia, in 1929, the son of a famous pianist. He joined the Communist Party in 1947, at the age of 18, one of a whole generation of idealistic and progressive young Czechs who welcomed the Communist takeover of their country in 1948. Two years later, however, he was expelled from the Party for, as he put it subsequently, saying 'something I would better have left unsaid'.[1] After working for some years as a labourer and jazz musician, Kundera was reinstated in the thaw that followed the 20th Party Congress in Moscow and Khrushchev's historic denunciation of Stalinism. He then became a teacher at the Prague Institute for Advanced Cinematographic Studies, where his students were the creators of the Czech New Wave in film. Kundera himself became a leader of the movement for greater intellectual and artistic freedom in his country. His first novel, *The Joke*, in which the spiritual and political history of post-war Czechoslovakia is reflected in a complex and ironic tale of love and sexual intrigue, was completed in 1965 and (delayed by state censors) published in 1967. It immediately became a bestseller, and a cult book of the Prague Spring of 1968, that brief moment when it seemed as if Czechoslovakia might achieve real independence from Soviet Russia under Dubček's liberal government. That fragile dream was shattered by the invasion of Russian tanks. Once more Kundera became *persona non grata*. He was expelled from the Party, deprived of his academic post, and had his writings proscribed. Meanwhile *The Joke* was translated into twenty languages, to general critical acclaim. The French translation carried a foreword by Louis Aragon which described it as 'one of the greatest novels of the century'. If *The Joke* made less impact in England, that was perhaps partly because the translation was a bad one, the text having been mutilated and rearranged without Kundera's knowledge. In 1975, after persistent persecution by the state, Kundera left Czechoslovakia and settled, with his wife, in France, where he still lives. His reputation continued to grow in Europe and America with the publication in translation of two prize-winning novels, *Life Is Elsewhere* (1973) and *The Farewell Party* (1976) and a collection of short stories, *Laughable Loves* (1974); it reached new heights with *The Book of Laughter and Forgetting*. This work, originally published in Czech in 1978, was translated and published in America in 1980, and in 1982 finally reached Britain, where many critics named it as their 'Book of the Year'. In 1983 Faber published a new, authorized translation of *The Joke*, which also achieved enthusiastic reviews, among them one by myself in the *Sunday Times* which prompted an invitation to write this article for the *Critical Quarterly*.

In the early 1960s, when the *Critical Quarterly* and I were young, and Milan Kundera was writing *The Joke* and wondering, no doubt, whether he would be allowed to publish it, it's very unlikely that I would have been asked, or, if asked, agreed, to write a critical article about a Czech novelist. The defiant, I-Like-It-Here provincialism of the Movement, the jealous guarding of the English Great Tradition by Leavis and his disciples, and the New Criticism's focus on stylistic nuance in literary texts, all militated against taking a professional interest in foreign writing. I was never under the spell of Leavis, but I was a literary child of the 1950s, and, as a critic, I was committed to the kind of close reading that, it seemed, could only be performed on and in one's mother tongue. In *Language of Fiction* (1966) I argued that meaning was as inseparable from verbal form in the novel as the New Criticism had shown it to be in lyric poetry; and that although prose fiction was more translatable than verse, since in it sound and rhythm were less important, nevertheless there was bound to be such a degree of alteration and loss of meaning in the translation of a novel that the critic could never 'possess' it with the necessary confidence.

I no longer hold this position with the puritanical rigour expressed in the first part of *Language of Fiction*. Exposure to the Continental European structuralist tradition of poetics and criticism has shown me that literary narrative operates several codes of communication simultaneously, and in most of them (for instance, enigma, sequence, irony, perspective) effects are readily transferable from one natural language to another (and even from one medium to another). A flashback is a flashback in any language; so is a shift in point of view, a peripeteia, or an 'open' ending.

This does not entail any downgrading of language in the novel. Kundera himself claims that total commitment to the novel as *verbal* art for which I tried to provide a theoretical justification in *Language of Fiction*. 'Ever since *Madame Bovary*', he observes in the preface to the new edition of *The Joke*, 'the art of the novel has been considered equal to the art of poetry, and the novelist (any novelist worthy of the name) endows every word of his prose with the uniqueness of the word in a poem.'[2] This does not mean that translation is impossible – if it did then a novelist like Kundera, writing in a minority language whose native speakers are forbidden access to his books, might as well shoot himself. Consider this characteristic comment, in *The Book of Laughter and Forgetting*, on the application of the word 'intellectual' in Czechoslovakia in the Stalinist period: 'All Communists hanged at the time by other Communists had that curse bestowed upon them.'³ The rhetorical force of this sentence derives chiefly from the repetition of the word 'Communists' as both subject and object of the verb 'to hang'; substitute 'dissidents' for the first mention, and the sense of outrage at the lunatic cruelty of the purges is considerably weakened. Another rhetorical device in the sentence is the ironic description of the epithet 'intellectual' as a 'curse'. Such tropes and figures are translatable between most Indo-European languages.

The problem of translation, then, is no longer a disincentive to addressing oneself to the critical consideration of a Czech novelist; and the conscious insularity of British literary culture in the 1950s has long since lost whatever justification it may once have had in encouraging a new wave of writers. But in the meantime, a new critical anxiety has arisen to threaten the project. To write on the fiction of 'Milan Kundera' is almost inevitably to accord that name the unity and substance of an historic individual, whose biography I briefly summarized at the outset: Milan Kundera, the author. But the liveliest and most innovative discourses of contemporary criticism, loosely describable as 'post-structuralist', have thrown the idea of the author very much into question.

Roland Barthes announced the 'Death of the Author' with characteristic Nietzschean relish back in 1968, at about the same time that Russian tanks were rolling into Czechoslovakia:

> The Author, when believed in, is always conceived of as the past of his own book: book and author stand automatically on a single line divided into a *before* and *after*. The Author is thought to *nourish* the book, which is to say that he exists before it, thinks, suffers, lives for it, is in the same relation of antecedence to his work as father to his child. In complete contrast, the modern scriptor is born simultaneously with the text, is in no way equipped with a being preceding or exceeding the writing, is not the subject with the book as predicate; there is no other time than that of the enunciation and every text is eternally written *here and now* . . . We know now that a text is not a line of words releasing a single 'theological' meaning (the 'message' of the Author-God) but a multidimensional space in which a variety of writings, none of them original, blend and clash.⁴

This proclamation, startling in 1968, is now a commonplace of academic criticism in the fashionable 'deconstructionist' mode, but has had little or no effect on the actual practice of writing outside the academy, which remains obstinately author-centred. Books are still identified and classified according to author. The value attributed to books brings kudos, prizes and royalties to their authors, who are the object of considerable public interest. Post-structuralist theorists, some of whom have been known to collaborate in this process, would no doubt explain it by saying that the institution of literature is still in thrall to bourgeois ideology. Michel Foucault, one of the most formidable of these theorists, prefers to speak of the author as a 'function' rather than as an origin of discourse: the era of bourgeois capitalism *required* the idea of the author as one who individualistically produced, owned and authenticated the literary text, but it was not always so, and it need not be so in the future.[5]

It is, of course, undeniable that the modern 'author' is a comparatively recent phenomenon. The further we peer back into history, the more anonymous and collective the production of stories, lyrics and drama appears. And Foucault is quite right to say that, looking in the opposite direction, 'We can easily imagine a culture where discourse would circulate without any need for an author'.[6] Whether one would wish to live in it is, however, another matter. George Orwell imagined such a culture in *Nineteen Eighty-Four*.

The idea of the author which Barthes and Foucault seek to discredit is the product of humanism and the Enlightenment as well as of capitalism. Collective, anonymous art belongs historically to eras when slavery and serfdom were deemed ethically acceptable. Copyright is only one of many 'rights' – freedom of speech, freedom of movement, freedom of religious worship – which the bourgeois ideology of liberal humanism has claimed for the individual human being. Only those who take such freedoms for granted in their daily lives could perhaps contemplate with satisfaction the obsolescence of the idea which sustains and justifies them.

Of course, the post-structuralist critique of the bourgeois or liberal humanist concept of individual man does not represent itself as totalitarian, but as utopian. 'Discourses, whatever their status, form or value, and regardless of our manner of handling them, would unfold in a pervasive anonymity', says Foucault in the passage cited above:

> No longer the tiresome repetitions, Who is the real author? Have we proof of his authenticity and originality? What has he revealed of his profound self in his language? New questions will be heard: What are the modes of existence of this discourse? Where does it come from, how is it circulated, who controls it? What placements are determined for possible subjects?[7]

It is however, difficult to understand how an anonymous discourse could ask of itself, who controls it. Certainly in *Nineteen Eighty-Four*, where only anonymous discourse is allowed to circulate, *none* of Foucault's questions is permitted, the second set no more than the first.

The Book of Laughter and Forgetting begins with an Orwellian story about the Czech Communist politician Clementis, who stood on a balcony beside his leader Gottwald on a cold day in February 1948, and in comradely spirit lent his fur hat to Gottwald, as they received the plaudits of the crowd at the inauguration of the Czech Communist State. Photographs of the occasion were widely circulated.

> Four years later Clementis was charged with treason and hanged. The propaganda section immediately airbrushed him out of history and, obviously, out of the photographs as well. Ever since, Gottwald has stood on that balcony alone. Where Clementis once stood, there is only bare palace wall. All that remains of Clementis is the cap on Gottwald's head.[8]

When *The Book of Laughter and Forgetting* was published, the government of Czechoslovakia deprived Milan Kundera of his citizenship *in absentia*. That a government should be stung into taking such revenge on an individual author is perhaps a good reason for wanting to defend the idea of authorship. If *The Book of Laughter and Forgetting* had been an anonymous discourse, like the anti-government jokes that circulate in all totalitarian states, the politicians would have found it easier to ignore.

One reason why the post-structuralist critique of the idea of the author has been so warmly welcomed in some quarters of academe is that it is presented as a liberation, a critical utopia. 'The Death of the Author, the Absolute Subject of literature, means the liberation of the text from the authority of a presence behind it which gives it meaning', says Catherine Belsey, enthusiastically paraphrasing Barthes. 'Released from the constraints of a single and univocal reading, the text becomes available for production, plural, contradictory, capable of change.'[9] Behind this argument is a quite false antithesis between two models of interpretation, one of which we are told we must choose: either (A) the text contains a single meaning which the author intended and which it is the duty of the critic to establish, or (B) the text is a system capable of generating an infinite number of meanings when activated by the reader. A historicist version of this antithesis, expounded by Barthes in the essay already cited, states that the classic text pretended it conformed to model A, and thus succeeded in placing certain limits on the reader's freedom to interpret, but the authentically modern text aspires to an infinite plurality of meaning as required by model B.

No one who is seriously engaged in the practice of writing fiction *and* familiar with modern critical theory (I speak personally, but also, I venture to think, for Kundera) could accept either of these positions as starkly stated here. Works of literature – in our era of civilization, at least – do not come into being by accident. They are intentional acts, produced by individual writers employing shared codes of signification according to a certain design, weighing and measuring the interrelation of part to part and parts to the developing whole, projecting the work against the anticipated response of a hypothetical reader. Without such control and design there would be no reason to write one sentence rather than another, or to arrange one's sentences in any particular order. There would be no ground, either, on which to object to censorship or to the kind of mutilation of an author's text by his publishers which Kundera suffered in respect of the first English edition of *The Joke*. To that extent, the model of composition which Barthes seeks to discredit – of the author *nourishing* his book as a father his child – is truer to experience (including, I would wager, Barthes's own experience) than the one he offers in its place. But once the child leaves home – the book is published – a different situation obtains. It is of the nature of texts, especially fictional ones, that they have gaps and indeterminacies which may be filled in by different readers in different ways, and it is of the nature of codes that, once brought into play, they may generate patterns of significance which were not consciously intended by the author who activated them, and which do not require his 'authorization' to be accepted as valid interpretations of the text.

The serious modern writer is, therefore, likely to be just as suspicious of position A, above, as of position B. He (or she) knows that the proponents of A are all too eager to discard the 'implied author'[10] of a text in pursuit of the 'real author', and to ask the latter what he 'meant' by his text instead of taking the trouble to read it attentively. The writer therefore finds ways of evading such questions, or confusing such questioners, by masks, disguises, obliquities and ambiguities, by hiding secret meanings in his text – secret, sometimes, even from himself.[11]

Milan Kundera seems to be a case in point. He was at the very outset of his literary career a victim of the intentional fallacy (a fallacy that is committed by imputing and inferring intentions on the basis of extra-textual evidence).[12] Here is a writer with a history of courageous resistance to the dominant ideology of a Communist state, finally forced into exile as the price of his intellectual independence. Must he not be labelled a 'dissident' writer? Since his books refer to the injustices and bad faith of the Communist régime in Czechoslovakia, must this not be what his fiction is *about*? That is precisely how *The Joke* has been received in the West. Kundera records, in the preface to the new edition, that, 'When, in 1980, during a television panel discussion devoted to my works, someone called *The Joke* "a major indictment of Stalinism", I was quick to interject, "Spare me your Stalinism, please. *The Joke* is a love story".'

This interjection is itself a statement of authorial intention, which we are not bound to accept. It is, indeed, a consciously simplistic description of *The Joke*, designed to head off a differently reductive reading of the text. But it does point us in the right direction. Kundera's work is ultimately more concerned with love – and death – than with politics; but it has been his fate to live in a country where life is willy-nilly conditioned by politics to an extent that has no equivalent in western democracies, so that these themes present themselves to his imagination inevitably and inextricably entangled with recent political history. But, as Kundera himself put it, repudiating the label of 'dissident writer':

If you cannot view the art that comes to you from Prague, Budapest or Warsaw in any other way than by means of this wretched political code, you murder it, no less brutally than the work of the Stalinist dogmatists. And you are quite unable to hear its true voice. The importance of this art does not lie in the fact that it pillories this or that political regime, but that, on the strength of social and human experience of a kind people here in the West cannot even imagine, it offers new testimony about mankind.[13]

As if to elude being read exclusively in the 'political code', Kundera concentrated subsequently on erotic comedy, often black comedy, in such works as *The Farewell Party* and *Laughable Loves*. In *The Book of Laughter and Forgetting* he returned to the explicit treatment of political material and dealt very directly with the effect of politics on his own life – but in a book so original, idiosyncratic and surprising in form that it offers the strongest possible resistance to a 'single, univocal reading'. Whereas in *The Joke* Kundera displayed, at the first attempt, his mastery of the modernist novel, *The Book of Laughter and Forgetting* is a masterpiece of post-modernist fiction, as I shall now attempt to show by comparing the forms of these books, by general consent Kundera's two most important productions.

The modernist novel is generally characterized by a radical rearrangement of the spatio-temporal continuity of the narrative line – what the Russian formalists called the *deformation* of the *fabula* in the *sjuzet*. The *fabula* is the story in the most objective, chronological form in which we can conceive it; the *sjuzet* is the representation of that story in an aesthetically motivated discourse, with all the gaps, elisions, rearrangements, repetitions and emphases which invest the story with meaning. *The Joke* is an exemplary case. A summary of the *fabula* of *The Joke* would begin in 1948 with the enthusiasm of the young Ludvik and his home-town friend Jaroslav for the Communist takeover of their country; then describe how Ludvik was expelled from his university because of a silly political joke and the treachery of his contemporary, Zamaneck. It would narrate Ludvik's wearisome penal military service, his ill-starred love-affair with the waif-like Lucie, and his rehabilitation after the post-1956 thaw, while Zamaneck cannily exploited the changing ideological climate and Jaroslav tried to forget the *ennui* of a safe Party job in a passion for folklore. It would explain how one day Ludvik was interviewed by a radio journalist called Helena, and on realizing that she was the wife of Zamaneck, determined to get his revenge on the latter by seducing her. Eventually our summary would reach the climax of the story, some time in the mid-1960s, when Ludvik returns to his home town for his assignation with Helena, who is reporting a folk ritual called the Ride of the Kings, in which Jaroslav's son is taking a leading part. Ludvik's revenge misfires when Helena tells him that she is estranged from her husband, while she is so shattered by the discovery of Ludvik's real indifference that she takes an overdose – fortunately (but humiliatingly) mistaking laxatives for sleeping pills. Jaroslav discovers that his son has tricked him over the Ride of the Kings, and suffers a heart attack.

Such a summary (drastically condensed here) would give some idea of the narrative content of *The Joke*, but, however detailed, would convey very little sense of what it is like to *read* the novel, in which the same information comes to the reader in an entirely different order and in an entirely different mode of discourse.

The novel opens, not with Ludvik's youth, but with his arrival as a middle-aged man in his home town to prepare for his assignation with Helena. The 'base time' of the narrative starts then and covers three days in the mid-1960s, leading up to the Ride of the Kings, Helena's suicide attempt and Jaroslav's heart attack. Everything else – the entire life histories of the characters before those few days – is retrospective narrative, or 'analepsis' to use Gérard Genette's term.[14] Furthermore, both the three-day action in the provincial town, and all the analepses, are mediated to the reader not by a reliable, impersonal authorial narrator, such as I pretended to be just now in summarizing the *fabula* – identifying and distinguishing between the characters, filling in the gaps in their knowledge, putting the reader in a privileged position of knowing more than any one of them knew – but through the interwoven monologues of four of these characters: Ludvik, Helena, Jaroslav and Ludvik's friend, Kostka.

These monologues do not pretend, like those of Stephen, Bloom and Molly in Joyce's *Ulysses*, to record thoughts and sensations as they occur, but are rather what Dorrit Cohn calls 'memory monologues',[15] like those of the characters in Faulkner's *The Sound and the Fury*. They are cast in the past tense, and are linguistically too well-formed to imitate the 'stream of consciousness' in Joycean fashion; on the other hand, they are not naturalized as journal or diary entries, or as oral anecdote or deposition. They are *interior* monologues, though they do have something of the quality of confession. The characters seem to be telling their stories, the story of the last few hours, and the story of their entire lives, to some absent Other, or to themselves, to their own consciences, in an effort to understand, justify or judge their own actions.

One important consequence of this method of narration is that it throws the reader, at the outset, into much the same doubt, confusion and uncertainty about the import of the tale as the characters experience in negotiating their lives. At first we seem to be presented with several life histories which have little or nothing to connect them. Only gradually, in a series of 'recognitions', do we perceive just how many connections there are – that, for instance, the woman Ludvik is planning to seduce is the wife of the man who masterminded his expulsion from the Party and the University many years ago – and the effect of these delayed recognitions is as powerful as are similar moments of recognition and reversal for the characters.

It must be said, too, that the coincidences upon which the narrative structure of *The Joke* heavily depends seem much less obvious and contrived when encountered in the *sjuzet* than they may appear in the clear light of the *fabula*. Another effect of the deformation of the original logic of events is that actions widely separated in time and space are juxtaposed in the text and interact semantically. Thus Ludvik's coldblooded preparations to seduce Helena are present to the reader's consciousness as he follows the story of the young Ludvik's more spontaneous but equally destructive attempt to possess Lucie. And as with all multiple-viewpoint novels, from Samuel Richardson's onwards, we are frequently afforded different subjective versions of the 'same' event, to ironic and instructive effect. The Ride of the Kings which seems so charged with poetry and magic to the consciousness of Jaroslav, because he has invested so much emotional and psychic capital in it, appears to Ludvik's eye as a rather shabby and perfunctory ritual, whose charm for himself consists precisely in its air of ideological 'abandonment' (pp. 217–21).

As we read *The Joke* we necessarily 'make sense' of the narrative by restoring the codes of causality and chronology which have been deliberately 'scrambled' in the text. But this is not to say that the meaning of the text is the *fabula* which we can disinter from the *sjuzet*. On the contrary, the meaning inheres in the hermeneutic process itself: the reader's activity in interpreting and making sense of the story, responding to the clues and cues provided by the text, constantly readjusting a provisional interpretation in the light of new knowledge, re-enacts the efforts of the characters to make sense of their own lives. Ludvik, especially, in spite of his scepticism, and with every excuse for cynicism, is convinced that 'everything in life that happens to me has a sense beyond itself, *means* something', if only he could discover what it is. Understandably he is obsessed with the disproportionate effects on his life of his 'joke'. What he has painfully to recognize is that this was one manifestation of a universal condition, that man is not master of his own fate. 'What if history plays jokes? . . . all at once I realized I was powerless to revoke my own joke: I myself and my life as a whole had been involved in a joke much more vast (all-embracing) and absolutely irrevocable' (p. 240). The novel is indeed full of 'jokes', tricks played on the characters by fate – the backfiring of Ludvik's revenge plan, the humiliating consequences of Helena's overdose, Jaroslav's deception by his son, to name but three – ingeniously juxtaposed and counterpointed in a text that manages to be both serious and moving, comic and ironic.

The Joke is manifestly a 'modern' novel, but it would be hard to believe that it was composed in the manner Roland Barthes attributes to the 'modern scriptor', who 'is born simultaneously with the text, is in no way equipped with a being preceding or exceeding the writing, is not the subject with the book as predicate'. On the contrary, we have in reading *The Joke* an overwhelming sense of a creative mind behind the text, its 'implied author', who constructed its labyrinth of meanings with love and dedication and immense skill over a long period of time, during which the design of the whole must have been present to his consciousness. *The Book of Laughter and Forgetting*, however, seems, in part, to fit Barthes's prescription/description of the modern text as a 'multidimensional space in which a variety of writings, none of them original, blend and clash'. It *is* 'original', but lacks the rich, 'deep', slowly emerging, satisfying aesthetic and thematic unity of *The Joke*. It is fragmentary, disjunctive, confused and confusing; it has an improvised air. Instead of telling a single, unified story, it tells several separate stories, only two of which concern the same character, a Czech political exile called Tamina, whose husband, Mirek, died shortly after they left their country. The chief character of the first story is a Czech dissident intellectual called Mirek – but it does not seem to be the same Mirek. The kind of 'recognitions' which illuminate *The Joke* are deliberately frustrated in the later book. We cannot, however, treat it as a collection of short stories. The seven parts do not have clear boundaries separating one from another. They flow or leak into each other, not via narrative continuity, but through the omnipresence of the authorial voice who comments, digresses and interjects, often in very personal and 'non-fictional' ways, and through the repetition-with-variation of certain themes and motifs. 'This entire book is a novel in the form of variations' (p. 165) an authorial voice tells us at one point. The closest equivalent I can think of is Kurt Vonnegut's *Slaughterhouse Five*, another post-modernist masterpiece, but even that artfully heterogeneous text, with its mixture of historical, fictional and metafictional discourses, has a single main character, and a single main storyline.

The method used to study the form of *The Joke* – inferring the *fabula* and comparing it with the *sjuzet* – will hardly do in this instance. There are too many discrete *fabulas* to cope with, and in any case they are narrated in a rather straightforward summary fashion. The 'deformation' of the *fabula* in the *sjuzet* consists not so much in the manipulation of chronology and point of view as in the disruption of the temporal–spatial continuity of the narrative by the intrusions and digressions of the authorial narrator. This narrator identifies himself quite unambiguously as 'Milan Kundera', and relates several apparently 'true' stories about his own life. Paradoxically, this overt appearance of the author in the text does not make it easier, but harder, to determine what it 'means'. The real author has, as it were, leapfrogged over the implied author, to appear as a trope in his own text, which makes it all the harder to identify the implied author's attitudes and values. These three versions of the author are, obviously, very closely related, but do not quite coincide with each other.

The only way to deal, critically, with *The Book of Laughter and Forgetting* is to review its textual strategies in the order in which they are experienced by the reader. I shall take as an example Part Three, entitled 'The Angels'. This begins:

Rhinoceros is a play by Eugene Ionesco during which people obsessed by a desire to be identical to one another gradually turn into rhinoceroses. Gabrielle and Michelle, two American girls, were doing an analysis of this play as part of a summer school course for foreigners in a small town on the Riviera. They were pets of Madame Raphael, their teacher, because they always kept their eyes on her and carefully wrote down her every word.

(p. 55)

The girls are baffled by their assignment until one of them ventures the opinion that ' "The author meant to create a comic effect!" ' . . . Then suddenly let out short, shrill, breathy sounds very difficult to describe in words' (p. 56). This, of course, is the sound of laughter.

The second section of 'The Angels' begins with a long quotation from a lyrical description of laughter – *'real laughter, beyond joking, jeering, ridicule'* – by 'one of those passionate feminists who have made their mark on our times'. It is a very vivid, engaging piece of writing, and Kundera comments, 'Only an imbecile could make fun of this manifesto of delight' (pp. 56–7). Yet, as he muses on the subject, this celebration of orgiastic, life-enhancing laughter is undermined by the introduction of the media-cliché of two lovers running hand in hand and laughing. 'All churches, all underwear manufacturers, all generals, all political parties have that laughter in common' (p. 58).

Section 3 consists of an apparently autobiographical account of how Kundera, deprived of his academic post after the Russian invasion of 1968, earned a little money, through the kind offices of a young woman friend (called R. in the text), by writing horoscopes under an assumed name for a magazine which she helped to edit. He did this so plausibly that the editor-in-chief asked for a personal horoscope, which Kundera duly supplied, taking advantage of the opportunity to encourage the editor to be more amiable to his colleagues. 'R. and I had a good laugh over it later. She claimed he had improved' (p. 61).

Section 4 is a kind of essay entitled, 'On two kinds of laughter'. Kundera proposes (how seriously?) that domination of the world is divided between demons and angels, and that an equilibrium between these two powers is desirable. 'If there is too much uncontested meaning on earth (the reign of the angels), man collapses under the burden; if the world loses all meaning (the reign of the demons) life is every bit as impossible' (p. 61). Laughter as an instrument of ridicule was an invention of the Devil. It was so effective that an angel sought to neutralize it by making the same sound but endowing it with the opposite meaning. 'There are two kinds of laughter, and we lack the words to distinguish them' (p. 62).

Section 5 begins by describing a photograph of youthful political demonstrators dancing in a circle, and the powerful appeal of this image and this activity. Mme Raphael, for instance, 'had cut the picture out of the magazine and would stare at it and dream. She too longed to dance in a ring' (p. 63). Dancing in a ring is subtly associated with the joyful laughter of her pupils, Michelle and Gabrielle.

Section 6 begins:

> I too once danced in a ring. It was the spring of 1948 . . . I took other Communist students by the hand, I put my arms around their shoulders, and we took two steps in place, one step forward, lifted first one leg and then the other, and we did it just about every month, there being always something to celebrate . . . Then one day I said something I would better have left unsaid. I was expelled by the Party and had to leave the circle.
>
> (p. 65)

He recalls 'another of those anniversaries of God knows what' in June 1950, when 'the streets of Prague were once again crowded with young people dancing in rings. I wandered from one to the next . . . but I was forbidden entrance' (p. 66). It happened to be the day after a politician called Milada Horokova had been hanged for alleged treason, along with the Czech Surrealist Zavis Kalandra, friend of André Breton and Paul Eluard, *doyen* of the French Communist literati. Bréton had called on Eluard to protest against the condemnation of Kalandra.

> But Eluard was too busy dancing in the gigantic ring encircling Paris, Moscow, Warsaw, Prague, Sofia, and Athens, encircling all the socialist countries and all the Communist parties of the world; too busy reciting his beautiful poems about joy and brotherhood. After reading Bréton's letter, Eluard took two steps in place, one step forward, he shook his head, refusing to stand up for a man who had betrayed the people . . . and instead, recited in a metallic voice
> *We shall fill innocence*
> *With the strength we have*
> *So long been lacking*
> *We shall never again be alone.*
>
> (pp. 66–7)

On this day in June 1950, Kundera actually witnessed Eluard reciting his utopian poetry in Prague to the rhythmic accompaniment of feet moving in a circular dance.

> Everyone was smiling, and Eluard leaned down to a girl he had his arm around and said,

A man possessed by peace never stops smiling

And she laughed and stamped the ground a little harder and rose a few inches above the pavement, pulling the others along with her, and before long not one of them was touching the ground, they were taking two steps in place and one step forward without touching the ground, yes, they were rising up over Wenceslaus Square, their ring the very image of a giant wreath taking flight, and I ran off after them down on the ground. I kept looking up at them and they floated on, lifting first one leg, then the other, and down below – Prague with its cafés full of poets and its jails full of traitors, and in the crematorium they were just finishing off one Socialist representative and one surrealist, and the smoke climbed to the heavens like a good omen, and I heard Eluard's metallic voice intoning,

Love is at work it is tireless

and I ran after that voice through the streets in the hope of keeping up with that wonderful wreath of bodies rising above the city, and I realised with anguish in my heart that they were flying like birds and I was falling like a stone, that they had wings and I would never have any.

(pp. 67–8)

This passage has the sublime perfection of a Joycean 'epiphany', but in its astonishing shift from the historical to the fantastic it strikes a characteristically 'post-modernist' note – one that has caused Milan Kundera to be linked with such writers as Gabriel Garcia Márquez, Günter Grass and Salman Rushdie, under the umbrella of 'magic realism'. Kundera uses this technique more modestly and sparingly (and perhaps for that reason more effectively) than they do, but with the same implied justification: that the contradictions and outrages of modern history are of such a scale that only the overt 'lie' of the fantastic or grotesque image can adequately represent them. The power and effectiveness of this passage could not, however, be conveyed by quoting it out of context. It brings together, with devastating rhetorical force, bits of information and symbolic motifs that have been previously introduced into the text with deceptive casualness. It is this periodic *convergence* of diverse and apparently disparate discourses that gives *The Book of Laughter and Forgetting* its unity. The story (such as it is) of Michelle and Gabrielle and Mme Raphael, ends with their resisting the demonic, derisive laughter of the rest of the class by laughing themselves and dancing in a circle until they rise into the air and disappear through the ceiling, 'leaving the stupefied students with nothing but the brilliant fading lights of these archangels from on high' (p. 74).

The story of Kundera's career as an astrologer ends more grimly: his identity is discovered, and R. loses her job. Kundera comes to the conclusion that he must leave the country to avoid endangering his friends. Meeting R. at a secret rendezvous to hear the story of her dismissal, Kundera is astonished to find that his strongest emotion is one of lust. 'I felt a violent desire to make love to her. Or to be more exact, a violent desire to rape her. To throw myself on her and take possession of her with all her intolerably exciting contradictions, her impeccable outfits, her rebellious insides, her reason and her fear, her pride and her misery' (p. 75). Although he suppressed the urge, his confession of it makes him hostage to 'those passionate feminists who have made their mark on our time'. Kundera has always resisted the temptation (one to which 'dissident' writers are especially prone) to claim, either in his own person, or vicariously through his fictional heroes, like Ludvik, a special moral authority or spiritual status just because he has suffered political persecution. He never pretends that he excluded himself from the charmed circle of ideological togetherness by a grand, premeditated gesture. It happens casually, accidentally, as the result of a joke, and provokes a sense of loss, rather than righteous self-justification, in the subject. 'The Angels' ends:

> Perhaps that wild desire to rape R. was merely a desperate attempt to grab at something during the fall. Because from the day they excluded me from the circle, I have not stopped falling, I am still falling, all they have done is give me another push to make me fall farther, deeper, away from my country and into the void of a world resounding with the terrifying laughter of the angels that covers my every word with its din.
>
> Sarah is out there somewhere, I know she is, my Jewish sister Sarah. But where can I find her?
>
> (p. 76)

Sarah is the name of an Israeli fellow-student of Gabrielle and Michelle, who expresses her contempt for them by kicking them on their behinds, though whether she is a 'real' or symbolic person remains unclear. *The Book of Laughter and Forgetting* contains many such enigmas, contradictions, ambiguities, which are not resolved. It never allows the reader the luxury of identifying with a secure authorial position that is invulnerable to criticism and irony. But that it is the work of a distinctive, gifted, self-conscious 'author' is never in doubt.

Chapter 12

Reading and writhing in a double-bind

> Stylistically, practical criticism works through a competing proliferation
> of 'personal' interpretations; it is therefore fundamentally a discourse of
> individual polemic (masked by that urbanity we all know so well from
> *The Times Literary Supplement*).

This observation was made in the course of a review, published in a journal
called *Screen Education*, of a book entitled *Screen Reader I*, edited by John
Ellis. Since *Screen Education* is an offshoot of *Screen* (a journal that has
been one of the principal mediators of the Lacanian – Althusserian – Marxist
school of literary semiotics in Britain), and *Screen Reader* derives from
Screen, it is not surprising that the review was a favourable one. The passage
quoted above is cited in the course of another review of another book: a
fiercely hostile review, written from the *Screen* position, and signed 'S.P.',
of *Reading Relations: Structures of Literary Production. A Dialectical Text/
Book*, by Bernard Sharratt, published by Harvester Press in 1982. This
review, in which the author's name is carelessly misspelled throughout, as
'Sharrett', 'Sharrott', 'Sherratt', etc., is incorporated in the final pages of
the book *Reading Relations* itself, together with an exasperated report on
the original manuscript by the publisher's reader, 'J.G.', who suggested
drastic cuts, several of which seem to have been carried out, and a so-
called 'paracritical review' by two friendly deconstructionists who identify
themselves as 'Marie and Bill' but are, like 'S.P.' and 'J.G.', fairly transparent
aliases for Dr Sharratt himself. These endpieces, gathered together under the
heading 'Suite-talk', anticipate and parody almost every possible evaluative
response to *Reading Relations*, just as the main body of the book parodies
and subverts its own procedures and the institutional practices and discourses to which it belongs. The book ends with a few pages of acknowledgements in which the author gravely thanks, among others, John Ellis, his
colleague at the University of Kent, and member of the editorial board of
Screen.

It is not only, therefore, the urbane lackey of the *TLS* who, invited to
review *Reading Relations*, is likely to approach his task in the spirit of a

man opening a strange-looking parcel with a Belfast postmark. The portrait of Dr Sharratt himself on the inside of the dust-jacket tends to reinforce such caution. He is posed against a rather bleak background that looks at first sight like the hard shoulder of the M1, but on closer examination is probably part of the Kent campus, a plateau overlooking the city of Canterbury. The author's handsome, tousled head is in three-quarters profile, and there is a frown just above the scholarly spectacles, and a faintly menacing thrust to the strong mouth and chin, which seem calculated to warn off potential assailants. That the eyes are narrowed and swivelled backwards as far as they can go may signify that he is more apprehensive of a stab in the back than of a frontal assault.

We may linger a little longer on the dust-jacket. It bears a glowing recommendation from Terry Eagleton – 'This is an absolutely important first-rate book' – from which we may safely infer, ignoring the distraction of that oddly placed 'absolutely', that *Reading Relations* will be in some sense a work of 'Marxist' criticism. It also bears a little rectangular, self-adhesive label on which is handwritten in blue ballpoint the price of the book, £18.95; and we may be struck by the irony of a work of Marxist criticism being entrammelled in the inflationary economics of contemporary publishing, which apparently deter the publisher from using his own technology to print the price of his product upon the cover for fear that it will be obsolete by the time it reaches the point of sale, thus imposing upon some unfortunate worker the alienating and repetitive task of inscribing and affixing thousands of individual price-tags by hand.

Opening the book, we find the contents divided up and categorized as if on a menu. *Apéritifs*: a clutch of quotations from Roland Barthes, S. T. Coleridge, T. S. Eliot, *et al. Crudités*: some rather personal, agonized reflections by the author about the paradoxes and contradictions of being a radical academic paid by a capitalist society to read books he would want to read anyway, in a world where political oppression and chronic social injustice are never more than a few hours' jet flight away. *Potage*: a conference paper 'about the relations between marxism and literary criticism, and, more generally, about politics and art', which takes a broad sweep through intellectual history from Plato to Marx and Lacan in a somewhat haphazard fashion (representative phrase: 'I want at this point to take a sudden jump to what may seem an entirely unrelated subject . . .'). *Poisson*: a review of Raymond Williams's *Marxism and Literature* – respectful but vaguely disappointed. *Brontë Entrée*: a rather routine essay on *Wuthering Heights* yoked forcibly to speculations about Trotsky . . .

At this point the reader may suspect that the flashy menu disguises a collation of warmed-up occasional essays and reviews. But the book suddenly changes shape in a manner reminiscent of eighteenth-century satire on scholarship and bookmaking. We are confronted with a new title page – *Reading Relations: A Study of the Reproduction of the Social Relations of the Production of Literature* by 'Anne Arthur' [an author – geddit?] published by 'Theoretical Parody Publications Ltd', and belatedly, a list of contents, which divides Ms Arthur's work into two parts. Part One consists of a lecture, a seminar and an examination paper with answers. The lecture is on 'Figures and models of marxist literary criticism' and consists of a critique of Marx, Goldmann, Althusser and Eagleton, trying to represent the relationship of literature to ideology and ideology to modes of production in a series of diagrams of increasingly baffling complexity, all boxes, arrows and connecting lines, of the kind that one has laboriously to translate back into discursive prose in order to understand.

The seminar, which begins promisingly with quotations from *The Goon Show* ('The letter is written in a disguised voice') and *Our Mutual Friend* ('He do the police in different voices') is perhaps the most original and substantial part of the book, though quite as trickily elusive of evaluation and interpretation as the rest of it. It begins with a somewhat laboured and over-ingenious analysis by 'Chris' of the 'reading-relations' between speaker, addressee and reader brought into play by the Dedication of Herbert's *The Temple*. Because of the rather special ontological status of the addressee in this instance (God) these relations are peculiarly complex, and hardly representative of 'literature' as a whole. The next speaker, Dai, makes this point, invoking the philosophical study of speech acts. Someone called LN, who seems to have stepped straight out of Posy Simmonds's *Guardian* strip cartoon, complains that 'what we need is a *theoretical framework* in which we can *precisely locate* the *concept* of literature. There are some *totally untheorised* terms playing across Chris's discourse . . .' and so on, until interrupted by Phil, a very recognizable type of seminar bully who drops highbrow names with a studiously common touch ('Yea, I've read me Derrida'). Phil is a Brechtian who believes in action rather than contemplation – writing and putting on a play about what happened to the printers of Herbert's *The Temple* in the political upheavals of the seventeenth century being to him a more meaningful exercise than fiddling about with the reading relations of the Dedication. Then George interestingly applies Gregory Bateson's concept of 'the double-bind' in the psychopathology of familial relations to relations of power and domination in the body politic, arguing that 'the point about at least some of these is that the "victim" puts himself into a double-bind insofar as he won't leave the field of contradictory injunctions because he will lose his *own* power'.

There follows a long contribution from Bert, remarkable both for its rambling structure, proceeding from topic to topic in a fashion more like free association than logical argument, and also for some striking observations on, for instance, discourse as an attempted denial of death:

> The fundamental 'repression' that shapes discourse is the repression of the knowledge of death, of final absence, the intellectual certainty that I

will die, very soon. Because the logic of 'difference' requires the logic of 'same', and what makes us all similar is the body; all bodies die; every body dies.

Bert also provides a fascinating commentary on the recent intellectual history of the left in Britain, focusing on the epistemological 'break' between the old humanist New Left represented by Raymond Williams and E.P. Thompson, and the new post-structuralist kind of Marxism imported from France in the 1960s and 1970s. Bert seems sentimentally nostalgic towards the former, though conscious of its theoretical weakness; and both fascinated and repelled by the latter, which in its denial of the autonomy of the individual self seems to him to give a theoretical blessing to the Stalinist totalitarianism which has done so much to discredit Marxism as a political philosophy in Western Europe.

Here we may feel that we are getting close to the position of the 'real' Dr Sharratt; but just when it looks as if he might stand up, he instead brings the seminar to an abrupt close, distributing, without comment, another gathering of quotations. (The plethora of quotations in this book – I write as the author of two of them – is not in itself to be deplored. On the contrary, they are one of its chief ornaments, testifying to the breadth and adventurousness of Sharratt's reading, and constituting quite an instructive course of education in themselves. It is only a pity that most of them are set in an eye-torturing eight-point type of the kind normally used for footnotes.)

The next part of the book consists of a take-home examination paper for a course entitled 'Studies in legal fiction' and some answers referring to such set texts as Poe's 'The mystery of Marie Roget', Chesterton's 'The blue cross', Camus's *The Fall*, Chandler's *The Big Sleep* and Kafka's *The Trial* (this one ends abruptly with the parenthetical note, 'Unfinished – no time'). There is some thoughtful and thought-provoking criticism in these pages about the relationship between the novel, especially the novel of crime and detection, and the ideological apparatus of the law in society at different historical periods.

And what comes after the final examination? Why, the postgraduate thesis, of course! Part Two of Ms Arthur's work consists of a doctoral thesis on nineteenth-century working-class autobiography, which it is no surprise to discover (from the Acknowledgements at the end of the book) was Sharratt's own PhD thesis, examined by Professor Raymond Williams. It is a decent, sensitive, slightly dull account, in the descriptive–ruminative manner of Williams himself, of some interesting but neglected literary materials, showing how the strains and tensions of being educated *and* working class in the Victorian period showed themselves in the writers' handling of the conventions of confessional and narrative writing. It seems entirely untouched by the influence of Continental post-structuralist theory.

Then comes the 'Suite-talk' which I referred to at the outset, from which one may infer Sharratt's own hopes and fears for the reception of his book. The most favourable estimate would be that he has found a way of renouncing the will-to-power which, some would argue, motivates, and vitiates, all discourse, even that which is ostensibly committed to interpret-ative free-play and plurality of meaning. By doing the critical police in different voices, he has divested them of their power to intimidate and repress, he has created spaces in his text into which the reader may insert himself in order to do his own 'work'. There is some suggestion that he has thus reinstated a Platonic (i.e. dialectical) model for criticism in place of the more totalitarian Aristotelian one. There is, however, no Socrates in *Reading Relations* – no speaker who acts as a leader, guide and teacher, ensuring that the dialectic progresses and produces knowledge. The only knowledge to be gained from *Reading Relations* is of the problems and contradictions that critics, especially Marxist critics, confront. Or, as 'S. P.' less sympathetically puts it: 'No possible *pattern* of thought, no procedure for *thinking* is ever preliminarily or provisionally established by this exercise in intellectual delinquency that it would be a misguided compliment to call derivatively Dadaist.' This writer has his own cruel explanation for the form of the book. Purporting to equate the *impasse* of Marxist theory with the *impasse* of working-class political movements in Western Europe, it in fact expresses only the vocational *impasse* of the radical academic:

> and, particularly, I suspect, the ex-'radical student' of the late 1960s, whose 'long march through the institutions', whose own extended politi-cal *rite de passage*, has turned into a slow revolve of university corridors and committees in the late 1970s, a game of professorial chairs in which the music gets more and more funeral and the strains of the *Red Flag* get ever fainter ... What the book *then* does to itself is to take the obvious next step: into self-destruction.

When one reflects that it is Sharratt himself that is writing this, the force of that 'self-destruction' becomes sufficiently strong to wipe the smile off the reader's face.

'S.P.' relents to the extent of suggesting that *Reading Relations* 'might best be read as. a typical instance of the self-conscious fiction of post-modernism'. The paracritical review by 'Marie and Bill', who admit that they are privy to the author's designing thoughts, certainly shows that there is more artfulness in the arrangement of the book's contents than one might suspect, but *Reading Relations* seems rather lacking in narrative interest to succeed as fiction.

The real motivation behind this remarkable enterprise might be sought in one of the quotations which the author tosses, without comment, to the participants in the seminar, on bringing this event to its close. The quotation is a long footnote to Perry Anderson's 1968 essay, 'Components of the national culture'.

> The novel has declined as a coherent genre, not – as is often alleged – because it was the product of the rising bourgeoisie of the nineteenth century and could not survive it. The true reason is that it has disappeared into the abyss between everyday language and the technical discourses inaugurated by Marx and Freud. The sum of objective knowledge within the specialised codes of the human sciences has decisively contradicted and surpassed the normal assumptions behind exoteric speech. The result is that a novelist, after Marx and Freud, has either to simulate an arcadian innocence or transfer elements of their discourse immediately into his work. Hence the entrenched bifurcation between pseudo-traditional and experimental novels. The ingenuousness of the former is always bad faith . . . The opposite solution – the inclusion of frontier concepts from Freud or Marx within the novel – has no viable outcome either . . . The novelist can only forge his art from the material of ordinary language. If there is a radical discordance between this and objective knowledge of man and society, the novel ceases. It has no ground between the naive and the arcane.

As a diagnosis of the state of fiction this seems, in the 1980s, unduly pessimistic. The serious literary novel is enjoying something of a boom; the polarity in British writing between 'traditional' and 'experimental' fiction is no longer as stark as it once was; and the success of a novel like D. M. Thomas's *The White Hotel* shows how a resourceful novelist may integrate the 'technical discourse' of Freud, for instance, into his fiction without losing touch with ordinary language. But if we substitute the words 'literary criticism' and 'literary critic' for 'novel' and 'novelist' in Anderson's note, then we get an exact formulation of the contemporary crisis in criticism, and of the vocational plight out of which Sharratt has written *Reading Relations*. It is literary criticism, not the novel, which has 'disappeared into the abyss between everyday language and the technical discourses inaugurated by Marx and Freud' (and, I would want to add, Saussure); which has bifurcated into the 'traditional' (literary history, literary biography, practical criticism) and the 'experimental' (structuralism, deconstruction, Bloom's poetics of misprision, etc.); which can find 'no ground between the naive and the arcane'.

The literary critic is thus placed in the classic double-bind, which according to Bateson consists of a 'primary negative injunction' (e.g. 'Do not exclude anybody seriously interested in literature from your discourse about literature'), a secondary injunction conflicting with the first at a more abstract level (e.g. 'Do acquaint yourself with the latest and most powerful tools of analysis available in the human sciences in spite of their mystifying jargon and counter-intuitive axioms') and a 'tertiary injunction prohibiting the victim from escaping from the field covered by the other two injunctions' (e.g. the academic job, with its dual obligation to teach and carry out research into 'literature').

Every sensitive and intelligent member of our profession must feel the pressure of this double-bind to some extent. For the Marxist, committed to an anti-élitist model of society and education, it represents a particularly cruel dilemma. As Bert puts it in the course of the seminar, Althusserian–Lacanian discourse is hardly the best way of hastening the Revolution, because 'your enemies don't read it and a lot of your allies *can't*'.

According to Bateson, the double-bind produces schizophrenia in the victim. *Reading Relations* is best described metaphorically as a schizophrenic book, in which the author's 'self' is split, fragmented, dispersed and demonized. The result, like real schizophrenia in the realm of human behaviour, is by turns fascinating, entertaining, irritating and intimidating to the putatively sane (or urbane). It is not entirely successful – but then the basic concept of the enterprise ruled out 'success'; it is certainly a very impressive, courageous and instructive kind of failure.

Chapter 13

A kind of business
The academic critic in America

Imre Salusinszky has compiled a book of interviews called *Criticism in Society*.[1] Though he questioned all his subjects about their biographies, he is remarkably reticent about his own. We learn, or infer, that he is a young Australian university teacher, that he considers Northrop Frye the greatest critic of the twentieth century, that he is obsessed with the question of 'the function of criticism', and that he took advantage of a Fulbright Fellowship to Yale in the mid–1980s to interview a number of distinguished literary critics on the East Coast of America concerning this perennial topic. That's about all, and perhaps it's enough for the purposes of the book. Mr Salusinszky himself says in his Introduction that 'the interviewer had to be a complete unknown, in order to be able to become a transparent cipher for the thoughts of the famous interviewees', but his tongue is in his cheek as he says it. If there is one thing modern criticism has taught us it is that there is no such thing as transparency in discourse. Mr Salusinszky is, in fact, as interviewers go, quite talkative, often to excellent effect.

The premise he started with was that the institution of literary criticism has increased in self-importance in direct proportion to its growing professionalization and socio-cultural marginalization. In other words, since serious literary criticism was virtually monopolized by the universities, it has become of all-absorbing interest to its practitioners and a matter of indifference or incomprehension to society at large. If true (and I think it is), this proposition has uncomfortable implications for academic critics who believe that universities have a generally civilizing mission to perform in society, and *a fortiori* for those who like to think of teaching and criticism as fields of significant political struggle. Mr Salusinszky touched this sensitive nerve as often as he could in the course of interviewing his subjects about their intellectual careers and present 'positions'. The result is a book that confirms its own premise: it is intensely interesting and entertaining to a reader who belongs to the same world as the interviewees, but will probably bore and baffle outsiders.

The title of the book may seem disproportionate to its actual scope: the 'criticism' under investigation is that practised in élite universities on the eastern seaboard of the United States, and the 'society' is American. The situation of criticism in that context is a very special case – but it is arguably what criticism all around the world is tending or aspiring towards, whether its practitioners admit it or not. Edward Said wryly recalls the remark of a UN official, 'The Third World leaders speak about Moscow, but in their hearts they all want to go to California.' The California of criticism is the network of top American literature departments, some of which – Berkeley, Stanford – are actually *in* California, but most of which are in the East – Yale, Harvard, Johns Hopkins, Cornell, Duke, Virginia, etc.

California gave us Hollywood and Hollywood created the star-system. Academic criticism in America is governed by a star-system as surely as the world of entertainment. Top-ranking critics are like the more independent film-stars or sports stars: they attract fans, they improve their earnings by transferring or threatening to transfer their services to other employers, they maintain a high public visibility (by attendance at conferences etc.) and suffer a high degree of anxiety about their performance and popularity relative to their peers. Of course, whereas famous actors and athletes have a mass audience, the audience of the top critics is tiny, consisting mostly of colleagues and graduate students; and the material rewards of their success are also negligible by the standards of secular American society (the highest salary for a Professor of English I have heard mentioned was $120,000, chickenfeed to a successful American doctor, lawyer or broker, never mind a film-star). Nobody becomes a university teacher in order to become world-famous or rich. What led us all into the profession in the first place was presumably a love of learning and an appreciation of the flexibility and freedom of the scholar's working conditions. But if you can manage to add to those simple, austere satisfactions a comfortable middle-class standard of living and the ego-gratification that comes from public success, you have a rather desirable life-style.

The world of American academic criticism is a small, insulated one, but it mirrors the macro-society in being highly competitive. In both worlds it is possible to succeed spectacularly, because it is also possible to fail. In other cultures, certainly in Britain, academic life has traditionally been organized so as to conceal or elide distinctions between excellence, competence and incompetence, once the ephebe has been elected to membership of the academy. Mr Salusinszky puts it harshly in conversation with Frank Lentricchia:

> you only have to spend ten minutes in a major British university to see what fantastic senses [*sic*] there are to American 'professionalism'. There, there is no professionalism. One effect of that, for example, is that jobs can still be handed out on an 'old boy' network, without regard to publication or productivity – not to say brains.
>
> (p. 197)

This is a little out of date – for one thing, there are no jobs to hand out at the moment – but it's true that in Britain we have always considered it rather vulgar to be overtly ambitious, and disloyal to call attention to the deficiencies of one's colleagues. The star-system cannot flourish in such a climate. Frank Kermode, who is a refugee from it, and the lone Brit among Mr Salusinszky's subjects, seemed to him to be 'the one least interested in generating a "position" that will identify him as the author of his own books', 'the most difficult . . . to "sum up", having neither formed his own school nor been incorporated into anyone else's'. Kermode himself says rather wistfully apropos of Harold Bloom, 'The world is full of Bloomians. There aren't any Kermodians in the world.' The last – indeed, the only – British academic critic who could be said to have had a following labelled by an adjectival form of his name was F. R. Leavis, and his image was antithetical to that of the film-star – it was the image of the saint. Leavis's authority and charisma depended crucially on his *not* having been given the conventional honours and rewards of academic distinction, and he paraded the slights he suffered from the Cambridge English Faculty like the stigmata all his life. The baggy clothes hanging from the small spare figure, the worn, suffering face above the open-necked shirt – all contributed to the ascetic, religious aura.

Just lately there has been a sudden change of climate in Britain: continuous professional assessment, more stringent criteria for probation and promotion in academic appointments, are being introduced in order to produce a leaner, more competitive system. But instead of pumping more money into the universities to provide incentives such as top American academics enjoy (enchanced salaries, light teaching loads, generous research grants, etc.), the Thatcher Government has drastically cut their funding over the last eight years, lowering the quality of life for everybody. In consequence British academics have had the worst of both worlds, finding it possible to fail, but not, in any significant sense, to succeed. Under a new pay deal reluctantly accepted by the Association of University Teachers there is going to be, in future, some system of merit awards and differential salaries, but it remains to be seen how this will work in practice. Meanwhile, it is hardly surprising that large numbers of literary scholars have recently left the universities either to freelance or to teach in America, that chairs are proving embarrassingly difficult to fill, and that the ambition of our brightest graduates these days is not to become university teachers but to go into the media.

All Mr Salusinszky's subjects are products of the American star-system or, like Derrida and Kermode, have been adopted by it. Frye, the oldest of them, has to some extent remained aloof and detached, loyal to his *alma mater*, the University of Toronto; but he makes frequent visits to the United States and his fame was largely created by the enthusiasm of his American admirers. Derrida frankly admits that he is more celebrated in America than in his native France, and this is presumably why he spends so much time in the former country. Significantly only Frye and Derrida among the interviewees mention the problem of obtaining public funds for the humanities. If Mr Salusinszky had interviewed a batch of British academic critics at the same time he would have heard about little else.

To even consider the question of the function of criticism is a luxury made possible by large amounts of money. In spite of its current economic difficulties, America is still so rich that it can afford, mainly through its private universities, to patronize and encourage intellectual activity like literary criticism which has no obvious utilitarian value and may actually be subversive of the aims and assumptions of society at large. This of course has always been a problem for teachers of the humanities under bourgeois capitalism – how can one in good conscience question the values of secular society while drawing one's income from it? (*Howards End* poses the same question in a non-academic context.) But the current obsession of literary scholars, especially in America, with 'theory' has given the question a sharper point. The ground on which university teachers of language and literature have traditionally justified their existence has been educational: that they were handing on a cultural heritage to the next generation, and teaching them to teach, directly or indirectly, others in their turn. This model sees the university as the apex of an educational pyramid which broadens out to connect seamlessly with secondary and primary education. But the age of 'theory' has made a drastic rupture between secondary and tertiary education, conceptually and methodologically. Not only has it questioned the idea of the canon and all the humanistic values associated with it, but it has done so in an arcane and jargon-ridden form of discourse that can only be understood after a long and strenuous initiation, if at all. Derrida, who more than any other single writer is responsible for this state of affairs, was startled by Salusinszky's simple question as to whether there is a place for deconstruction in secondary school teaching. After some hesitation he admits that there isn't; indeed he 'cannot say that there could be a deconstructive teaching, even in the university. I think that deconstruction, to the extent that it's of some interest, must first insinuate itself everywhere, but not become a method or a school' (p. 14).

There are of course those on the intellectual left who see something sinister in this insinuation, a collusion by literary scholars in the sins of Reagan's administration by default, by withdrawal into a hermetically sealed world of texts about texts. Salusinszky quotes an observation of Edward Said that 'it is no accident that the emergence of so narrowly defined a philosophy of pure textuality and critical non-interference has coincided with the ascendancy of Reaganism, or for that matter with a new cold war, increased militarism and defence spending, and a massive turn to the right on matters touching the economy, social services, and organized labour' (pp. 126–7). (It is a point of view that has recently received specious but potent support from the revelation that the late Paul de Man, the highly revered guru of Yale deconstructionism, wrote many newspaper articles in occupied Belgium in the early 1940s urging cultural collaboration with Nazi Germany.)

Said's intellectual development is an interesting story, as complex and tortuous as his ethnic and social background (he is a Palestinian, from a well-off right-wing Christian family, educated in British schools in the Near East and later at an American university). His first book was a phenomenological study of Joseph Conrad, *Joseph Conrad and the Fiction of Autobiography* (1966). The essays collected in *Beginnings* (1975) and *The World, the Text and the Critic* (1983) traced his fascinated and ultimately disillusioned exploration of structuralism and deconstruction, and *Orientalism* (1978) marked his plunge into a politically engagé style of criticism, applying Foucault's analysis of discourse as a field of power-relations to western writing about the East. He is a member of the Palestine National Council and the chief intellectual spokesman for the Palestinian cause in the United States – a somewhat lonely eminence requiring not a little courage, given the strength of the Jewish constituency and Zionist lobby in America. But Said's life-style is a long way from Yasser Arafat's. When Salusinszky met him he frankly admitted to being 'surprised at the New York persona: urbane and rather assimilated' (p. 127).

Said, along with Fredric Jameson, Frank Lentricchia and Stephen Greenblatt, has inspired a recent 'turn' in American academic criticism, away from Derridean deconstruction, towards a Foucauldian or Marxist focus on literature in its social and ideological contexts. Something called the New Historicism is all the rage – so much so that J. Hillis Miller felt obliged to assert the continuing need for deconstructive reading in his Presidential Address to the MLA in 1986. (My attention was drawn to this fascinating document by John Sutherland, in a mordant commentary on the current critical scene in America, 'Ivory Institutes', *TLS*, 18–24 December, 1987.) It would be quite misleading, however, to see this debate in terms of the old opposition between 'formalism' and 'relevance', theory and praxis. The New Historicism is just as heavily theorized, and almost as impenetrable to the layman, as the deconstructionist school it it seeking to supplant. Only in a theoretical sense (or a purely emotive sense) has it politicized the professional practice of criticism.

Harold Bloom, for many years a kind of heterodox fellow-traveller with the Yale school of deconstructionists, travesties the new historicism in the course of a wonderfully funny, outrageously Wildean performance in front of Salusinszky's tape recorder:

> I'll tell you, dear Imre: what I understand least about the current academy, and current literary scene of criticism, is this lust for social enlightenment; this extraordinary and, I believe, mindless movement towards proclaiming our way out of all introspections, our way out of guilt and

sorrow, by proclaiming that the poet is a slum-lord – whether he wants
to be or not – and that there is no distinction between Yale University
– or the University of Melbourne – and the New York Stock
Exchange . . . This is clap-trap . . . I am weary of this nonsense, and will
not put up with it. It has nothing to do with *my* experience of reading
poetry, of writing criticism and teaching other people how to read poetry
and write criticism. If they wish to alleviate the sufferings of the exploited
classes, let them live up to their pretensions, let them abandon the academy and go out there and work politically and economically and in a
humanitarian spirit. They are the hypocrites, the so-called Marxist critics,
and all of this rabblement that follows them now in the academies. They
are the charlatans, they are the self-deceivers and deceivers of others . . .
I am a proletarian; they are not. I'm almost the only person I know at
Yale who was born and raised in a working-class family. I'm the son of
a New York garment worker, who was an unwilling member of the
International Ladies Garment Workers' Union, which he always
despised. These critics are American versions of that Parisian intellectual
and social disease I can least abide . . . which is the high bourgeoisie being
unable to stand its status as the high bourgeoisie, while continuing to
enjoy it in every possible respect. I am more than weary of this, and I'm
especially weary of the self-righteousness that goes with their hypocrisy.
How is it that they don't bore themselves to death? . . . The only critical
wisdom I know is that there is no method except yourself. Everything
else is imposture. There is only oneself.

(pp. 66–7)

One of the novel features of Salusinszky's book is that he showed each of
his subjects transcripts of the preceding interviews, thus inviting them to
comment on each other's contributions. Frank Lentricchia, though disowning the label 'Marxist', is the advocate (in his *After the New Criticism*
[1980] and *Criticism and Social Change* [1983]), of a politically progressive,
historicising approach to criticism, and was evidently stung by Harold
Bloom's remarks:

Those who speak cynically of left intellectuals should examine the implications of suggesting that the university is not a good place to pursue
social change. What the fuck are they doing? If they believe that, they
should resign their jobs.

(p. 190)

When Salusinszky restates Bloom's position – 'I think he would say that the
authentic thing is to stay within the academy and admit that criticism, like
literature, is a form of self-exploration, self-discovery and self-exfoliation'
– Lentricchia makes a rather subtler response:

Whose self? Where is this self? The reader's self? Harold's self? My self?

Where did this self come from? Was Harold self-born? Was he self-originated? This is the problem with Harold's theory: with all of its historical, self-conscious sophistication, it carries buried within itself a radical desire for self-origination. I wish that Harold would pursue his sense of himself as the only proletarian at Yale.

(p. 195)

Aficionados of this sort of debate will admire the dexterity with which Lentricchia turns against Bloom one of the orthodoxies of post-structuralism, common to all its sects and schools – the delusoriness of 'origins'. But there is a certain factitiousness about the counter-attack, betrayed by the familiar 'Harold'. Nearly all the interviewees refer to each other, even when expressing strong disagreement, by first names – Harold, Geoffrey, Jacques, etc. (though not 'Northrop' – in this as in other respects, Frye is the odd man out. I wonder if anyone dares to call him Northrop). This style of naming again reminds one of the world of sport, where top athletes who compete fiercely against each other on the football field or tennis court share a kind of professional camaraderie at other times, a mutual respect based on their sense of belonging to a professional élite.

There is surely a hidden link between the professionalism of the American academic world and the eagerness with which it has devoured, domesticated and developed European theory. The very difficulty and esotericism of theory make it all the more effective for purposes of professional identification, apprenticeship and assessment. It sorts out the men from the boys, or, to put it another way, speeds the tribal process by which boys become young men and push out the old men. Whereas the methods of traditional humanistic scholarship have hardly altered since the nineteenth century, the rules of the theory game are changing all the time, and you have to be fast as well as smart to keep up. Lentricchia worries about this in an interesting and revealing way, both disapproving of the phenomenon and acknowledging that he is inescapably implicated in it:

> let's face it, one of the ways to get noticed, to get published, to become important in literary-critical circles in this country is to be perceived as being on the avant-garde edge of certain movements. Right now, the thing everywhere is politics and history, with a strong dash of Marxism and feminism. I just distrust the whole enterprise, because I guess I think it *is* an enterprise: there's a kind of business going on here.

When Salusinszky shrewdly observes, 'In the United States . . . there is an almost instant intermixing of any new idea or approach with professional ends', Lentricchia says:

> You're using 'professionalism' in its horrid sense . . . which is a powerful sense . . . that, since this is what we do, we need a certain language and terminology to do it, we need to publish our stuff, we need to further

our careers . . . Professionalism in a democratic context (in a US context) has one fantastic sense for me. To go back to Michael Novak's little word, it allows the 'pigs' in. The pigs have a chance.

(p. 197)

By 'pigs', Lentricchia (and Novak) means the ethnic minorities despised and for so long repressed by American WASP society. That is to say, the professionalism of American academic life, and its 'star-system', have enabled Lentricchia, the son of poor Italian-American parents, the grandson of Calabrian peasants, to become a well-paid professor at the prestigious English Department at Duke. (This institution, incidentally, is itself a striking illustration of the same system. In the mid-1980s Duke, a rich but not particularly distinguished university in North Carolina, decided to buy its way into the top league of English departments. Lentricchia was hired in 1984, followed in 1985 by Stanley Fish, brilliant exponent of reader-oriented critical theory, the Americanist Jane Tompkins, and Fred Jameson, the leading American Marxist critic. The dynamic Fish was made chairman of the Department and, bankrolled by the Duke administration, quickly recruited Annabel and Lee Patterson and Barbara Herrnstein Smith. All these men and women occupy very different and probably incompatible positions in the ideology of English studies; what they have in common is high-profile professional distinction. The Duke department was soon acknowledged as one of the top departments in the country. Just so can an unsuccessful baseball or football team become champions in a season or two, by a shrewd expenditure of large amounts of money on top-class players. It's a pity Salusinszky didn't find an opportunity to interview Stanley Fish.)

To return to Lentricchia: indignant as he is at the social injustice his forebears suffered, much as he wants to integrate that awareness into his criticism, and conscientiously as he scatters slang and four-letter words in his conversation to establish his working-class credentials, he cannot bring himself to knock the system that enabled him to achieve, on a modest but not negligible scale, the American Dream.

I like teaching at Duke and making the salary I make. I don't have the theory of Marxism that what Marx wants for the world is for everyone to be poor. I like Garcia Marquez's notion of Marx much better: what we need is for everybody to be able to drink wine, to drive a decent car, and so on.

(p. 192)

This is a very American idea of the Revolution: not just a car for everyone, but a *decent* car – and no nitpicking about the social and ecological consequences.

Perhaps it is clear by now that the primary interest of this book, at least for me, is not so much the critics' accounts of their respective intellectual positions, which most readers will know already from their published work, but the incidental insights which one obtains into aspects of their lives and characters not revealed in the printed word: their styles of impromptu speech, their sociological backgrounds, personal histories, hopes, anxieties, dreams and self-images. Derrida's response to a question about his intellectual life ('I don't know what my "intellectual life" is. How could I separate my intellectual life from my life?') for instance, is a kind of epiphany of what it means to be a Parisian intellectual. When he says in an aside, 'my deepest desire being to write literature, to write fiction', much that seems wilfully obscure and self-indulgent in his writing becomes instantly more explicable. (Frank Kermode, incidentally, disarmingly confesses to having read Derrida's *Grammatologie* with total bafflement only to discover some time later that his copy had many crucial pages missing.) When Said confides that although he still admires Conrad, 'now it's almost unbearable for me to read him', one cannot help wondering whether that isn't because of Conrad's scorn for politically motivated violence, so powerfully expressed in works like *The Secret Agent* and *Under Western Eyes*.

Given the preoccupation of these men and a solitary woman (a rather subdued Barbara Johnson – the feminist perspective on Criticism in Society is somewhat under-represented in this book) with the underlying and often suppressed conventions of various kinds of discourse, it is suprising that none of them thought to put the interview itself, as a discursive form, under theoretical scrutiny. It is a very modern genre, intimately linked to the development of electric and electronic media, related to and yet different from the literary tradition of the reported 'conversation' which goes back through works like Boswell's *Johnson*, and Drummond of Hawthornden's *Conversations* with Ben Jonson, ultimately to Plato's dialogues. The distinctive feature of the interview is what Harold Bloom would call its 'agonistic' element: the object of the interviewer is to get the interviewee to reveal or betray his authentic self, whereas the aim of interviewee is, usually, to *construct* a self that he wishes the world to see. Imre Salusinszky is always probing for contradictions, gaps and fissures between the public persona implied by the critical text and the living breathing person; while his subjects – even the deconstructionists among them – seem anxious to defend the wholeness and integrity of their life-work as if it were a classic realist narrative text. If Harold Bloom's is the most enjoyable *performance* in the book it may be because there really isn't much difference between what we think of him and what he thinks of himself – he really is as vain, self-obsessed and perversely brilliant as he seems to be from the books, and he has not the slightest interest in ingratiating himself by pretending otherwise. J. Hillis Miller also seems wholly consistent with his published persona, but that self is more reasonable and professional than Bloom's, hence less amusing.

As well as showing his subjects the transcripts of preceding interviews,

Imre Salusinszky tried to give some continuity to his book by showing each of them a poem by Wallace Stevens, 'Not Ideas about the Thing, but the Thing Itself', and inviting them to comment on it. A surprising number of them, he points out, are particularly devoted to Stevens (the exception is Said, who observes epigrammatically that Stevens' poems are like 'an orchestra tuning up, but never actually playing'). The exercise lends an additional agonistic element to the interviews, since each critic is on his or her mettle to cap or go beyond the comments of their predecessors in the sequence of interviews. J. Hillis Miller, coming last, has an opportunity to demonstrate his superiority over all of them, and siezes it with relish: 'Since I knew that you were going to ask me this, I've read [the poem] a little, which means that if I really gave you an answer it would take another hour and a half' (p. 234). Even his short answer is easily the longest speech in the book. 'Your discussion was so clear that I didn't feel the need to interrupt,' says an impressed Salusinszky at the end. It is indeed a formidably clever reading of the poem, but its very thoroughness is slightly chilling. What would it have been like, one wonders with a certain awe, if Miller had read the poem more than just a little?

J. Hillis Miller is shrewdly placed at the end of the book, for he is the complete American professional, who sees criticism as a struggle for mastery: mastery of the critic over the text, of the critic over his peers, of one school of criticism over another, of one critical culture over another. In that remarkable 1986 Presidential Address to the MLA, Miller said, without obvious irony, that 'Although literary theory may have its origin in Europe, we export it in a new form all over the world – as we do many of our scientific and technological inventions, for example the atom bomb'; and put forward a frankly combative model of the critical enterprise: 'I am for diversity . . . not for a permissive pluralism that says anything goes, but for a fair and open fight for survival that is not even sure the fittest will survive but recognizes such an open fight as our only hope' (*PMLA*, 102 [1987] pp. 287 and 290). He also named sixteen young literary theorists whom he expected to make the running in the immediate future. Sixteen! Imagine being a young American literary theorist and *not* being on the list! What humiliation! As for the lucky ones, Sutherland cynically observed that Miller's endorsement probably added thousands of dollars to their market value at a stroke. In Lentricchia's words, 'there's a kind of business going on here'. It is rather shocking to those brought up in a more genteel tradition of scholarship; but it is also what makes America the most interesting, exciting and challenging place in the world, at the moment, in which to practise academic literary criticism. If that's what you want to do.

Notes

Introduction

1 Katerina Clark and Michael Holquist, *Mikhail Bakhtin*, Cambridge, Mass., 1984, p. vii.
2 Quoted by Tzvetan Todorov, *Mikhail Bakhtin: The Dialogic Principle*, Manchester, 1984, p. 4.
3 Nicholas Bachtin, *Lectures and Essays*, Birmingham, 1963.
4 See Clark and Holquist, op. cit., pp. 19–20.
5 I. A. Richards, *Principles of Literary Criticism*, 1924, p. 25.
6 David Lodge, *Language of Fiction*, 1966, p. 47.
7 Mark Schorer, 'Technique as discovery', in *Critiques and Essays on Modern Fiction 1920–51*, ed. J. W. Aldridge, New York, 1952, pp. 67–8.
8 Roman Jakobson and Morris Halle, *Fundamentals of Language*, The Hague, 1956, p. 78.
9 Mikhail Bakhtin, *Problems of Dostoevsky's Poetics*, ed. Caryl Emerson, Manchester, 1984, pp. 200–1.
10 Quoted by Todorov, op. cit., p. 68.

1 The novel now

1 Catherine Belsey, *Critical Practice*, 1980, pp. 7ff.
2 Roland Barthes, *Image–Music–Text*, 1977, pp. 145–6.
3 Paul de Man, *Blindness and Insight*, 1983, p. 17.
4 Graham Greene, *Ways of Escape*, 1980, p. 134.
5 Ibid., p. 77.
6 Lennard J. Davis, *Factual Fictions: The Origins of the English Novel*, New York, 1983, pp. 42ff.
7 Martin Amis, *Money*, Harmondsworth, Middx, 1985, pp. 87–8.
8 Lennard J. Davis, *Resisting Novels: Ideology and Fiction*, New York, 1987, p. 5. All page references are to this edition.
9 D. H. Lawrence, *Selected Literary Criticism*, ed. Anthony Beal, 1956, p. 105.
10 Katerina Clark and Michael Holquist, *Mikhail Bakhtin*, Cambridge, Mass., 1984, pp. 11–12.
11 Mikhail Bakhtin, *The Dialogic Imagination*, Austin, Tx, 1981, p. 280.
12 Mikhail Bakhtin, *Problemy tvorčestva Dostoevskogo*, Leningrad, 1929.
13 Mikhail Bakhtin, *Problems of Dostoevsky's Poetics*, Manchester, 1984, p. 200.
14 Ibid., p. xxii.
15 D. H. Lawrence, *Reflections on the Death of a Porcupine*, Philadelphia, Pa, 1925, pp. 106–7.

16 See ch. 4 of this book.

2 Mimesis and diegesis in modern fiction

1 Fay Weldon, *Female Friends*, 1977, pp. 163–4.
2 Gérard Genette, *Introduction à l'architexte*, Paris, 1979, pp. 14–15.
3 *Great Dialogues of Plato*, trans. W. H. D. Rouse, New York, 1956, p. 190.
4 Ibid., p. 191.
5 Homer, *The Iliad*, trans. E. V. Rieu, Harmondsworth, Middx, 1950, pp. 23–4.
6 Gérard Genette, *Narrative Discourse*, trans. Jane E. Lewin, Oxford, 1980, p. 170.
7 Samuel Johnson, *The History of Rasselas, Prince of Abissinia*, Carlton Classics edn, 1923, p. 23.
8 Sir Walter Scott, *The Heart of Midlothian*, Everyman edn, 1909, p. 265.
9 *Readings in Russian Poetics*, ed. Ladislav Matejka and Krystyna Pomovska, Cambridge, Mass., 1979, p. 155. It is almost certain that the section of *Marxism and the Philosophy of Language* included in this anthology, which deals with the typology of narrative discourse, is directly or indirectly the work of Mikhail Bakhtin.
10 George Eliot, *Middlemarch*, Penguin English Library edn, Harmondsworth, Middx, 1965, p. 32.
11 *Readings in Russian Poetics*, pp. 155–6.
12 James Joyce, *Ulysses*, ed. Walter Gabler, 1986, p. 3. All page references are to this edition.
13 James Joyce, *A Portrait of the Artist as a Young Man*, New York, 1964, p. 215.
14 For an explanation of this term, see p. 49.
15 Claudia Jameson, *Lesson in Love*, Mills & Boon, 1982, p. 76.
16 *Readings in Russian Poetics*, p. 188. My account of Bakhtin's discourse typology is based mainly on this extract from Bakhtin's first book, *Problems of Dostoevsky's Art* (1929), later revised and expanded as *Problems of Dostoevsky's Poetics* (1963).
17 E. M. Forster, *Howards End*, Harmondsworth, Middx, 1953, p. 13.
18 Ibid., p. 174.
19 D. H. Lawrence, *Lady Chatterley's Lover*, The Hague, 1956, p. 139.
20 Mikhail Bakhtin, *The Dialogic Imagination*, ed. Michael Holquist, trans. Caryl Emerson and Michael Holquist, 1981, p. 55.
21 Ibid., p. 54.
22 Ibid., pp. 171–3.
23 Virginia Woolf, 'Modern fiction', reprinted in *Twentieth Century Literary Criticism: A Reader*, ed. David Lodge, 1972, p. 89.
24 Dorrit Cohn, *Transparent Minds: Narrative Modes for Presenting Consciousness*, Princeton, NJ, 1978, pp. 247–55.
25 Graham Greene, *Collected Essays*, 1969, p. 116.
26 Margaret Drabble, *The Middle Ground*, 1980, pp. 246–7.
27 Joseph Heller, *Good as Gold*, 1980, p. 321.
28 Kurt Vonnegut, *Slaughterhouse Five*, New York, 1969, p. 109.

3 *Middlemarch* and the idea of the classic realist text

1 Barbara Hardy (ed.), *Middlemarch: Critical Approaches to the Novel*, 1967, p. 3.

2 Ibid., pp. 94–5.

3 Henry James, *The House of Fiction*, ed. Leon Edel, 1962, p. 267.

4 J. Hillis Miller, 'Optic and semiotic in *Middlemarch*', in *The Worlds of Victorian Fiction*, ed. Jerome Buckley, 1975, p. 127.

5 Readers seeking further light on these matters might consult the following sources, listed in an order corresponding roughly to a progressive shift of focus from structuralism to post-structuralism: Robert Scholes, *Structuralism in Literature*, London, 1974; Terence Hawkes, *Structuralism and Semiotics*, London, 1977; Jonathan Culler, *Structuralist Poetics*, London, 1978; *Structuralism and Since*, ed. John Sturrock, Oxford, 1979; and Catherine Belsey, *Critical Practice*, London, 1980. The last of these is closest to Colin MacCabe's position, the theoretical bases of which are also expounded in his own book.

6 Colin MacCabe, *James Joyce and the Revolution of the Word*, 1979, p. 4.

7 'Metalanguage: a language or system of symbols used to discuss another language or system', Collins *New English Dictionary*.

8 MacCabe, op. cit., p. 100.

9 Ibid., p. 14.

10 Ibid., p. 27.

11 See pp. 28–9 above.

12 Gérard Genette has traced this process from Plato and Aristotle to the present day in his monograph, *Introduction à l'architexte*, Paris, 1979, arguing that in developing Plato's distinction between three modes of poetic utterance into a theory of three basic genres (lyric, drama, epic), later poeticians not only misrepresented the classical authors, but created a good deal of confusion in poetics. For a short account in English of this work, see James Kearns, 'Gérard Genette: a different genre', *The Literary Review*, 1981, no. 33, pp. 21–3.

13 Gérard Genette, *Narrative Discourse*, trans. Jane E. Lewin, Oxford, 1980, p. 164.

14 Mikhail Bakhtin, 'Discourse typology in prose' (an extract from *Problems of Dostoevsky's Poetics*, Leningrad, 1929) in *Readings in Russian Poetics*, ed. Ladislav Matejka and Krystyna Pomorska, Ann Arbor, Mich., 1978, p. 193. This anthology also contains an extract, entitled 'Reported speech', from Volosinov's *Marxism and the Philosophy of Language*, Leningrad, 1930. For a survey of Bakhtin's work, and a discussion of the vexed question of his relationship to Volosinov, see Ann Shukman, 'Between Marxism and formalism: the stylistics of Mikhail Bakhtin', *Comparative Criticism: A Yearbook*, ed. E. S. Shaffer, Cambridge, 1980, vol. II, pp. 221–34.

15 Hardy, op. cit., pp. 67–9.

16 MacCabe, op. cit., p. 15.

17 *Middlemarch*, Penguin English Library edn, Harmondsworth, Middx, 1965, p. 217.

18 Farebrother's allusions to the various versions of the Hercules myth are indeed full of proleptic irony in application to Lydgate, whose 'resolve' to make a contribution to medical science will be sacrificed to Rosamund's feminine and domestic desires (equivalent to 'holding the distaff'), and who will eventually wear the Nessus shirt of failure and disillusionment in his professional and emotional life.

19 See particularly *Surprised by Sin, The Reader in Paradise Lost*, 1967; *Self-Consuming Artefacts: The Experience of Seventeenth-Century Literature*, Berkeley and Los Angeles, 1972; and *Is There a Text in this Class? The Authority of Interpretative Communities*, London, 1981.

20 MacCabe, op. cit., p. 19.
21 Hillis Miller, op. cit., p. 128.
22 Steven Marcus, 'Human nature, social orders, and nineteenth-century systems of explanation: starting in with George Eliot', *Salmagundi*, 1975, vol. XXVI, p. 21.
23 Graham Martin, '*The Mill on the Floss* and the unreliable narrator', in Anne Smith, (ed.), *George Eliot: Centenary Essays and an Unpublished Fragment*, 1980, p. 38.

4 Lawrence, Dostoevsky, Bakhtin

1 See pp. 34–40.
2 The following English language editions have been used: M. Bakhtin, *Problems of Dostoevsky's Poetics*, ed. and trans. Caryl Emerson, Introduction by Wayne Booth, Manchester, 1984; V. N. Volosinov, *Marxism and the Philosophy of Language*, trans. L. Matejka and I. R. Titunk, 1973; M. Bakhtin, *Rabelais and His World*, trans. Helene Iswolsky, 1968; M. Bakhtin, *The Dialogic Imagination*, ed. Michael Holquist, trans. Caryl Emerson and Michael Holquist, 1981.
3 See pp. 46–7.
4 David Lodge, *The Modes of Modern Writing*, 1977, p. 161.
5 E.g. '[J. M. Robertson]'s an arrant ass to declare *Crime and Punishment* the greatest book – it's a tract, a treatise, a pamphlet compared with Tolstoi's *Anna Karenina* or *War and Peace*', *The Letters of D. H. Lawrence*, vol. I, ed. James T. Boulton, Cambridge, 1979, pp. 126–7. The remarks about Dostoevsky, and Lawrence's Preface to *The Grand Inquisitor*, collected together in *Selected Literary Criticism*, ed. Anthony Beal, 1961, pp. 229–41, though largely hostile, show how well acquainted he was with the Russian novelist's work.
6 D. H. Lawrence, *Women in Love*, Harmondsworth, Middx, 1960, p. 263. All page references are to this edition.
7 Frank Kermode, 'D. H. Lawrence and the apocalyptic types', in *Continuities*, 1968.
8 Frank Kermode, *Lawrence*, 1973, p. 74.
9 James Joyce, *A Portrait of the Artist as a Young Man*, 1942, p. 115.
10 'Things' was first published in *The Bookman* (New York), August 1928. Page references are to D. H. Lawrence, *The Princess and Other Stories*, ed. Keith Sagar, Harmondsworth, Middx, 1971. My attention was first drawn to this story by Professor John Preston, who discusses its 'dialogic' structure, with a reference to Volosinov (though not Bakhtin), in 'Narrative procedure and structure in a short story by D. H. Lawrence', *Journal of English Language and Literature* (Korea), 1983, vol. XXIX, pp. 251–6.
11 D. H. Lawrence, *Mr Noon*, ed. Lindeth Vasey, Cambridge, 1984. All page references are to this edition.
12 Ibid., p. xxii.
13 D. H. Lawrence, *The Lost Girl*, ed. John Worthen, Cambridge, 1981, p. xxix. All page references are to this edition.
14 For a valuable exploration of this aspect of Bakhtin's work, see Peter Stallybrass and Allon White, *The Politics and Poetics of Transgression*, Ithaca, NY, 1986.

5 Dialogue in the modern novel

1 David Lodge, *Language of Fiction*, 1966, p. 47.
2 Mikhail Bakhtin, *Problems of Dostoevsky's Poetics*, ed. and trans. Caryl Emerson, Manchester, 1984, pp. 200–1.
3 Evelyn Waugh, *A Handful of Dust*, Harmondsworth, Middx, p. 7.
4 V. Volosinov, 'Discourse in life and discourse in poetry: questions of sociological poetics', *Russian Poetics in Translation*, 1983, vol. 10, pp. 5–29.
5 Laurence Sterne, *Tristram Shandy*, 1903, p. 117.
6 Jacques Derrida, *Of Grammatology*, Baltimore, Md, 1976.
7 David Lodge, *The British Museum is Falling Down*, Harmondsworth, Middx, 1965.
8 Evelyn Waugh, *Vile Bodies*, 1947, pp. 176–7.
9 Henry Green, *Nothing*, 1979, p. 18.
10 Roman Jakobson, 'Closing statement: linguistics and poetics', in *Style in Language*, ed. Thomas E. Sebeok, Cambridge, Mass., 1960, pp. 350–77.
11 Evelyn Waugh, *Decline and Fall*, Harmondsworth, Middx, 1937, p. 14.
12 Ivy Compton-Burnett, *A God and His Gifts*, 1966, pp. 159–60.
13 George Eliot, *Middlemarch*, Harmondsworth, Middx, 1965, p. 50.
14 Mikhail Bakhtin, *The Dialogic Imagination*, 1981, p. 280.
15 Bakhtin, *Problems of Dostoevsky's Poetics*, p. 196.

6 After Bakhtin

1 Thomas A. Sebeok (ed.), *Style in Language*, Cambridge, Mass., 1960.
2 Charles E. Osgood, 'Some effects of motivation on style of encoding', in Sebeok, op. cit., pp. 293–306.
3 E.g. 'Deconstruction is not a dismantling of the structure of a text but a demonstration that it has already dismantled itself'; J. Hillis Miller, 'Stevens' rock and criticism as cure, II', *The Georgia Review*, 1976, vol. XXX, p. 341.
4 Stanley Fish, *Is There a Text in this Class? The Authority of Interpretive Communities*, Cambridge, Mass., 1980.
5 Paul de Man, 'Dialogue and dialogism', *Poetics Today*, 1983, vol. IV, pp. 99–107.
6 V. N. Volosinov (M. M. Bakhtin), *Marxism and the Philosophy of Language*, trans. Ladislav Matejka and I. R. Titunik, New York, 1973, pp. 85–6.
7 Morris Zapp, in the present writer's novel, *Small World: An Academic Romance*, 1984, pp. 25–6.
8 M. M. Bakhtin, *The Dialogic Imagination*, ed. Michael Holquist, trans. Caryl Emerson and Michael Holquist, Austin, Tx, and London, 1981, p. 280.
9 The question has, of course, been posed before. See, for instance, the interesting exchange between Ken Hirschkop, 'A response to the forum on Mikhail Bakhtin', and Gary Saul Morson, 'Dialogue, monologue, and the social: a reply to Ken Hirschkop', in *Critical Inquiry*, 1985, vol. XI, pp. 672–86. The most lucid and balanced discussion is probably to be found in Tzvetan Todorov, *Mikhail Bakhtin: The Dialogic Principle*, Manchester, 1984, pp. 66–8 and *passim*.
10 M. M. Bakhtin, *Problems of Dostoevsky's Poetics*, ed. and trans. Caryl Emerson, Manchester, 1984, p. 200.
11 Bakhtin, *The Dialogic Imagination*, p. 416.
12 Bakhtin, *Problems of Dostoevsky's Poetics*, pp. 200–1.
13 F. W. Bateson and B. Shahevitch, 'Katherine Mansfield's *The Fly*: a critical exercise', *Essays in Criticism*, 1982, vol. XII, pp. 39–53.
14 Katherine Mansfield, *The Collected Stories*, Harmondsworth, Middx, 1981, p.

412. 'The fly' was first collected in Katherine Mansfield's *The Dove's Nest and Other Stories*, 1923.

15 Bateson and Shahevitch, op. cit., p. 49.
16 See chapter 4 of this book.
17 D. H. Lawrence, *Studies in Classic American Literature*, New York, 1964, p. 165.
18 Bakhtin, *Problems of Dostoevsky's Poetics*, p. 166.
19 Katerina Clark and Michael Holquist, *Mikhail Bakhtin*, Cambridge, Mass., 1984, p. 276.
20 Bakhtin, *The Dialogic Imagination*, p. 39.
21 Clark and Holquist, op. cit., p. 293.
22 Bakhtin, *The Dialogic Imagination*, pp. 327–8.
23 M. M. Bakhtin, 'The problem of text in linguistics, philosophy, and the other human sciences: an essay of philosophical analysis', quoted by Todorov, op. cit., p. 68.
24 See, for example, Richard Ohmann, 'Speech, action, and style', in *Literary Style*, ed. Seymour Chatman, London and New York, 1971, pp. 241–59.
25 Roland Barthes, *Image – Music – Text*, trans. Stephen Heath, 1977, p. 142.

7 Crowds and power in the early Victorian novel

1 Elizabeth Gaskell, *North and South*, ed. Dorothy Collin, with an Introduction by Martin Dodsworth, Harmondsworth, Middx, 1970, pp. 226–7. All page references are to this edition.
2 Raymond Williams, *Culture and Society*, 1958, ch. 5.
3 Humphrey House, *The Dickens World*, 1960, p. 207.
4 Charlotte Brontë, *Shirley*, Harmondsworth, Middx, 1974, p. 505.
5 Elias Canetti, *Crowds and Power*, trans. Carol Stewart, 1962. All page references are to this edition.
6 Charles Kingsley, *Alton Locke*, 1967, p. 94.
7 J. A. Froude, *Thomas Carlyle*, 1884, vol. 1, p. 93. Cited by Kathleen Tillotson, Introduction to *Barnaby Rudge*, by Charles Dickens, Harmondsworth, Middx, 1973, p. 22n.
8 Hilaire Belloc, Introduction to Thomas Carlyle, *The French Revolution*, 1906, vol. i, p. xvi.
9 Ibid., pp. xvi–xvii.
10 Thomas Carlyle, *The French Revolution*, 2 vols, 1906, vol. I, p. 170. All page references are to this edition.
11 Charles Dickens, *Barnaby Rudge*, Harmondsworth, Middx, 1973, p. 475. All page references are to this edition.
12 Charles Dickens, *A Tale of Two Cities*, Harmondsworth, Middx, 1959, pp. 245–6. All page references are to this edition.
13 George Rudé, *The Crowd in the French Revolution*, Oxford, 1959, p. 4n.
14 Edmund Burke, *Reflections on the Revolution in France*, Harmondsworth, Middx, 1982, pp. 164–5.
15 See Peter Stallybrass and Allon White, *The Politics and Poetics of Transgression*, Ithaca, NY, 1986.
16 Mikhail Bakhtin, *Rabelais and His World*, Cambridge, Mass., 1968, p. 89.
17 Ibid., p. 119.
18 Mikhail Bakhtin, *Problems of Dostoevsky's Poetics*, ed. and trans. Caryl Emerson, Manchester, 1984, p. 124.
19 Quoted by Kathleen Tillotson, op. cit., p. 29.

20 Benjamin Disraeli, *Sybil or: The Two Nations*, Harmondsworth, Middx, 1954, p. 271. All page references are to this edition.
21 Georg Lukács, *The Historical Novel*, trans. Hannah and Stanley Mitchell, Harmondsworth, Middx, 1969, p. 20.
22 *Coriolanus*, in which this theme is particularly prominent, is cited and discussed in two of the Condition of England novels: Charlotte Brontë's *Shirley* (chapter 6) and George Eliot's *Felix Holt* (chapter 30).

8 Composition, distribution, arrangement

1 All page references to Jane Austen's novels are to the third editions of the texts edited by R. W. Chapman, Oxford, 1932–4.
2 Arnold Kettle, *An Introduction to the English Novel*, 1962, p. 100.
3 Roman Jakobson, 'Two aspects of language and two types of linguistic disturbances', in Roman Jakobson and Morris Halle, *Fundamentals of Language*, The Hague, 1956. See also my *The Modes of Modern Writing*, London, 1977.
4 Mark Schorer, 'The humiliation of Emma Woodhouse', reprinted in *Emma: A Casebook*, ed. D. Lodge, 1968.
5 Introduction to *Emma*, Oxford, 1971, pp. xiv–xvi.
6 Gérard Genette, *Narrative Discourse*, trans. J. E. Lewin, Oxford, 1980.
7 F. R. Leavis, *The Great Tradition*, 1948, p. 19n.
8 Henry James, *The House of Fiction*, ed. Leon Edel, 1957, p. 207.

9 The art of ambiguity

1 Leon Edel, *The Life of Henry James*, Harmondsworth, Middx, 1977, vol. 2, p. 15.
2 Ibid., pp. 137–52.
3 *The Notebooks of Henry James*, ed. F. O. Matthiessen and Kenneth B. Murdock, New York, 1961, p. 208.
4 Ibid., p. 138.
5 Wayne Booth, *The Rhetoric of Fiction*, 1961, p. 159.
6 Philip L. Greene, 'Point of view in *The Spoils of Poynton*', *Nineteenth-Century Fiction*, 1967, vol. 21, p. 368.
7 Nina Baym, 'Fleda Vetch and the plot of *The Spoils of Poynton*', *PMLA*, 1969, vol. 84, p. 106.
8 William Bysshe Stein, 'The method at the heart of madness: *The Spoils of Poynton*', *Modern Fiction Studies*, 1968, vol. 14, pp. 198 and 202.
9 John Lucas, '*The Spoils of Poynton*: James's intended uninvolvement', *Essays in Criticism*, 1966, vol. 16, p. 482. (A reply to the article by Bellringer cited in the next note.)
10 A. W. Bellringer, '*The Spoils of Poynton*: James's unintended involvement', *Essays in Criticism*, 1966, vol. 16, p. 185.
11 Tzvetan Todorov, 'The secret of narrative', in *The Poetics of Prose*, Oxford, 1971, pp. 143–78; Ralf Norrman, *Techniques of Ambiguity in the Fiction of Henry James*, Abo, Finland, 1977, and *The Insecure World of Henry James's Fiction*, London, 1982; Shlomith Rimmon, *The Concept of Ambiguity: The Case of Henry James*, London, 1977; Christine Brooke-Rose, *A Rhetoric of The Unreal*, Cambridge, 1981, chs 6–8.
12 All page references for quotations from the novel, James' Preface of 1908, and relevant passages in his Notebooks, are to *The Spoils of Poynton*, ed. David Lodge, Harmondsworth, Middx, 1987.

13 Matthiessen and Murdock, op. cit., p. 251.
14 Arnold Edelstein, 'The tangle of life: levels of meaning in *The Spoils of Poynton*', *Hartford Studies in Literature*, 1970, vol. 2, pp. 133–50.
15 Stein, op. cit., p. 193.
16 *The Spoils of Poynton*, ed. Bernard Richards, London, 1982, p. 189.
17 Robert C. McLean, 'The subjective adventure of Fleda Vetch', in *Henry James: Modern Judgements*, ed. Tony Tanner, 1968, pp. 204–21.
18 Ibid., p. 220.
19 The suggestion of C. B. Cox, *The Free Spirit*, 1963, pp. 52–3, who cites Henry James's endorsement of the pragmatic philosophy of his brother William.
20 Norrman, *The Insecure World of Henry James's Fiction*.
21 Richards, op. cit., p. 185.
22 See the relevant articles in *A Dictionary of Political Thought* by Roger Scruton, 1982.
23 In the Postscript to his book *Appreciations*, 1889, Walter Pater referred to 'that *House Beautiful* which the creative minds of all generations – the artists and those who have treated life in the spirit of art – are always building together, for the refreshment of the human spirit . . .' I am indebted to Ian Small for this information.

10 Indeterminacy in modern narrative

1 Seymour Chatman, *Story and Discourse: Narrative Structure in Fiction and Film*, Ithaca, NY, 1978, pp. 147–51.
2 W. K. Wimsatt Jr with Monroe C. Beardsley, 'The intentional fallacy', in *The Verbal Icon*, Lexington, Ky, 1954, pp. 3–18.
3 'All I carried away from the magic of Auckland was the face and voice of a woman who sold me beer at a little hotel there. They stayed at the back of my head till ten years later when, in a local train of the Cape Town suburbs, I heard a petty officer from Simonstown telling a companion about a woman in New Zealand who "never scrupled to help a lame duck or put her foot on a scorpion." Then, precisely as the removal of the key-log in a timber-jam starts the whole pile – those words gave me the face and voice at Auckland, and a tale called "Mrs Bathurst" slid into my mind, smoothly and orderly as floating timber on a bank-high river'; Rudyard Kipling, *Something of Myself*, 1937, p. 135.
4 Wolfgang Iser, *The Act of Reading: A Theory of Aesthetic Response*, Baltimore, Md, and London, 1978.
5 Roland Barthes, *S/Z*, trans. Richard Miller, 1975.
6 Page references to 'Mrs Bathurst' are to *Traffics and Discoveries* in the Sussex Edition of Kipling's *Complete Works*, 1937–9.
7 Elliott L. Gilbert, *The Good Kipling: Studies in the Short Story*, Manchester, 1972, pp. 110–11n. Gilbert is indebted to J. M. S. Tompkins, *The Art of Rudyard Kipling*, London, 1959, p. 145, for the suggestion that Vickery stood up to attract the lightning, though Tompkins unwarrantably assumes that the second figure is female. C. A. Bodelsen, who rashly claims that 'the story *must* have a definite meaning, and it must be possible to get at it, if only one picks up the right trail', argues inexplicably that the second figure is Mrs Bathurst's ghost. See his *Aspects of Kipling's Art*, Manchester, 1964, pp. 127 and 145. Another enigma in the story, first pointed out to me in a seminar discussion of this paper, concerns Hooper's remark to Pritchard, 'If you don't mind I'd like to hear a little more o' your Mr Vickery', *before* the name has been uttered

in the conversation (p. 348). One can infer either that Hooper knows more about Vickery than he pretends, and betrays this to the alert reader (but not to the characters, including the narrator), or that Kipling the implied author is responsible for the slip. It is of the nature of the story that it is impossible to decide between these alternative explanations.

11 Milan Kundera, and the idea of the author in modern criticism

1 Milan Kundera, *The Book of Laughter and Forgetting*, trans. Michael Henry Heim, 1982, p. 65. All page references are to this edition, which was reprinted by Penguin Books in 1983.
2 Milan Kundera, *The Joke*, trans. Michael Henry Heim, 1983, p. xi. All page references are to this edition.
3 Kundera, *The Book of Laughter and Forgetting*, p. 5.
4 'The death of the author', in Roland Barthes, *Image–Music–Text*, trans. Stephen Heath, 1977, pp. 145–6.
5 Michel Foucault, *Language, Counter-memory, Practice*, ed. and trans. Donald F. Bouchard with Sherry Simon, Ithaca, NY, 1977, pp. 113–38.
6 Ibid., p. 138.
7 Ibid., p. 138.
8 Kundera, *The Book of Laughter and Forgetting*, p. 3.
9 Catherine Belsey, *Critical Practice*, 1980, p. 134.
10 The term was coined by Wayne Booth in his *Rhetoric of Fiction*, 1961, and has since achieved wide circulation in criticism of the novel. I use it to designate the creative mind to whom we attribute the production of the text, and whom we encounter only in the text, as distinct from the actual human being who physically wrote it, and who has an existence outside the text.
11 See Frank Kermode's *Essays on Fiction*, 1983, especially the Prologue and the essay 'Secrets and narrative sequence' for some characteristically suggestive thoughts on this subject.
12 See 'The intentional fallacy', in *The Verbal Icon*, by W. K. Wimsatt Jr with Monroe C. Beardsley, Lexington, Ky, 1954, pp. 3–18.
13 Milan Kundera, 'Comedy is everywhere', *Index on Censorship*, 1977, vol. 6, p. 6.
14 Gérard Genette, *Narrative Discourse*, trans. Jane E. Lewin, Oxford, 1972, p. 40.
15 Dorrit Cohn, *Transparent Minds: Narrative Modes for Presenting Consciousness in Fiction*, Princeton, NJ, 1978, pp. 247ff.

13 A kind of business

1 Imre Salusinszky, *Criticism in Society: Interviews with Jacques Derrida, Northrop Frye, Harold Bloom, Geoffrey Hartman, Frank Kermode, Edward Said, Barbara Johnson, Frank Lentricchia, and J. Hillis Miller*, Methuen, New York and London, 1987.

Index